S0-BRS-364

Analysis and Design of Information Systems

Second Edition

Springer

New York
Berlin
Heidelberg
Barcelona
Hong Kong
London
Milan
Paris
Singapore
Tokyo

Arthur M. Langer

Analysis and Design of Information Systems

Second Edition

 Springer

004.21
L276

Arthur M. Langer
Division of Continuing Education
    and Special Programs
203 Lewisohn Hall
Columbia University
2970 Broadway
New York, NY 10027
USA

Library of Congress Cataloging-in-Publication Data
Langer, Arthur M.
    Analysis and design of information systems / Arthur M. Langer.—2nd ed.
        p.   cm.
    Rev. ed. of: The art of analysis, © 1997.
    Includes bibliographical references and index.
    ISBN 0-387-95038-9 (alk. paper)
        1. Computer software—Development.   2. System analysis.   I. Langer, Arthur M.
    Art of analysis.   II. Title.
    QA76.76.D47L37   2000
    004.2´1—dc21   00-040046

Printed on acid-free paper.

The first edition was published in 1997 by Springer-Verlag New York, Inc., as *The Art of Analysis.*

© 2001 Springer-Verlag New York, Inc.
All rights reserved. This work may not be translated or copied in whole or in part without the
written permission of the publisher (Springer-Verlag New York, Inc., 175 Fifth Avenue, New
York, NY 10010, USA), except for brief excerpts in connection with reviews or scholarly
analysis. Use in connection with any form of information storage and retrieval, electronic
adaptation, computer software, or by similar or dissimilar methodology now known or here-
after developed is forbidden.
The use of general descriptive names, trade names, trademarks, etc., in this publication, even
if the former are not especially identified, is not to be taken as a sign that such names, as
understood by the Trade Marks and Merchandise Marks Act, may accordingly be used freely
by anyone.

Production managed by Lesley Poliner; manufacturing supervised by Joe Quatela.
Photocomposed copy prepared from Microsoft Word files supplied by the author.
Printed and bound by Maple-Vail Book Manufacturing Group, York, PA.
Printed in the United States of America.

9 8 7 6 5 4 3 2 1

ISBN 0-387-95038-9   SPIN 10767206

Springer-Verlag   New York Berlin Heidelberg
A member of BertelsmannSpringer Science+Business Media GmbH

To the ongoing pursuit of knowledge.
There is no greater power.

Preface

Analysis continues to be one of the most challenging and popular subjects at conferences on information development and business process reengineering. With the growing popularity of open systems development, the Web, and e-commerce, there is more pressure than ever for an approach to analysis that will ensure high-quality maintainable systems that meet end-user and business expectations. Although there are many new buzzwords in the industry, the term "analysis" continues to encompass the broad challenge of how information system professionals can document and design requirements to fit user needs.

Many books written on this subject tend to focus on the simple mechanics of how to do analysis, rather than on the art of performing analysis most successfully. For indeed, the act of analysis is an art. The most successful analysts are not necessarily the best technicians, but rather are gifted individuals who have the ability and insight to extract information from users and transfer it into a logical system specification. The field of analysis is no longer new, and the time has come for education to focus on doing analysis well, not just adequately. This book seeks to cultivate the skills and insights that distinguish a truly successful analyst.

The book identifies many alternative modeling tools that an analyst can use. It emphasizes how and when the analyst can best apply them and what benefits can be derived from their application. The book's approach suggests that analysts can and should make their own choices about which modeling methodologies to apply when meeting the needs of an organization. It may come as a surprise to many lay readers to learn that such an approach is unique among analysis textbooks. Yet the fact is that most such books teach only a single method of analysis and advocate the use of that method alone in all situations. In suggesting that analysts may find success in mixing methodologies, this book breaks important new ground.

New to the Second Edition

This second edition expands the scope of analysis into many new areas, particularly those involved with designing Web-based electronic commerce systems. Five new chapters have been added that address client/server, Internet, Intranet, and contemporary network requirements that are required to meet the needs of today's global business economy. In addition, a new chapter has been added that focuses on how to approach and design graphic screens for Web browsers. Finally, previous chapters have updated content, are reorganized in a different presentation order, and have more exercises.

The Aim of This Book

The risks involved in performing analysis are significant: Those projects that involve reengineering activities have a failure rate over 70 percent. With the expansion of the Internet as a vehicle for electronic commerce, the stakes are even higher than before, and identifying the sources of failure can be invaluable. In general, failures can be attributed to two kinds of risks: those associated with the process of change and those relating to the technology itself. I am confident that the success rate can be dramatically improved if we focus less on the methodology and more on the ability of the analyst to perform the work. This book is therefore meant as a "practitioner's guide" to doing analysis through every facet of developing software solutions.

The book defines the word "analyst" to include any individual involved in establishing the requirements and design of a system. For this reason, the book includes subjects like joint application development (JAD) and prototyping, which may not always be performed by analysts but which nevertheless fall within the confines of the definition.

My enthusiasm for writing this book was supported by many of my students who found that existing books on analysis are:

- *very theoretical*. Although they explain the methodologies, they do not provide enough examples of their actual application.

- *too procedural*. They do not deal with the "human" aspects of developing requirements and thus do not provide a complete understanding of how to be successful. After all, the whole point of analysis is to service human enterprises, not just to create systems for their own sake. The human side of analysis is as important as the technical side.

- *lacking simple but effective case examples*. The examples do not demonstrate the concepts effectively or are too complex for practice study.

- *too one-sided in their views*. It is important to establish all available methodologies, even those that conflict with each other. Putting opinions into perspective and leaving many of the ultimate decisions to the practitioner is a significant part of the analyst's education.

The Intended Audience for This Book

This book assumes a reasonable understanding of computer concepts and terminology. The material is presented to be used in a first-level analysis course or university program. In addition, it can be used by practicing information systems professionals or executives who are managing information technology and need an in-depth understanding of the principles of the analysis and design process, particularly as it relates to Web-based development. Furthermore, many programmers who are also performing analysis may find this book a way of developing a useful approach to structured and object methodologies.

Acknowledgments

Although I developed this book on my own, my colleagues, students, and clients provided invaluable information. My colleague at Columbia Amanda Douglas contributed many of her lecture notes and exercises from her GUI design course. My workshop instructors Cynthia Hernandez and Greg Vimont developed many new exercises and case studies.

Most of all, I must continue to thank the students of Columbia University for their inspiration and dedication to learning. It is wonderful to participate in the cognitive development of another. I know we are building a better future.

Arthur M. Langer
New City, NY
August, 2000

Contents

1
Introduction

What Is, Is

Thirty years of developing requirements for systems have taught us that the only successful approach to analysis is to accept what exists in the user's environment, however far from ideal those conditions may be, and work within those limitations. It may be very tempting to use analysis time to try to re-focus how the user does business. Yet efforts to re-design or reengineer, unless specifically requested by the user, will typically be a waste. Although your assessment may be correct and your suggestions potentially useful, being correct is less important in this situation than being wise and understanding the ability of your users to successfully implement and utilize what they need. Analysts tend to ignore this simple wisdom, much to their own distress and that of their clients.

Looking at a typical example of an analysis situation will help to illustrate this point. Let us assume that an enterprise needs a relational database model to gather information about a subject area of the business. There are 200 offices that will need to connect into a nationally provided service. Users disagree on the mission of the applications and cannot determine what reports or query information they want. Some offices are automated, but they do not have the same software and hardware. There is little expertise in the user community to determine the data requirements and file layouts (identifying elements in each file). Management has requested that the analyst establish a specification which identifies the requirements of the system as well as the necessary hardware and software.

Faced with so unwieldy a task, many analysts will adopt the following approach in an attempt to impose order on a disorderly situation:

1. Force users to define all requirements. Since they are unable to do so, this insistence will probably result in their guessing or providing incomplete information.
2. Determine the hardware and software configuration, despite having inaccurate or incomplete requirements.
3. Ignore the political environment.

    4.   Establish a project plan that everyone knows will fail, but push ahead with it anyway.

It should be clear that this approach is the wrong one, on a number of different counts. Yet such an approach is all too typical for analysts confronted with a less-than-ideal working environment. Happily, there is a better approach for all concerned, one that recognizes and responds to the conditions actually present at the users' site. In this case it is evident that the users are not positioned to provide the requirements for a system, largely because they do not fully understand their own needs and because they do not agree on what those needs are. What the analyst must understand in such a situation is that because of this lack of knowledge and organization, user needs will tend to change during the process of product analysis and design. Such changes are to be expected; they are simply part of the life cycle for this particular implementation. To ignore the situation and try to implement a system is to invite failure. Put simply then, what is, is. The task of the analyst is to work with what is rather than trying to change it or—even worse—simply denying it. Once you as an analyst understand that reality, you understand that your solution must accommodate what will inevitably occur.

Here is a more sensible approach to the situation described above:

1.   Focus on designing a model that can provide the users with the capability they want. Create a project plan that assumes that the database will be incomplete during phase I because of the users' inability to define the correct information. The process will therefore be iterative and thus will be finalized during the later parts of the development life cycle.

2.   Do not try to identify hardware before it is clear what the usage requirements are, such as peak-time processing, number of users, and so on. It will be more beneficial to establish the operating system or architectural environment that you want to support, pending the results of the analysis.

3.   Utilize a software system or CASE tool that will allow users to generate new scenarios such that they can see how these scenarios relate to the entire system.

4.   Set up a pilot program. This will require that certain offices agree to be test sites for the early versions of the software. The function of the pilot is to provide feedback on the effectiveness and shortfalls of the product. It is important to state clearly the objectives of the pilot and the format of the feedback in order to ensure the success of the exercise.

5.   Formulate a plan that depicts a schedule for getting the entire enterprise implemented and live on the new system. Be sensitive to the politics of the situation, and use a realistic approach that will not require a cultural change in order to implement software in the existing environment.

The essence of this approach is to develop a strategy that fits the reality of the environment rather than force the environment to change. Throughout this book, we will explore this simple but crucial concept. No two system development projects are identical, and the more familiar the analyst is with the environment, the more successful the project will be. This book will also argue against the conventional wisdom that suggests using an approach based on only a single methodology (e.g., Yourdon, Martin, Booch, etc.). The mixing of methodologies allows the analyst a wider range of tools. Hands-on experience shows that this kind of mixing of methodologies can be done quite successfully and that it is appropriate in a large number of analysis situations.

Just What Is a Complex Project?

Most analysts, project team members and users worry about the complexity of their projects. Their requirements seem entirely unique to them, and therefore a very special approach seems to be required. How many times have you heard: "the tools and approaches used elsewhere just won't work in this environment"?

The truth, however, is very different: the only truly complex projects are those that people make so! It is important for the analyst to recognize that the procedures utilized, regardless of the size of the project, should remain fundamentally the same. As we have discussed above, the analyst's approach to the implementation of each project should be tailored individually; however, the procedures for this implementation should remain constant. Very often the organization of interviews, the utilization of techniques such as Joint Application Development (or JAD), discussed later in this chapter) or the simple addition of more analysts to the project can solve what appear to be insurmountable problems.

In fact, most of the myriad problems that arise in product development can be traced to two fundamental issues:

1. People are trying to solve the wrong problem, i.e., the identified problem is not really what is wrong.
2. The solution to the real problem is often much simpler than it first appears to be.

Because we have failed to recognize these issues, the industry's frustration with developing appropriate software solutions has been chronic, and this situation has not really improved over the last twenty-five years! The question is why?

To put it bluntly, analysts often fail to do their jobs properly! We tend to put together plans and schedules that are doomed from the start to fail, an issue treated in more detail later. The ultimate goal of the analyst must take into account the reality of the environment in which the work is occurring. Remember, work within the environment. Let users decide what degree of change is appropriate for their own operation; do not take it upon yourself to demand that they change.

For example, how many times have you seen a Gantt Chart[1] for a project schedule that resembles the one below?

Activity		March	April	May	June	July	August	Sept	Oct
Feasibility		☐							
Analysis			☐						
Design				☐					
Development					☐				
Quality Assurance							☐		
Implementation								☐	

Figure 1.1 Sample Gantt Chart.

It looks nice, but in reality the plan it depicts could never happen. Focus in particular on the intersection of Development and Quality Assurance (QA) activities. The plan shows that once Development is finished, the materials are forwarded to QA for testing. The sequence assumes, however, that QA will never find an error and that therefore the materials will never be returned to Development! Any analyst knows that this scenario is very unlikely to occur. Such poor planning results in deficient allocation of resources to the project. Should the development schedule be met, programming resources most probably will be allocated to other projects. Thus, if QA finds errors (which they undoubtedly will), reallocating these programming resources becomes difficult and problematic. And remember: programmers do not like returning to an "old" program to do maintenance or error fixing.

Figure 1.2 reflects a more realistic view of the life cycle of the project:

The difference in approach is striking. The question is, as sensible as this plan appears to be, why don't we always do it this way? Quite frankly, this plan does not look as nice—as neat and tidy—as the previous plan. But of course simply denying the pain of reality—the inevitable inconveniences and delays—does not make that reality go away. In defense of the previous configuration, some developers might suggest that the iterations of efforts between testing and fixing the software are assumed to be included in the QA time. Maybe, but don't count on it! Just look at the second schedule and you will see how the results of this proper allocation added to the delivery time of the project. It is clear that the original plan was simply incorrect.

---

[1] A Gantt Chart is a tool that depicts progress of tasks against time. It was developed by Henry L. Gantt in 1917.

Activity		March	April	May	June	July	August	Sept	Oct
Feasibility									
Analysis									
Design									
Development									
Quality Assurance									
Implementation									

Figure 1.2 Modified Gantt chart reflecting realistic project activity behavior.

There is absolutely no reason that a schedule should not reflect the reality of what will most probably occur. The results are clear: Realistic planning provides a more reliable schedule. Among the many benefits of such a schedule are the confidence and respect gained by both the users and the development staff. There is nothing like producing a schedule that reflects what everyone is confident will occur.

At this point, experienced analysts are no doubt wondering what happens when management dictates how much time we have and shows no flexibility about running behind schedule. This problem is unfortunately not uncommon, and typically fits into one of three scenarios:

1. Management is ignorant of the analysis and construction of systems and simply has no idea how much time is required to complete the project. In this case the analyst will need to develop a convincing presentation for management about how systems are designed and developed. The presentation should be carefully documented to refer to the industry statistics for similar projects in similar companies. This kind of documentation adds much credibility to the discussion. You can also consider having an independent source, such as a respected consulting firm, support your position.

2. Management has little confidence in Development. They feel that picking a date and sticking to it is the best method of getting the project finished. Yes, this is the bully technique! It usually results from bad experiences, probably from looking at those unrealistic Gantt Charts. In this situation, the analyst must take steps to gain the management's confidence. Using the suggestions above would be a good start. In addition, you will need to research and to understand the history of what your predecessors did to encourage this type of distrusting and dictatorial attitude from management, and you will need to find a tactful way to address those issues.

3. Unfortunately, bad management does exist. If you cannot win any concessions or understanding from management, you may have reached what is known as the "no-win scenario." Management is simply unwilling to allot adequate time for the completion of the project and to be persuaded otherwise. When this situation exists in the workplace, the advice is straightforward: You can leave, or you can find some way to deal with this constraint. In either case, be aware that under the no-win scenario there is little hope that the project will result in the development of quality software. This perspective is not cynical, but instead realistic: some projects are doomed to fail before they begin. What is important is that the analyst recognize as early in the life cycle as possible that the project cannot be successful.

The Tiers of Software Development

The lifecycle of software development continues to evolve, particularly with the advent of the object paradigm (discussed in Chapter 9). The lifecycle of development inevitably affects the way analysis and design are accomplished. Indeed, it seems only natural that the rapid changes in software methodologies would be accompanied by parallel development in analysis and design. Unfortunately, such is not the case, and the advances in software development continue to overshadow the importance of analysis and design.

As the software industry focuses on electronic commerce (e-commerce) through robust Web-based development, it becomes vitally important for the analyst to use the appropriate sequence of tiers to arrive at requirements. Developers cannot expect good results from taking shortcuts, tempting as it may be to do so. The recommended sequence of tiers is outlined below.

User Interface

Regardless of the type of software applications being developed, systems cannot be effectively designed without an appropriate user interface. The user interface tier acts as the foundation for the project: Without a solid foundation at this level, the project is at risk of collapsing at some point during development. Despite its importance, the user-interface tier is often overlooked: Many software projects today move too quickly into development without the effort having been spent to determine what is really needed from the user community. Successful analysts are aware of the critical importance of the user interface phase of any project. Chapter 2 focuses on methods of formulating user interfaces that can significantly improve software development.

Tools

Software systems require that analysts have the appropriate tools to do their job. Furthermore, an even more significant challenge is understanding which of the many available tools to use at any given point. Software development tools are often designed for specialized use rather than for general application, and using the wrong tool can potentially cause significant damage. Finally, the sequence of use for each specialized tool is also critical to success. Indeed, the order of operation, as well as the relationship among specialized analysis tools, must be mastered to ensure success. Chapters 3 and 4 focus on which tools are needed to accomplish which tasks. The chapters also outline the advantages and disadvantages of each tool.

Productivity Through Automation

Having the appropriate tools and knowing how and when to use them is only part of the formula for success. Analysts must also be productive—and productivity can be accomplished only through the use of automation. Automation is implemented using integrated computer aided software engineering (CASE) products. These products provide the analyst with an automated and integrated toolbox of features that are centralized through a core data dictionary and repository.

Object Orientation

Successful projects employ the concepts of object orientation (OO). Whether or not software systems are OO compliant, analyzing systems using the object method builds better systems that are more cohesive, reusable, and maintainable (see Chapter 9). More cohesive code is "tighter" code, and is more easily fixed and maintained. It is also the foundation of the reusable components that can be incorporated into other applications later. Without the OO construct, systems tend to have pieces that are recoded and hard to maintain. With the advent of the enterprise solutions and e-commerce transactions that will be vital to business strategies, building object-based systems has become more a requirement than an option. However, as this book will show, businesses and organizations cannot just jump into OO, but rather they must create the foundations first through the previous tiers of development. Put another way, it is more important to understand the concepts of OO during analysis and design than it is to have the OO scheme actually programmed. This idea is discussed further in Chapter 9.

Client/Server

Today's software is still governed by client/server processes. While client/server has become more widespread, it has not necessarily become better understood. As with the OO paradigm, client/server software development is often confused with network hardware strategy. While client/server hardware topology is an important issue in itself, it has little to do with the process of deciding how software modules should interact across the network and where such modules should be placed. Such decisions will be driven by issues that arise during the process of analysis. Client/server software processing, in its true implementation, involves the interaction of objects and defining the way in which they will communicate with each other. Thus, analysts must first be versed in the laws governing OO if they are to pursue the client/server model. Incidentally, almost all Web-based applications that use JAVA, Active-X and other controls are designed essentially under the guidelines of interaction objects in a client/server environment.

Internet/Intranet

The advent of Web-based technology, sometimes known as Internet/Intranet processing, has led the industry to the use of a new breed of software applications. This new breed requires more robust processing and involves careful design and placement of pictures that provide users with a true "cafeteria" style of operation. These new applications bring new challenges to analysts and designers. Increasingly, it is not programmers who are designing the interface; rather, analysts themselves are beginning to work with commercial advertisers and marketing departments to create a "look and feel" that will be critical to the survival of many businesses. E-commerce, a result of the Internet/Intranet boom, represents another level of analysis. I believe that in the future, e-commerce will exert the strongest shaping influence on the analyst's profession—a profession destined to become tomorrow's integrators of systems development. Indeed, programming tools will continue to become easier to develop and more abundant in precoded forms. There will, undoubtedly, be less distribution of development teams, that is, companies will find more and more outsourced solutions to fill their needs. Notwithstanding the "automation" of code, the need for integrators who can communicate with executives and with line management and operations personnel will ultimately be the most significant forces in the development of strategic-based systems over the Internet.

Internet/Intranet processing requires that analysts have mastered the client/server paradigm. Indeed, many professionals have dubbed Internet development as "client/server grown up." While this may or may not be the best definition of Internet/Intranet development, it is another statement that supports the tier concept, the concept that underlies the approach of this book.

•   •   •

This introduction is focused on presenting the steps necessary to success as a professional analyst. I call each of these steps tiers because of their building-block nature and their dependencies on each other. I believe, therefore, that to learn to become an effective analyst, one must master the specifics within each of these tiers and must pass critical information to the next level. Rather than look at analysis sequentially, I would present the steps as levels as depicted in Figure 1.3.

Tier	Analyst Application
6	Internet/Intranet—Web-based transaction processing, media, and graphics
5	Client/server—breaking down objects to their client and server applications
4	Object orientation—selection of objects and classes
3	CASE—automation and productivity of tier 2
2	Structured Tools—DFD, PFD, ERD, STD, process specification, data repository
1	User Interface—interviewing skills, JAD, RAD

Figure 1.3 Tiers of analysis and software application development.

The table graphically shows how each tier must be dependent on the other. There is a profound message in this diagram that suggests that no tier can be developed or exist without the previous one. To ensure success on a project, everyone involved in the design and development of application software must fully understand the interdependent nature of these tiers. Analysts must be able to convey to their colleagues that to do Internet/Intranet development, organizations must first have excellent user interfaces, mastery of a structured tool-set, a vehicle for automation so that the process will be productive, an understanding of the concept of objects, and a way to deploy these objects in a client/server environment. It all sounds so simple, and in many ways it is. The question answered by this new edition is *how?*

Problems and Exercises

1. Professionals often refer to software projects as being very complex. Explain why this complexity might be overstated and misunderstood.
2. What is a Gantt chart? How are Gantt charts used and why is it important that they be realistic estimates of how the project will proceed?
3. Explain what is meant by "tiers of software development."
4. The user interface represents the first critical step to obtaining the proper needs of users. Provide five examples of different user positions that might be critical to interview.
5. Discuss the importance of using the appropriate analysis tool when interviewing users and building specifications.
6. How is productivity obtained in analysis? What tool is best used?
7. Explain why object orientation is beneficial to software developers.
8. What is the use of client/server with respect to software development?
9. Why is Internet/Intranet processing so important to today's Web development?

2
The User Interface

Establishing User Interfaces

The success factors in analysis start with the established interfaces from day one. What does this mean? You must start the process by meeting with the right people in the organization. In the best projects, the process is as follows:

1. *Executive interface*: There needs to be an executive-level supporter of the project. Without such a supporter, you risk not being able to keep the project on schedule. Most important, you need a supporter for the political issues that you may need to handle during the project (discussed in detail later). The executive supporter, sometimes known as a *sponsor* (JAD reference), should provide a preliminary schedule advising the organization of what is expected and the objectives of the project. The executive supporter should attach a letter to the preliminary schedule and send it to the project team members. The letter must put the importance of the project into perspective. Therefore, it is strongly recommended that you draft this letter yourself or at least have influence over its content, since doing so can ensure that the message is delivered appropriately. The executive supporter should also establish regular reviews with the analyst and the user community to ensure that objectives are being met.

2. *Department head or line manager interface*: If appropriate, the department head should provide guidance about which individuals should represent the department needs. If several people are involved, the analyst should consider a JAD-like approach. Depending on the size of the organization, the department head might also establish review sessions to ensure compliance.

3. *Functional user interface*: Perhaps the most important people are the ones who can provide the step-by-step needs of the system. Figure 2.1 shows a typical organization interface structure.

Figure 2.1 Established interface layers.

Forming an Interview Approach

Your primary mission as an analyst or systems designer is to extract the physical requirements of the users and convert each to its logical equivalent (see Chapter 3 for a full discussion of the concept of the logical equivalent). The most critical step in this mission is the actual interview, in which you must establish a rapport with the user(s) that will facilitate your obtaining the information you need. Your approach will dramatically change based on the level and category of the individual being interviewed. Therefore, prior to meeting with any user, it is critical to understand the culture of the company, its past experiences with automation, and most important its organizational structure.

The following five-step procedure will help guide you more smoothly through the interview process.

Step 1: Get The Organization Chart

Few things are more useful in understanding the chain of command and areas of responsibility than the organization chart. Depending on the size of the enterprise and the scope of the project, the organization chart should start at the executive supporter level and work down to the operational users.

Step 2: Understand Everyone's Role in the Organization Chart

If there are any individuals not involved in the project who should be, given their position in the organization, first ask why and then make a notation for yourself that they are not to be included. Management may assume an individual or role should not be included and may often overlook their importance. Do not be afraid to ask why a person is not deemed necessary for the analysis of the system, and determine if you are satisfied with the reasons for their exclusion. Remember, you can still control and change the approach at this point, and management will probably respect you for doing so.

Step 3: Assume the Situation Is Political

Be sure you understand the personalities with which you will have to deal. In almost any implementation, politics among people becomes part of the process. To ignore its existence—and the constraints it is likely to impose—is to invite failure. The question is how to obtain information about internal politics. The best approach is to start as high up in the organization as possible, typically at the executive supporter level. You might be surprised at the amount of information they have. Of course, you should not explicitly ask about the politics but rather phrase your question as follows: "Can you give me some perspective on potential department and personnel conflicts that may occur during the interview cycle and that I should be aware of?" You may not always get the answer you need, but if you keep asking the question during every interview, you will discover a great deal about the way the organization functions. And remember, only people make projects complex!

Step 4: Obtain Information About User Skill Sets

Starting an interview without knowledge of the user's technical skills puts the analyst at a huge disadvantage. Having this information will allow you to formulate a plan of questions and to determine the best approach to the interview. If the user has no knowledge, the questions should be tailored to include a minimum of technical content. The following guidelines for preparing for interviews reflect a common sense approach, yet it is amazing how many analysts fail even to consider such strategies!

1. Gather information before the session to allow the user—as well as yourself—to be prepared and to give you both a much clearer understanding of what will be covered during the interview.
2. Develop a questionnaire. Technical questions should be phrased differently depending on the level of knowledge the user possesses.
3. Determine whether the interview will provide enough input to obtain the necessary information. This is not always the case; however, it happens more often than you might think. Understanding user capabilities before the interview may not only change the scope of the meeting but also suggest who, in addition to the user, should attend the interview.

Step 5: Arrange for a Pre-Meeting with the User

A pre-meeting may not always be possible. In any case it must be a short meeting, perhaps half an hour. The session should be designed to be high-level and provide a general idea of what will be covered during the actual interview. But more important, it will allow you to get a snapshot of the user. You might say you are obtaining a "comfort level" (or "discomfort level") for that user, and such meetings can provide you with an idea of what to expect and how to finalize your approach. What do you look for? Here is some direction.

1. The pre-meeting should give you enough feedback to place or confirm the user's technical level.

2. Look at everything in the user's office or his or her environment. Is it sloppy? Is it tidy and organized? The state of the user's environment will often be consistent with the way he or she provides information. The insight you gain from observing the environment should give you guidance about the types of questions to ask this individual.

3. Look for signs of attitude. The user's level of interest should be evident. Does he or she view the upcoming session as a waste of time, or is he or she excited about the meeting ?

The information gleaned in the pre-meeting can provide you with helpful hints about what to expect from the interview and from the user in general.

Dealing with Political Factions

The importance of internal politics at the user's site should never be underestimated. Perhaps the most common question raised by both professionals and student analysts is how to provide quality analysis when office politics get in the way. Here are some guidelines.

1. First, assess whether you are in the no-win scenario. Many of us hate to admit that the no-win scenario does indeed exist in many environments, but you should be on the lookout for the signs. If your manager will not support you, if the company is underpaying you, if the users hate you, if there are no automated tools to do the analysis, and if upper management doesn't care, then you are in a difficult position. If you cannot change the situation, you must inform management that the results of your analysis will be significantly impaired by the lack of support and tools to complete the project properly. The techniques offered in this book assume that all parties are interested in providing the best solution possible, not in providing a system that is barely adequate.

2. On the other hand, do not be too quick to assume that you are in the no-win scenario. Most politically hampered projects need some strategy to get them on course, and most problems can be overcome if you know how to approach them. Here is a typical example of such a problem and some ideas you can apply to solve it.

Problem

The users who currently operate the system won't talk to me. They are afraid either that the new system might replace them or that their jobs will significantly change. In short, they fear change.

Recommended Solution

Most operational users are managed by a supervisor or "in-charge." Sometimes, even a line manager can be directly responsible for production workers. In any event, you must determine who is responsible and meet with that person. The purpose of the meeting is to gain their support. This support is significant, since you might find that the supervisor was once in operations and will be able to understand the problems you may encounter. If the meeting is successful, the supervisor may be able to offer a strategy. This strategy can vary from a general meeting with the users, to individual discipline, to escalation to upper management. Whatever you do, do not allow such a situation to continue and do not accept abuse; to do so will ultimately reflect on you and your abilities.

Obviously, if the supervisor is also a problem, then you have no choice but to go to upper management. However, this option is not a desirable one from the analyst's viewpoint. Upper management's reaction may not be helpful, and it could be damaging. For example, they might be indifferent to your problem and instruct you to deal with it yourself, or they might simply send the supervisor a letter. In some cases you may be fortunate and the supervisor's responsibilities regarding the system will be given to another manager. Consider, though, how unpleasant the consequences may be if you appeal to upper management and get no support: You may be left working with an already unhelpful supervisor who has been made even more so by your complaint. It is important to remember that once you go to upper management, the line has been drawn. Supervisors typically are responsible for the day-to-day operation. They usually know more about the entire operation than anyone else, and therefore you are well advised to find a way to get them on your side. A supportive supervisor can be invaluable in helping you overcome problems, as long as you are not shy about suggesting ways to get the users comfortable.

Categories and Levels of Users

Establishing user interfaces represents the vehicle to formulate much of the interview approach. It is necessary, however, to go further into the characteristics of the people particularly with respect to the *category* and *level* they have within the organization. Figure 2.1 established the three general categories, called executive, department head or line manager, and functional. It is important to explore their characteristics. In order that we better understand each category, I have always asked the following question: *What would be their interest in the success of the project, that is, what would make them happy with the new system?* Let's apply this question for each user category.

1. *Executive users:* Individuals at this layer are most interested in the concept of return on investment (ROI). ROI basically focuses on whether an investment will provide a financial return that makes the effort worthwhile to the organization. While there are many comprehensive formulas that are often applied to the study of ROI, our context pertains to the short- and long-term benefits of investing in building new software. There are generally five reasons why executives agree to fund software development. They are listed in order of significance to the investor.

    a. *Monetary return:* Simply put, this means that the software will generate dollar revenue. An example might be the Internet software that supports on-line ordering systems such as Amazon has for book shipments. Their system not only provides the functionality to handle shipments, but provides a Web interface that can be directly associated with revenues provided by book orders through the Internet.

    b. *Increased productivity:* Many software systems are unable to demonstrate direct monetary benefits. However, many of them are developed to increase productivity. This means that the system will allow organizations to actually produce and deliver more. Thus, the system allows the organization to derive higher revenues through increased productivity of its resources.

    c. *Reducing costs:* Software projects are approved so that organizations can reduce their existing overhead costs. This typically relates to the replacement of manual activities with computer ones. While reducing costs appears to be similar in nature to increasing productivity, they are often implemented for different reasons. Increased productivity usually relates to organizations that are growing and are looking for ways to improve output because of very high demand. Reducing costs, on the other hand, can represent a defensive measure, where an organization is seeking to find ways to cut costs because of a shrinking market.

    d. *Competition:* Software systems are created because the competition has done so. Therefore, producing software for competitive reasons is a defensive measure against someone else who has demonstrated its value. An example of this is in the banking sector. Citibank was one of the first banks to introduce automated teller machines (ATM). Other banks soon followed because of the success that Citibank had with proliferating ATMs throughout New York State. This does not imply, however, that competitive systems are always defense mechanisms. Indeed, many commercial Web sites are being introduced based simply on market forecasts for their potential to increase business.

e. *For the sake of technology:* While not the most popular reason, some organizations will invest in new systems because they think that it is time to do so or they are concerned that their technology is getting old. This way of supporting new systems development is rare, as it suggests the spending of money without a clear understanding of its benefits.

Therefore, the executive category of users is one that is interested in the value of the investment. These users have a global view of needs as opposed to the details. In fact, they may know little of how things are really done. The value of the executive interface is to provide the scope and objectives of the project against the perceived value they intend to get from the software. Another popular phrase for this is the *domain* of the system. Domain often refers to *boundaries.* Ultimately, what makes them happy is a system that delivers what was promised or the expected ROI.

2. *Department head or line manager users:* These users represent two main areas of user input. First, they are responsible for the day-to-day productivity of their respective departments. Thus, they understand the importance of meeting the objectives of the organization as set forth by the executives. Indeed, they often report to the executives. On the other hand, department heads and line managers are responsible to their staff. They must deal with the functional users and prescribe ways to improve both their output and their job satisfaction. These users perhaps provide what I call *the best bang for the buck,* a phrase that usually means for the time invested, you get the most payback. One can see that the department heads and line managers are responsible for most of what happens every day in an organization. Another phrase that can be used to describe them is your *most valuable players (MVPs).* However, beware: MVPs are the hardest to find and get for the interviews. What makes department heads and line managers happy is the most complex. They want a system that produces the output that they are expected to provide and they need a system that keeps their staff happy and productive.

3. *Functional users:* Also known as the users in the trenches, these people essentially do the operational activities. While they know a lot about their processes, they usually care little about the productivity and expected ROI. I often see these users as people who want little pain, and just want to work the hours they need to. Thus, fancy systems are of little interest to them unless they provide no pain—and no pain to these users means having a system that makes their job easier.

The next area to understand about users is their level. By level, I mean their understanding of computers. There are three levels of users:

1. *Knowledgeable:* The determination of knowledge can be tricky and is certainly based on someone's opinion. I define knowledge in reference to experience. An experienced user can be defined as a person who "has been through it before." A user who has been through the development of a new system can therefore be defined as "knowledgeable" within this context.

2. *Amateur:* The definition of an amateur is based not so much on experience, but rather on the type of experience the user has. Amateurs can be thought of as hobbyists who enjoy working with computers at home, but have no professional experience in developing software in an organization. In this perspective, I believe that the meaning of amateur is globally defined as one who does not get paid for the work they perform.

3. *Novice:* These users have no experience with computers. While there are fewer such users than there were ten years ago, they still exist. A better way of perceiving a novice user is to consider my definition of knowledgeable. In this context, a novice user is one who has never been part of the implementation of a new system in a professional environment.

Perhaps the most problematic of the above levels is the amateur. I have found that users who are knowledgeable provide benefit to projects. They in many ways act as a checkpoint for the analyst in that they can ask good questions and particularly remember historical problems that actually can help the development process. Novice users add little value and also add few problems. They tend to do what you ask of them. Amateurs, on the other hand, tend to know enough to be dangerous. They also tend to have such a profound interest in the topic that they often go off on tangents about the technology instead of concentrating on the particulars of the project.

What is most important is the mapping of these categories and levels. An analyst might interview a knowledgeable executive, or a novice functional user. Each permutation can affect the way interviews are conducted. For example, an interview with a group of amateurs would focus the analyst on ensuring that the agenda is very specific. Otherwise, discussions could easily get off track. Therefore, the understanding about user levels and categories can only assist in the development of effective interview approaches.

Joint Application Development (JAD)

JAD is a process that was originally developed for designing computer-based systems. JAD centers on a three-to five-day workshop that brings together business area people (users) and IS (Information Systems) professionals. Under the direction of a facilitator, these people define anything from high-level strategic plans to detailed system specifications. The products of the workshop can include definitions of business processes, prototypes, data models, and so on.

Simply put, JAD is a method for holding group sessions with users, instead of individual sessions. You may have no choice but to use JAD when there are simply too many users to interview. JAD is also an excellent tool for use in highly political situations where obtaining consensus among users is difficult. JAD significantly differs from standard analysis in that it requires an up-front commitment from the user community. Specifically, the users must ultimately run the sessions themselves and make commitments to provide the requirements of the system. Finally, if prototypes are used, JAD is an excellent means of applying rapid application development (RAD). Both prototyping and RAD will be discussed in greater detail later.

The most important part of implementing JAD is the management of the process and the determination of the appropriate individuals to be involved. The standard roles used in JAD are as follows:

- *executive sponsor*: This individual effectively plays the same role as the executive supporter introduced earlier in this chapter. This person is typically at the vice-president level and ultimately has the responsibility for the business area. The ideal person for this role is someone to whom users will have to report if they plan to miss a session and who can reprimand them if they do. This thinking may seem harsh or cynical, but the risk is high that users may find more important things to do when the sessions begin. Such absenteeism can entirely undermine the process, and IS should not be called upon to police users.
- *facilitator*: In the best situations, the facilitator should not come from either the user community or IS, but rather from an independent area or consulting firm. This arrangement allows the session to be independent. That is, the facilitator of the JAD must be impartial and have overall responsibility for controlling the flow of the sessions. In the ideal scenario, the facilitator should report to the executive sponsor.

- *scribe*: This person is designated to record minutes and decisions and in many cases actually produces the models using a computer-aided software engineering (CASE) tool (see Chapter 6). A good scribe has knowledge of the business area, good analytical skills, and knowledge of CASE software. For these reasons, scribes often come from IS.
- *IS representatives:* IS personnel should be in the meetings not to provide requirements but rather to answer questions about the existing hardware and software. This information can be critical when discussing physical constraints of the existing systems and what data are currently available.
- *participant:* These are the users who have been selected to represent their respective areas. They attend the JAD sessions and are expected to come prepared to voice their opinions about what the system must do to accommodate the needs of their business unit. Participants are thus part of the "agree-to-agree" process and are empowered to vote on the actual specifications incorporated into the final software specification.
- *session leader:* This user is a participant who has been selected to lead the discussion on a particular subject. Such users must be prepared to provide specific topic issues so that the participants can openly discuss their opinions about what the session leader presents. The session leader may be asked to lead the discussion in a particular direction, or in some instances may have some preliminary work and may advocate a position on what the system should do. In these instances, the session leader may come to the meeting to ask for ratification from his/her peers.
- *observer:* These are users who attend the session to observe what is occurring, or in some cases to answer specific questions that may arise during the course of discussion. Observers are not empowered to talk unless they are asked. IS personnel, executives, and other interested parties typically attend JAD sessions to understand the process and learn from it. A special role exists when an observer serves as a "tie-breaker." In this capacity, the observer can be called upon, either by the facilitator or the session leader, to make a final judgment on a deadlocked issue. While this role is effective in getting decisions made, it can damage the democratic process under which JAD sessions are suppose to operate.

Below is an example of an 11-phase implementation outline for a JAD session with approximately 60 users in 10 different business areas.

Phase I: Define JAD Project Goals

The purpose of these sessions will be to meet with senior management and other key organization people in order to:

- get a clear understanding of the history of the project;
- finalize the scope and time frame requirements of the existing plan;
- understand the current organization and whether political or other constraints exist;
- jointly determine the number and size of the JAD sessions to be held;
- determine the best role of Information Systems in the JAD;
- define which key users and other managers should be interviewed individually prior to the JAD.

Produce a management guide after Phase I. Its purpose will be to define management's purpose, scope and objectives of the project. That is, it communicates management's direction and commitment. The management guide will be approved and issued by upper management to the participating users and information system personnel.

Phase II: Meet with Key Users and Managers

Estimate that you may need to interview about 20 people from key organizations prior to the JAD. These key users and managers should typically represent three levels of the organization. The purpose of these meetings will be to:

- get familiar with the existing systems;
- validate the number of sessions and specific participants needed;
- assess the technical expertise of the participating users;
- determine what specific information can be gathered by the users prior to the JAD sessions;
- gather previous analysis and design materials and documents that may exist and explain user requirements;
- discuss types of agendas and length of sessions;
- focus on specific requirements of certain users.

Schedule interviews to last about 60 to 90 minutes and prepare an agenda that will put the purpose and scope of the interview into perspective.

Phase III: Meet with Information Systems

Get a technical overview of the existing analysis performed and state of all working documents. Gather information on:

- project history;
- potential problems envisioned in implementing the new system;
- proposed hardware to support the new system (if relevant);
- IS representatives to participate in the JAD sessions;

- models and information that can be used in the JAD sessions.

Phase IV: Prepare JAD Approach

Prepare a complete JAD program that will outline recommendations for the number and types of sessions to be held. The JAD approach will also consider the modeling tools to be used and the methods for getting user sign-off. You should focus on the following specific issues:

- the number and type of preparation sessions necessary to get users familiar with the modeling terminology;
- what business processes have already been previously modeled and can be reviewed during the sessions. This is done to avoid discussing pro-cesses that users feel have already been defined from previous analysis sessions;
- the number and types of sessions along with specific users in atten-dance at each session;
- a Work Document of the proposed agendas for each type of session;
- overview of materials to be used such as overheads, flip charts and room requirements;
- proposed format of the user sign-off documents.

You should meet with upper management to review the proposed approach for implementation.

Phase V: Finalize JAD Organization Structure

Assign JAD Facilitators to specific sessions along with information systems support personnel (scribes, etc.). Determine the number of JAD facilitators required. You may need one JAD project leader to take overall responsibility for the entire engagement. A detailed timeline of specific deliverables and re-views should be produced for the entire project, including reports to upper management on the JAD session progress.

Phase VI: Hold Overview Training Sessions

Depending on the results of Phase IV, hold any necessary sessions to get users familiar with the methods that will be used during the JAD. This is typically a one-day course on analysis and includes an overview of modeling lingo and tools such as:

- business area analysis,
- process flow diagrams (data flows),
- entity relational diagrams and normalized data modeling,
- process specifications,
- activity matrices,

- state transition diagrams,
- decomposition models,
- object-oriented techniques,
- prototyping.

Phase VII: Hold JAD Workshop Sessions

Prior to these sessions, participants will be asked to come prepared with certain information they will need to assist in the process. This information may typically include sample forms and reports that they use or need. The workshop sessions will be held with a set time frame and an agenda of items typically including:

- *examine assumptions*: These will be reviewed with the users and opened for discussion. An assumption will either:
  - stay as it is,
  - be revised,
  - become an *open issue* (if consensus cannot be reached).
- *design business processes*: Review the collection of activities relating to the business and the system.
- *define data requirements*: Data are defined to support the business process. Data models are used, developed, and reviewed as necessary.
- *design screens*: The screens will typically use a series of menus or other branching techniques to define how users need to access the various functions. This is usually accomplished by identifying main menu and submenu selections.
- *design reports*: Report names are collected and completed with detailed report descriptions. These normally include
  - report name,
  - description,
  - frequency,
  - number of copies,
  - distribution list,
  - selection criteria,
  - sort criteria,
  - data elements.
- *identify open issues*: These issues are added throughout the sessions. Open issues are those that are not resolved after a period of discussion. These are kept on a separate chart.

Throughout the above processes, the scribe will be tracking minutes of the meeting as well as the open issues and new diagramming requirements.

Phase VIII: Resolve Open Issues

Prior to subsequent sessions, all open issues must be resolved, either by smaller work groups or if necessary by upper management. In any event, it is critical that this is managed by both the facilitator and upper management prior to moving to the next level sessions.

Phase IX: Prepare Materials for Workshop Review Sessions

The facilitator should produce a sign-off level document for review. Process and data models and process specifications will be reviewed and finalized. These sessions can also include prototype screens and reports.

Phase X: Hold Sign-Off Workshops

These workshops will be designed to review the results of the initial JAD sessions. The process and data models will be reviewed. If prototypes are used, the sessions will utilize screen walkthroughs as a method of gaining user acceptance. The exact number of review sessions will depend on the complexity of the system as well as the number of screens and reports to be prototyped.

During these sessions, user acceptance test plans may also be discussed and outlined for eventual submission to the responsible QA organization. This will typically involve a discussion of the minimum acceptance testing to be validated against the product and the mechanism for testing in the field.

Phase XI: Finalize Specification Document

After review sessions are completed, the Facilitator will prepare the final document to be submitted for approval and eventual implementation. If prototypes are used, the screens and reports can be moved into the software development (construction) phase. There should also be post-JAD reviews with the development teams to clarify information supplied in the final system specification document.

JAD is introduced and discussed in this chapter because of its generic inclusion in the user-interface phase of analysis. However, it should be noted that the above outline can be integrated with many of the subjects contained in later chapters of this text. The analyst may, therefore, wish to review this outline again after completing the book in order to determine how the other concepts of analysis can be used in a JAD session.

Problems and Exercises

1. Why is it so critical for the analyst to understand the "culture" of the organization?
2. Management support is a key component of the success of any project. Sometimes management may unfairly dictate the terms and deadlines of projects. Provide examples of different possible management opinions and how analysts can prepare effective responses to them.
3. What are the benefits of obtaining an Organization Chart prior to conducting interviews with users?
4. How does politics affect the role of the analyst and his/her approach to the information-gathering function of the interviews?
5. Why does understanding user skills provide the analyst with an advantage during interviews?
6. Explain how meeting a user in their office or place of work can assist the analyst in developing a better approach prior to the interview.
7. What is the purpose of JAD sessions? How do they compare to individual interviewing? Discuss the advantages and disadvantages of JAD.
8. Define each of the roles necessary for effective JAD sessions.
9. What is the purpose of a Management Guide?
10. Develop a proforma JAD outline for a project of 20 users in 3 business locations.
11. Name and explain what is meant by user categories.
12. How do user levels assist the analyst when preparing for user interviews?

Mini-Project

You have been assigned by your boss to interview Mr. Smith. Mr. Smith runs a department within Human Resources that essentially provides two tasks: (1) assigning employee identification numbers to new employees, and (2) sending applications for individual insurance to the firm's insurance provider.

The following is a list of processes that were learned about Mr. Smith's department procedures. It is dated January 1, 1999:

- The hiring department sends a copy of the hire letter to the department to notify them about a new hire.
- New employees must report to the department on their first day. The employee must bring the original hire letter.
- New employees are validated and asked to fill out a new hire employee form. The form contains the necessary information needed by the department.

- After the form is filled out, employees receive an identification card. Every identification card has a unique ID number.
- The insurance form information (on the new employee) is sent to the insurance company.
- The insurance company must accept all applications.
- The insurance company has 30, 60, or 90 days to respond to an application. The number of days depends on the employee's level.
- The department will follow up on late acceptance verifications.

Insurance confirmations are returned to the department, but the actual insurance package is sent to the individual.

All information on the employee collected by the department is filed in an employee folder.

Mr. Smith has been running this operation manually for over 25 years.

Assignment

Prepare 15 questions that you would ask Mr. Smith during the interview.

3
Overview of Analysis Tools

The Concept of the Logical Equivalent

The primary mission of an analyst or systems designer is to extract the physical requirements of the users and convert them to software. All software can trace its roots to a physical act or a physical requirement. A physical act can be defined as something that occurs in the interaction of people, that is, people create the root requirements of most systems, especially those in business. For example, when Mary tells us that she receives invoices from vendors and pays them thirty days later, she is explaining her physical activities during the process of receiving and paying invoices. When the analyst creates a technical specification which represents Mary's physical requirements, the specification is designed to allow for the translation of her physical needs into an automated environment. We know that software must operate within the confines of a computer, and such systems must function on the basis of logic. The logical solution does not always treat the process using the same procedures employed in the physical world. In other words, the software system implemented to provide the functions which Mary does physically will probably work differently and more efficiently than Mary herself. Software, therefore, can be thought of as a logical equivalent of the physical world. This abstraction, which I call the concept of the *logical equivalent* (LE), is a process that analysts must use to create effective requirements of the needs of a system. The LE can be compared to a schematic of a plan or a diagram of how a technical device works.

Your success in creating a concise and accurate schematic of the software that needs to be developed by a programmer will be directly proportional to how well you master the concept of the Logical Equivalent. Very often requirements are developed by analysts using various methods that do not always contain a basis for consistency, reconciliation and maintenance. There is usually far too much prose used as opposed to specific diagramming standards that are employed by engineers. After all, we are engineering a system through the development of software applications. The most critical step in obtaining the LE is the understanding of the process of Functional Decomposition. Functional Decomposition is the process for finding the most basic parts of a system, like defining all the parts of a car so that it can be built. It would be possible not from looking at a picture of the car, but rather at a schematic of all the functionally decomposed parts. Developing and engineering software is no different.

Below is an example of an analogous process using functional decomposition, with its application to the LE:

In obtaining the physical information from the user, there are a number of modeling tools that can be used. Each tool provides a specific function to derive the LE. The word "derive" has special meaning here. It relates to the process of Long Division, or the process or formula we apply when dividing one number by another. Consider the following example:

The above example shows the formula that is applied to a division problem. We call this formula long division. It provides the answer, and if we change any portion of the problem, we simply re-apply the formula and generate a new result. Most important, once we have obtained the answer, the value of the formula steps is only one of documentation. That is, if someone questioned the validity of the result, we could show them the formula to prove that the answer was correct (based on the input).

Now let us apply long division to obtaining the LE via functional decomposition. The following is a result of an interview with Joe, a bookkeeper, about his physical procedure for handling bounced checks.

> Joe the bookkeeper receives bounced checks from the bank. He fills out a Balance Correction Form and forwards it to the Correction Department so that the outstanding balance can be corrected. Joe sends a bounced check letter to the customer requesting a replacement check plus a $15.00 penalty (this is now included as part of the outstanding balance). Bounced checks are never re-deposited.

The appropriate modeling tool to use in this situation is a Data Flow Diagram (DFD). A DFD is a tool that shows how data enters and leaves a particular process. The process we are looking at with Joe is the handling of the bounced check. A DFD has four possible components:

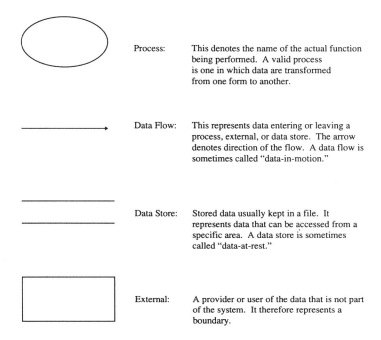

Process: This denotes the name of the actual function being performed. A valid process is one in which data are transformed from one form to another.

Data Flow: This represents data entering or leaving a process, external, or data store. The arrow denotes direction of the flow. A data flow is sometimes called "data-in-motion."

Data Store: Stored data usually kept in a file. It represents data that can be accessed from a specific area. A data store is sometimes called "data-at-rest."

External: A provider or user of the data that is not part of the system. It therefore represents a boundary.

Now let us draw the LE of Joe's procedure using DFD tools:

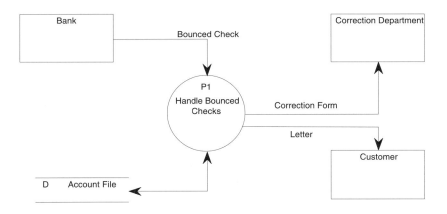

Figure 3.1 Data flow diagram for handling bounced checks.

The above DFD shows that bounced checks arrive from the bank, the Account Master file is updated, the Correction Department is informed and Customers receive a letter. The Bank, Correction Department and Customers are considered "outside" the system and are therefore represented logically as Externals. This diagram is considered to be at the first level or "Level 1" of functional decomposition. You will find that all modeling tools employ a method to functionally decompose. DFDs use a method called "Leveling."

The question is whether we have reached the most basic parts of this process or should we level further. Many analysts suggest that a fully decomposed DFD should have only one data flow input and one data flow output. Our diagram currently has many inputs and outputs and therefore it can be leveled further. The result of functionally decomposing to the second level (Level 2) is as shown in Figure 3.2.

Notice that the functional decomposition shows us that Process 1: Handling Bounced Checks is really made up of two sub-processes called 1.1 Update Balance and 1.2 Send Letter. The box surrounding the two processes within the Externals reflects them as components of the previous or parent level. The double sided arrow in Level 1 is now broken down to two separate arrows going in different directions because it is used to connect Processes 1.1 and 1.2. The new level is more functionally decomposed and a better representation of the LE.

Once again we must ask ourselves whether Level 2 can be further decomposed. The answer is yes. Process 1.1 has two outputs to one input. On the other hand, Process 1.2 has one input and one output and is therefore complete. Process 1.2 is said to be at the Functional Primitive, a DFD that cannot be decomposed further. Therefore, only 1.1 will be decomposed.

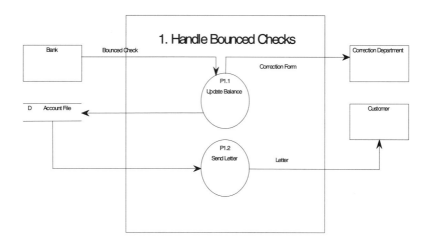

Figure 3.2 Level 2 data flow diagram for handling bounced checks.

Let us decompose 1.1 as follows:

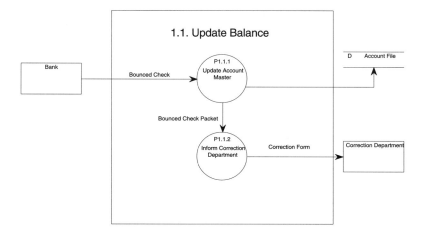

Figure 3.3 Level 3 data flow diagram for handling bounced checks.

Process 1.1 is now broken down into two sub processes: 1.1.1 Update Account Master and 1.1.2 Inform Correction Department. Process 1.1.2 is a Functional Primitive since it has one input and one output. Process 1.1.1 is also considered a Functional Primitive because the "Bounced Check Packet" flow is between the two processes and is used to show connectivity only. Functional decomposition is at Level-3 and is now complete.

The result of functional decomposition is the following DFD:

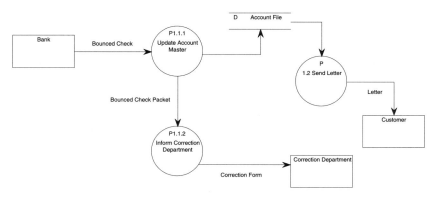

Figure 3.4 Functionally decomposed level-3 data flow diagram for handling bounced checks.

As in long division, only the complete result, represented above, is used as the answer. The preceding steps are formulas that we use to get to the lowest, simplest representation of the logical equivalent. Levels 1, 2 and 3 are used only for documentation of how the final DFD was determined.

The logical equivalent is an excellent method that allows analysts and systems designers to organize information obtained from users and to systematically derive the most fundamental representation of their process. It also alleviates unnecessary pressure to immediately understand the detailed flows and provides documentation of how the final schematic was developed.

Tools of Structured Analysis

Now that we have established the importance and goals of the logical equivalent, we can turn to a discussion of the methods available to assist the analyst. These methods serve as the tools to create the best models in any given situation, and thus the most exact logical equivalent. The tools of the analyst are something like those of a surgeon, who uses only the most appropriate instruments during an operation. It is important to understand that the surgeon is sometimes faced with choices about which surgical instruments to use; particularly with new procedures, there is sometimes disagreement among surgeons about which instruments are the most effective. The choice of tools for analysis and data processing is no different; indeed, it can vary more and be more confusing. The medical profession, like many others, is governed by its own ruling bodies. The American Medical Association and the American College of Physicians and Surgeons, as well as state and federal regulators, represent a source of standards for surgeons. Such a controlling body does not exist in the data processing industry, nor does it appear likely that one will arise in the near future. Thus, the industry has tried to standardize among its own leaders. The result of such efforts has usually been that the most dominant companies and organizations create standards to which others are forced to comply. For example, Microsoft has established itself as an industry leader by virtue of its software domination. Here, Might is Right!

Since there are no real formal standards in the industry, the analysis tools discussed here will be presented on the basis of both their advantages and their shortcomings. It is important then to recognize that no analysis tool (or methodology for that matter) can do the entire job, nor is any perfect at what it does. To determine the appropriate tool, analysts must fully understand the environment, the technical expertise of users and the time constraints imposed on the project. By "environment" we mean the existing system and technology, computer operations, and the logistics—both technically and geographically— of the new system. The treatment of the user interface should remain consistent with the guidelines discussed in Chapter 2.

The problem of time constraints is perhaps the most critical of all. The tools you would ideally like to apply to a project may not fit the time frame allotted. What happens, then, if there is not enough time? The analyst is now faced with selecting a second-choice tool that undoubtedly will not be as effective as the first one would have been. There is also the question of how tools are implemented, that is, can a hybrid of a tool be used when time constraints prevent full implementation of the desired tool?

Making Changes and Modifications

Within the subject of analysis tools is the component of maintenance modeling, or how to apply modeling tools when making changes or enhancements to an existing product. Maintenance modeling falls into two categories:

1. *Pre-Modeled*: where the existing system already has models that can be used to effect the new changes to the software.
2. *Legacy System*: where the existing system has never been modeled; any new modeling will therefore be incorporating analysis tools for the first time.

Pre-Modeled

Simply put, a Pre-Modeled product is already in a structured format. A structured format is one that employs a specific format and methodology such as the data flow diagram.

The most challenging aspects of changing Pre-Modeled tools are:

1. keeping them consistent with their prior versions, and
2. implementing a version control system that provides an audit-trail of the analysis changes and how they differ from the previous versions. Many professionals in the industry call this Version Control; however, care should be taken in specifying whether the version control is used for the maintenance of analysis tools. Unfortunately, Version Control can be used in other contexts, most notably in the tracking of program versions and software documentation. For these cases, special products exist in the market which provide special automated "version control" features. We are not concerned here with these products but rather with the procedures and processes that allow us to incorporate changes without losing the prior analysis documentation. This kind of procedure can be considered consistent with the long division example in which each time the values change, we simply re-apply the formula (methodology) to calculate the new answer. Analysis version control must therefore have the ability to take the modifications made to the software and integrate them with all the existing models as necessary.

Being Consistent

It is difficult to change modeling methods and/or CASE tools in the middle of the life cycle of a software product. One of our main objectives then is to try avoid doing so. How? Of course, the simple answer is to select the right tools and CASE software the first time. However, we all make mistakes, and more importantly, there are new developments in systems architecture that may make a new CASE product attractive. You would be wise to foresee this possibility and prepare for inconsistent tools implementation. The best offense here is to:

- ensure that your CASE product has the ability to transport models through an ASCII file or cut/paste method. Many have interfaces via an "export" function. Here, at least, the analyst can possibly convert the diagrams and data elements to another product.
- keep a set of diagrams and elements that can be used to establish a link going forward, that is, a set of manual information that can be re-input to another tool. This may be accomplished by simply having printed documentation of the diagrams; however, experience has shown that it is difficult to keep such information up to date. Therefore, the analyst should ensure that there is a procedure for printing the most current diagrams and data elements.

Should the organization decide to use different tools, e.g., process-dependency diagrams instead of data flow diagrams, or a different methodology such as crows'-foot method in Entity Relational Diagramming, then the analyst must implement a certain amount of reengineering. This means mapping the new modeling tools to the existing ones to ensure consistency and accuracy. This is no easy task, and it is strongly suggested that you document the diagrams so you can reconcile them.

Version Control

This book is not intended to focus on the generic aspects of version control; however, structured methods must have an audit trail. When a new process is changed, a directory should be created for the previous version. The directory name typically consists of the version and date such as: xyz1.21295, where xyz is the name of the product or program, 1.2 the version and 1295 the version date. In this way previous versions can be easily re-created or viewed. Of course, saving a complete set of each version may not be feasible or may be too expensive (in terms of disk space, etc.). In these situations, it is advisable to back up the previous version in such a manner as to allow for easy restoration. In any case, a process must exist, and it is crucial that there be a procedure to do backups periodically.

Legacy Systems

Legacy systems usually reside on mainframe computers and were developed using 3GL[2] software applications, the most typical being COBOL. Unfortunately, few of these systems were developed using structured tools. Without question, these are the systems most commonly undergoing change today in many organizations. All software is comprised of two fundamental components: processes and data. Processes are the actual logic and algorithms required by the system. Data, on the other hand, represent the information that the pro-cesses store and use. The question for the analyst is how to obtain the equivalent processes and data from the legacy system. Short of considering a complete rewrite, there are two basic approaches: the *data approach* and the *process approach.*

The Data Approach

Conversion of legacy systems for purposes of structured changes requires the modeling of the existing programs to allow for the use of analysis tools. The first step in this endeavor is the modeling of the existing files and their related data structures. Many 3GL applications may not exist in a relational or other database format. In either case, it is necessary to collect all of the data elements that exist in the system. To accomplish this, the analyst will typically need a conversion program that will collect the elements and import them into a CASE tool. If the data are stored in a relational or database system, this can be handled through many CASE products via a process known as reverse engineering. Here, the CASE product will allow the analyst to select the incoming database, and the product will then automatically import the data elements. It is important to note that these reverse-engineering features require that the incoming database is SQL (Structured Query Language) compatible. Should the incoming data file be of a non-database format (i.e., a flat file[3]), then a conversion program will need to be used. Once again, most CASE tools will have features that will list the required input data format.

Figure 3.5 is a sample of the reengineering capabilities of the System Architect product by Popkin Software and Systems.

---

[2] 3GL stands for "Third Generation Language." These programming languages belong to a family of design that typically uses compilers to transform a higher-level language into assembly code for the target computer.

[3] A file consisting of records of a single record type, in which there is no embedded structure information governing relationships between records. Microsoft Press, *Computer Dictionary*, 2nd ed., p. 169.

Figure 3.5 Reverse engineering using System Architect.

Once the data has been loaded into the CASE product, the various data models can be constructed. This process will be discussed further in Chapter 8.

Although we have shown above a tool for loading the data, the question still remains: How do we find all the data elements? Using COBOL as an example, one could take the following steps:

1. Identify all of the File Description (FD) tables in the COBOL application programs. Should they exist in an external software product like Librarian, the analyst can import the tables from that source. Otherwise the actual file tables will need to be extracted and converted from the COBOL application program source. This procedure is not difficult; it is simply another step that typically requires conversion utilities.

2. Scan all Working Storage Sections (see Figure 3.6) for data elements that are not defined in the File Description Section. This occurs very often when COBOL programmers do not define the actual elements until they are read into a Working Storage Section of the program. This situation, of course, requires further research, but it can be detected by scanning the code.

3. Look for other data elements that have been defined in Working Storage that should be stored as permanent data. Although this can be a

difficult task, the worst case scenario would involve the storing of redundant data. Redundant data is discussed further in Chapter 4.

4. Once the candidate elements have been discovered, ensure that appropriate descriptions are added. This process allows the Analyst to actually start defining elements so that decisions can be made during logic
data modeling (Chapter 5).

```
WORKING-STORAGE SECTION.
01 PAYROLL-RECORD.
    05      NAME.
            10      INITIAL-1                       PIC X.
            10      LAST-NAME                       PIC X(20).
    05      DATE-OF-HIRE.
            10      MONTH-OF-HIRE       PIC 99.
            10      DAY-OF-HIRE         PIC 99.
            10      YEAR-OF-HIRE        PIC 99.
    05      PAY-NUMBER                  PIC 9(6).
```

Figure 3.6 Working Storage Section of a COBOL program.

The Process Approach

The most effective way to model existing programs is the most direct way, that
is, the old-fashioned way: start reading and analyzing the code. Although this
approach may seem very crude, it is actually tremendously effective and productive. Almost all programming languages contain enough structure to allow
for identification of input and output of files and reports. By identifying the
data and reports, the analyst can establish a good data flow diagram as shown
in Figure 3.7.

```
DATA DIVISION.
FILE SECTION.
FD          PAYROLL-FILE
LABEL RECORDS ARE OMITTED.
01          PAYROLL-RECORD.
  05        I-PAYROLL-NUMBER                    PIC X(5).
  05        I-NAME                              PIC X(20).
  05        I-HOURS-WORKED                      PIC 99V9.
  05        FILLER                              PIC XXX.
  05        I-PAYRATE                           PIC 99V999.
  05        I-DEPENDENTS                        PIC 99.
  05        FILLER                              PIC X(20).


FD          REPORT-FILE
LABEL RECORDS ARE OMITTED.
01          REPORT-RECORD.
  05        O-PAYROLL-NUMBER                    PIC X(5).
  05        FILLER                              PIC XX.
  05        O-NAME                              PIC X(20).
  05        FILLER                              PIC XX.
  05        O-HOURS-WORKED                      PIC 99.9.
  05        FILLER                              PIC XX.
  05        O-PAYRATE                           PIC 99.999.
  05        FILLER                              PIC XX.
  05        O-DEPENDENTS                        PIC 99.
  05        FILLER                              PIC XX.
  05        O-GROSS-PAY                         PIC 999.99.
  05        FILLER                              PIC XX.
  05        O-TAX                               PIC 999.99.
  05        FILLER                              PIC XX.
  05        O-NET-PAY                           PIC 999.99.
```

Figure 3.7 Input data and report layouts of a COBOL program.

The above example shows two File Description (FD) tables defined in a COBOL program. The first table defines the input file layout of a payroll record, and the second is the layout of the output payroll report. This is translated into a DFD as shown in Figure 3.8.

In addition, depending on the program language, many input and output data and reports must be defined in the application code in specific sections of the program. Such is true in COBOL and many other 3GL products. Furthermore, many 4GL products force input and output verbs to be used when databases are manipulated. This is very relevant to any products that use embedded SQL to do input and output. The main point here is that you can produce various utility programs ("quick & dirty," as they call them) to enhance the accuracy and speed of identifying an existing program's input and output processing.

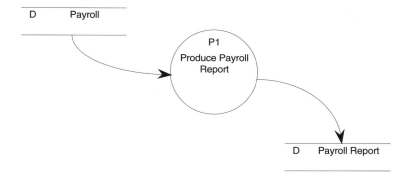

Figure 3.8 Translated COBOL file descriptions into a data flow diagram.

Once the flows in the data flow diagram are complete, the next step is to define the actual program logic, or what is typically called the *process specifications* (discussed later in this chapter). Once again there is no shortcut to save your going through the code program by program. There are some third-party software tools on the market that can provide assistance, but these tend to be very programming-language specific. Although the manual method may seem overwhelming, it can be accomplished successfully and will often provide great long-term benefits. Many companies will bring in part-time college interns and other clerical assistance to get this done. It should be noted that a CASE tool is almost always required to provide a place to document logic. This is especially important if the CASE tool will be used to generate actual program code.

Specification Formats

An ongoing challenge for many IS and software firms is determining what a good specification is. Many books written about analysis tools tend to avoid answering this question directly. When addressing the quality of a process specification, we must ultimately accept the inevitable prognosis that we can no longer be exclusively graphical. Although Yourdon and DeMarco[4] argue that structured tools need to be graphical, the essence of a specification is in its ability to define the algorithms of the application program itself. It is therefore impossible to avoid writing a form of pseudocode. Pseudocode is essentially a

---

[4] Ed Yourdon, *Modern Structured Analysis*, Yourdon Press, and Tom DeMarco, *Structured Analysis and System Specification*, Yourdon Press, focus on the importance of using graphic diagrams wherever possible.

generic representation of how the real code must execute. Ultimately, the analyst must be capable of developing clear and technically correct algorithms. The methods and styles of process specifications are outlined on the following pages. The level of technical complexity of these specifications varies based on a number of issues:

1. the technical competence of the analyst. Ultimately, the analyst must have the ability to write algorithms to be most effective.

2. the complexity of the specification itself. The size and scope of specifications will vary, and as a result so will the organization of the requirements.

3. the type of the specifications required. There are really two levels of specifications: business and programming. The business specification is very prose-oriented and is targeted for review by a non-technical user. Its main purpose is to gain confirmation from the user community prior to investment in the more specific and technical programming specification. The programming specification, on the other hand, needs to contain the technical definition of the algorithms and is targeted for technical designers and programmers.

4. the competence of the programming staff as well as the confidence that the analyst has in that staff. The size and capabilities of the programming resources will usually be directly proportional to the emphasis that the analyst will need to place on the specifics and quality needed for a process specification.

Although the alternative techniques for developing a Process Specification are further discussed in Chapters 4 and 7, the chart below should put into perspective the approach to deciding the best format and style of communication. It is important to understand that overlooking the process specification and its significance to the success of the project can have catastrophic effects on the entire development effort. The table below reflects the type of specification suggested based on the technical skills of the users:

High-Level, Nontechnical Users	Technically Literate Users	Very Technical Users or MIS Personnel
Business specification in prose	Business specification in prose	No need for separate business specification
Do not show programming specification	Show and review programming specification	Incorporate business specification with programming specification

Figure 3.9 Types of process specifications based on user computer literacy.

Figures 3.10 and 3.11 are sample business and programming specifications, respectively, that depict the flow from a user specification to the detailed program logic.

Client:	Date: 9/5/99
XYZ Corporation	
Application:	Supersedes:
Operations Database	
Subject:	Author:
Contact Management	A. Langer
Process:	Page:
Overview - Business Spec	1 of 2

Overview

The contact management process will allow users to add, modify or delete specific contacts. Contacts will be linked to various tables including Company. A contact refers to a person who is related to XYZ for business reasons. It can be a client, a vendor, a consultant, a person involved in a negotiation, etc.

Contact General Information:

The database must allow for the centralization of all the contacts handled by all the departments in XYZ.
The database and screens will be focused on the following information component groupings:

Basic Information

This is the minimum data requirement and includes such elements as Name, Title, Organization, Phone, Fax, Address, Country, etc.

Contact Profile Information

Further qualification and related elements. Relations include:

- department
- type of client
- nature of client (primary, technical)
- interest of prospect
- importance of client
- memberships (FTUG)
- FT employee

This is a business specification that reflects the overall requirements in prose format. Its focus is to provide the user who is not technical with a document that he or she can authorize. This business specification should then point to the detailed programming logic that is shown in Fig. 3.11.

Figure 3.10 Sample Business Specification.

Client: XYZ Company	Date: 9/15/99
Application: Contact Management	Supersedes: 9/5/99
Subject: Program Specification Detail	Author: A. Langer
Spec-ID FTCM01 - Add/Modify Screen Processing	Page: 1 of 1

Process Flow Description:
The user will input information in the top form. At a minimum, at least the Last Name or Contact ID will be entered. The system must check a Security indicator prior to allowing a user to modify a Contact. The Security will be by Department or Everyone. Therefore, if the Modify button is selected and the user is restricted by a different department, Display:
      " Access Denied, not eligible to modify, Department Restriction"

If Security authorized, the Add/Modify Button will activate the following business rules:

      If Contact-ID (cntid) not blank
      Find match and replace entered data into record
      If no match display "Invalid Contact-ID" and refresh cursor

> This area actually states the algorithm required by the program. It is in a format called Pseudocode" meaning "false code." This type of logic resembles Cobol format. (see Chapter 4)

    If Contact-ID (cntid) Blank and Last-Name (cntlname) Blank then
      Display " Contact-ID or Last-Name must be entered"
      Place Cursor at Contact-ID (cntid) entry.

      If Contact-ID (cntid) Blank and Last-Name (cntlname) + First-Name (cntfname) is Duplicate
      Display Window to show matches so that user can determine if contact already in system
      If user selects the Add Anyway button
            assume new contact with same name and assign new Contact-ID (cntid)
      else
            upon selection bring in existing data and close window.
    Else
      Create new record with all new information fields and assign Contact-ID (cntid)

    If Company button activated
      Prompt user for Company-ID (cmpcd) and/or Company-Name (cmpna)
      If duplicate
            link foreign-key pointer to matched company
      else
            add Company-Name (cntcmpna) to Contact Table only
            Display "You must use Company Screen to Link, Company Master File Not Updated"

Figure 3.11 Sample Programming Specification.

Problems and Exercises

1. Describe the concept of the logical equivalent as it relates to defining the requirements of a system.
2. What is the purpose of functional decomposition? How is the leveling of a DFD consistent with this concept?
3. How does Long Division depict the procedures of decomposition ? Explain.
4. What is a legacy system ?
5. Processes and data represent the two components of any software application. Explain the alternative approaches to obtaining process and data information from a legacy system.

6. What is reverse engineering? How can it be used to build a new system?
7. Why is analysis version control important?
8. Explain the procedures for developing a DFD from an existing program.
9. What is the purpose of a process specification? Explain.
10. Outline the differences between a business specification and a programming specification. What is their relationship, if any?

4
Process-Based Tools

Data Flow Diagrams

Chapter 3 discussed the concept of the logical equivalent, justifying and defining it by showing a functional decomposition example using data flow diagrams (DFD). In this section, we will expand upon the capabilities of the DFD by explaining its purpose, advantages and disadvantages (described later as the Good, the Bad and the Ugly) and most important: how to draw and use it.

Purpose

Yourdon's original concept of the DFD was that it was a way to represent a process graphically. A process can be defined as a vehicle that changes or transforms data. The DFD therefore becomes a method of showing users strictly from a logical perspective how data travels through their function and is transformed. The DFD should be used in lieu of a descriptive prose representation of a user's process. Indeed, many analysts are familiar with the frustrations of the meeting where users attend to provide feedback on a specification prepared in prose. These specifications are often long descriptions of the processes. We ask users to review it, but most will not have had the chance to do so before the meeting, and those who have, may not recollect all the issues. The result? Users and analysts are not in a position to properly address the needs of the system, and the meeting is less productive than planned. This typically leads to more meetings and delays. More important, the analyst has never provided an environment in which the user can be walked through the processes. Conventional wisdom says that people remember 100% of what they see, but only 50% of what they read. The graphical representation of the DFD can provide users with an easily understood view of the system.[5]

The DFD also establishes the boundary of a process. This is accomplished with two symbols: the terminator (external) and the data store. As we will see, both represent data that originate or end at a particular point.

---

[5] Ed Yourdon, *Modern Structured Analysis*, pp. 134–35.

The DFD also serves as the first step toward the design of the system blue-print. What do we mean by a *blueprint*? Let us consider the steps taken to build a house. The first step is to contact a professional who knows how to do design. We call this individual an *architect*. The architect is responsible for listening to the homebuilder and drawing a conceptual view of the house that the homebuilder wants. The result is typically two drawings. The first is a prototype drawing of the house, representing how the house will appear to the homebuilder. The second is the blueprint, which represents the engineering requirements. Although the homebuilder may look at the blueprint, it is meant primarily for the builder or contractor who will actually construct the house. What has the architect accomplished? The homebuilder has a view of the house to verify the design, and the builder has the specifications for construction.

Let us now translate this process to that of designing software. In this scenario, the analyst is the architect and the user is the homebuyer. The meeting between the architect and the homebuyer translates into the requirements session, which will render two types of output: a business requirements outline and prototype of the way the system will function, and a schematic represented by modeling tools for programmers. The former represents the picture of the house and the latter the blueprint for the builder. Designing and building systems, then, is no different conceptually from building a house. The DFD is one of the first—if not *the* first—tools that the analyst will use for drawing graphical representations of the user's requirements. It is typically used very early in the design process when the user requirements are not clearly and logically defined.

Figures 4.1 and 4.2 show the similarities between the functions of an architect and those of an analyst.

Designing the House

| Drawing | Architect | Blueprint |

Figure 4.1 The interfaces required to design and build a house.

Designing the System

| Prototype | Analyst | DFD |

Figure 4.2 The interfaces required to design and build a system.

How do we begin to construct the DFD for a given process? The following five steps serve as a guideline:

1. Draw a bubble to represent the process you are about to define.
2. Ask yourself what thing(s) initiate the process: what is coming in? You will find it advantageous to be consistent in where you show process inputs. Try to model them to the left of the process. You will later be able to immediately define your process inputs when looking back at your DFD, especially when using them for system enhancements.
3. Determine the process outputs, or what things are coming out, and model them to the right of the process as best you can.
4. Establish all files, forms or other components that the process needs to complete its transformation. These are usually data stores that are utilized during processing. Model these items either above or below the process
5. Name and number the process by its result. For example, if a process produces invoices, label it "Create Invoices." If the process accomplishes more than one event, label it by using the "and" conjunction. This method will allow you to determine whether the process is a functional primitive. Ultimately, the name of the process should be one that most closely associates the DFD with what the user does. Therefore, name it what the user calls it! The number of the process simply allows the analyst to identify it to the system and most important to establish the link to its children levels during functional decomposition.

Let us now apply this procedure to the example below:

Vendors send Mary invoices for payment. Mary stamps on the invoice the date received and matches the invoice with the original purchase order request. Invoices are placed in the Accounts Payable folder. Invoices that exceed thirty days are paid by check in two-week intervals.

Step 1: Draw the Bubble

Figure 4.3 A process bubble.

Step 2: Determine the inputs

In this example we are receiving an invoice from a Vendor. The Vendor is considered a Terminator since it is a boundary of the input and the user cannot control when and how the invoice will arrive. The invoice itself is represented as a data flow coming from the Vendor terminator into the process:

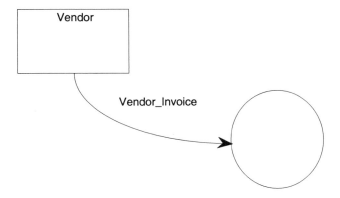

Figure 4.4 Terminator sending invoice to the process.

Step 3: Determine the outputs of the process

In this case the result of the process is that the Vendor receives a check for payment:

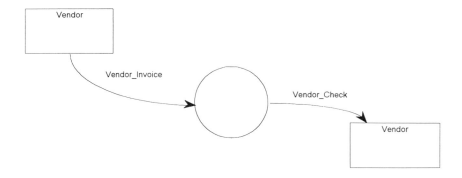

Figure 4.5 DFD with output of check sent to vendor.

Step 4: Determine the "processing" items required to complete the process

In this example, the user needs to:

- match the invoice to the original purchase order;
- create a new account payable for the invoice in a file; and
- eventually retrieve the invoice from the Accounts Payable file for payment.

Note that in Figure 4.6 the Purchase Order file is accessed for input (or retrieval) and therefore is modeled with the arrow coming into the process. The Accounts Payable file, on the other hand, shows a two-sided arrow because entries are created (inserted) and retrieved (read). In addition, arrows to and from data stores may or may not contain data flow names. For reasons that will be explained later in the chapter, the inclusion of such names is not recommended.

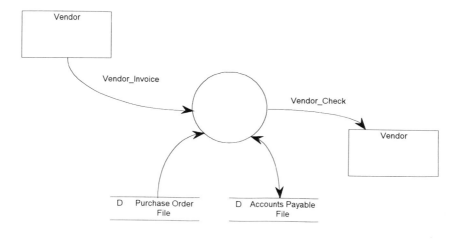

Figure 4.6 DFD with interfacing data stores.

Step 5: Name and number the process based on its output or its user definition.

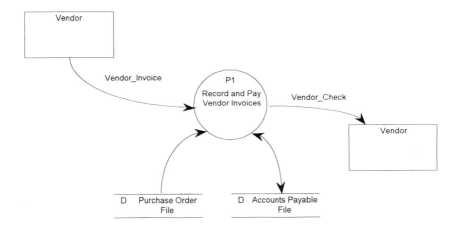

Figure 4.7 Final named DFD.

The process in Figure 4.7 is now a complete DFD that describes the event of the user. You may notice that the procedures for stamping the invoice with the receipt date and the specifics of retrieving purchase orders and accounts payable information are not explained. These other components will be defined using other modeling tools. Once again, the DFD reflects only data flow and boundary information of a process.

The DFD in Figure 4.7 can be leveled further to its functional primitive. The conjunction in the name of the process can sometimes help analysts to discover that there is actually more than one process within the event they are modeling. Based on the procedure outlined in Chapter 3, the event really consists of two processes: Recording Vendor Invoices and Paying Vendor Invoices. Therefore, P1 can be leveled as shown in Figure 4.8.

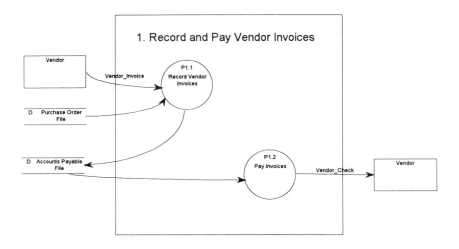

Figure 4.8 Leveled DFD for Record and Pay Invoices process.

Advantages of the DFD

Many opponents of the DFD argue that this procedure takes too long. You must ask yourself: What's the alternative? The DFD offers the analyst several distinct advantages. Most fundamentally, it depicts flow and boundary. The essence of knowing boundary is first to understand the extent of the process prior to beginning to define something that may not be complete or accurate. The concept is typically known as *top-down*, but the effort can also be conceived as step-by-step. The analyst must first understand the boundary and flows prior to doing anything else. The steps following this will procedurally gather more detailed information until the specification is complete.

Another important aspect of the DFD is that it represents a graphical display of the process and is therefore a usable document that can be shown to both users and programmers, serving the former as a process verification and the latter as the schematic (blueprint) of the system from a technical perspective. It can be used in JAD sessions and as part of the business specification documentation. Most important, it can be used for maintaining and enhancing a process.

Disadvantages of the DFD

The biggest drawback of the DFD is that it simply takes a long time to create: so long that the analyst may not receive support from management to complete it. This can be especially true when there is a lot of leveling to be performed. Therefore, many firms shy away from the DFD on the basis that it is not practical. The other disadvantage of the DFD is that it does not model time-dependent behavior well, that is, the DFD is based on very finite processes that typically have a very definable start and finish. This, of course, is not true of all processes, especially those that are event driven. *Event-driven systems* will be treated more thoroughly when we discuss State Transition Diagrams later in this chapter.

The best solution to the time-consuming leveling dilemma is to avoid it as much as possible. That is, you should avoid starting at too high a summary level and try to get to the functional primitive as soon as you can. If in our example, for instance, the analyst had initially seen that the DFD had two processes instead of one, then the parent process could have been eliminated altogether. This would have resulted in an initial functional primitive DFD at Level 1. The only way to achieve this efficiency on a consistent basis is through practice. Practice will eventually result in the development of your own analysis style or approach. The one-in, one-out principle of the logical equivalent is an excellent way of setting up each process. Using this method, every event description that satisfies one-in, one-out will become a separate functional primitive process. Using this procedure virtually eliminates leveling. Sometimes users will request to see a summary-level DFD. In these cases the functional primitives can be easily combined or "leveled-up."

Process Flow Diagrams

While the data flow diagram provides the analyst with the LE of a process, it does not depict the sequential steps of the process, which can be an important piece of information in analyzing the completeness of a system. Understanding the sequence of steps is especially important in situations where the information gathered from users is suspect or possibly inaccurate. A process flow diagram (PFD) can reveal processes and steps that may have been missed, because it requires users to go through each phase of their system as it occurs in its actual sequence. Having users go through their process step by step can help them remember details that they might otherwise have overlooked. Therefore, using process flows provides another tool that can test the completeness of the interview and LE.

Because of this advantage of the PFD, many methodologies, such as the James Martin technique,[6] suggest that analysts should always use PFDs instead of DFDs. However, it is my opinion that these two models not only can coexist but may actually complement each other. This section will focus on how a process model is implemented and balanced against a DFD.

What Is a PFD?

PFDs were derived originally from flowcharts. Flowcharts, however, while they are still valuable for certain diagramming tasks, are too clumsy and detailed to be an effective and structured modeling tool. The PFD represents a more streamlined and flexible version of a flowchart. Like a DFD, the PFD suggested here contains processes, externals, and data flows. However, PFDs focus on how externals, flows, and processes occur in relation to sequence and time, while DFDs focus only on the net inputs and outputs of flows and the disposition of data at rest.

The diagram on the following page is an example of a process flow.

---

[6] The James Martin technique is a methodology that replaces data flow with process flows as its vehicle to depict events as opposed to Yourdon's method of data flow diagrams.

Editorial Directory Design Process Flow

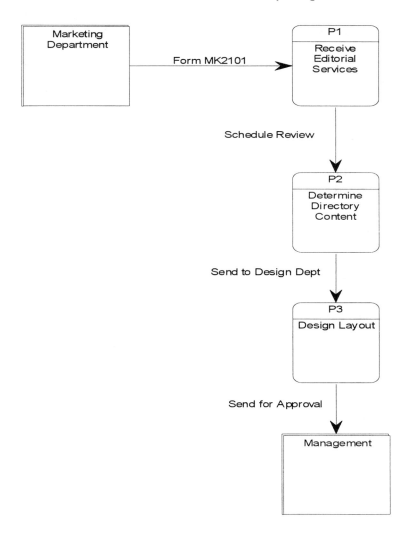

Figure 4.9 Sample process flow diagram.

The above figure shows how a PFD depicts flows from one task to another. As with a DFD, externals are shown by a rectangle. Flows are labeled and represent information in transition. Unlike DFDs, process flows do not necessarily require labeling of the flow arrows, and the processes themselves reflect descriptively what the step in the system is attempting to accomplish, as opposed to necessarily defining an algorithm.

Perhaps the most significant difference between a DFD and a process flow is in its integration as a structured tool within the data repository. For example, a labeled data flow from a DFD must create an entry into the data dictionary or repository. Flow arrows from PFDs do not. Furthermore, a functional primitive data flow points to a process specification; no such requirement exists in a process flow. Figure 4.10 represents a DFD depiction of the same process shown in Figure 4.9 above.

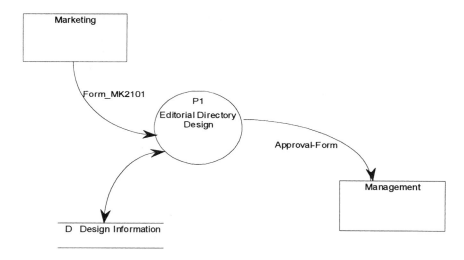

Figure 4.10 PFD in DFD format.

Note that the PFD and the DFD share the same boundaries of externals (i.e., Marketing and Management). The DFD flows, however, must be defined in the data dictionary or repository and therefore contain integrated formulas. The other notable difference lies in the interface of the data store "Design Information," which will eventually be defined as an entity and decomposed using logic data modeling techniques.

What are the relative benefits of using a PFD and a DFD? The answer lies in the correspondence between the process rectangle and the DFD process bubble. Process rectangles actually represent sequential steps within the DFD. They can be compared to an IF statement in pseudocode or a simple statement to produce a report or write information to a file. The PFD, in a sense, can provide a visual depiction of how the process specification needs to be detailed. One functional primitive DFD can thus be related to many process rectangles.

Based on the above analysis, therefore, a PFD can be justified as a tool in support of validating process specifications from within a DFD. In addition, the PFD might reveal a missing link in logic that could result in the creation of a new DFD. Based on this argument, the process flow can be balanced against a DFD and its functional primitives. Finally, the PFD has the potential to provide a graphic display of certain levels of logic code. The corresponding PFD for the DFD shown in Figure 4.8 is illustrated in Figure 4.11.

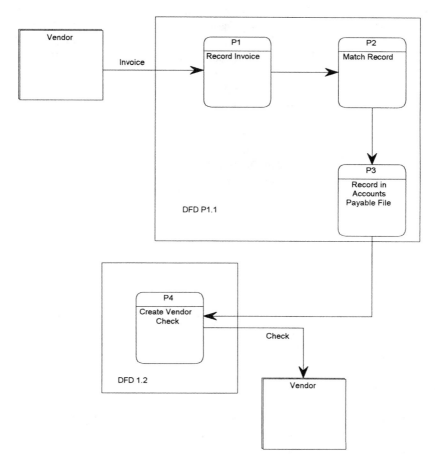

Figure 4.11 PFD and DFD cross-referenced.

Sequence of Implementation

If both a DFD and a PFD are to be created, which should be done first? While the decision can be left to the preference of the analyst, it is often sensible to start with the DFD. A DFD can be created very efficiently, and it is useful to be able to compare the DFD children against the sequential flow of the PFD. Creating the DFD first also supports the concept of decomposition, since the PFD will inevitably relate to the process specification of a functional primitive DFD. While this approach seems to be easier in most cases, there is also justification for creating a PFD first, especially if an overview flow diagram provides a means of scoping the boundaries of an engineering process.

Data Dictionary

The data dictionary (DD) is quite simply a dictionary that defines data. We have seen that the data flow diagram represents a picture of how information flows to and from a process. As we pick up data elements during the modeling design, we effectively "throw" them into the data dictionary. Remember, all systems are comprised of two components: Data and Processes. The DD represents the data portion.

There is a generic format followed by analysts, called DD notation. The conventional notations are listed below:

=	Equivalence
+	Concatenation
[ ]	Either/Or Boundary
/	Either/Or separator
( )	Optional
{ }	Iterations of
**	Comment

Equivalence (=):

The notion of equivalence does not express mathematical equality but rather indicates that the values on the right side of the equal sign represent all the possible components of the element on the left.

Concatenation (+):

This should not be confused with or compared to "plus"; it is rather the joining of two or more components. For example: Last_Name + First_Name means that these two data elements are being pieced together sequentially.

Either/Or with Option Separator ([/]):

Means "one of the following" and therefore represents a finite list of possible values. An example would include the definition of Country = [USA/Canada/United Kingdom/etc.].

Optional ( ):

The value is not required in the definition. A very common example is middle initial: Name = Last_Name + First_Name + (Middle_Init).

Iterations of { }:

The value between the separators occurs a specific or infinite number of times. Examples include:

1{X}5	The element "X" occurs from one to five times
1{X}	The element "X" occurs from one to infinity
3{X}3	The element "X" must occur three times.

Comments (**)

Comments are used to describe the element or point the definition to the appropriate process specification should the data element not be definable in the DD. We will explain this case later in this section.

Now that we have defined the components of the DD, it is important to expand on its interface with other modeling tools, especially the DFD. If we recall the example used earlier to describe drawing a DFD, the input data flow was labeled "Vendor_Invoice" (see Figure 4.4). The first DD rule to establish is that all labeled data flow names must be defined in the DD. Therefore, the DFD interfaces with the DD by establishing data element definitions from its labeled flows. To define Vendor_Invoice, we look at the physical invoices and ascertain from the user the information the system requires. It might typically be defined as follows:

Vendor_Invoice=   Vendor_Invoice+Invoice_Number+Vendor_Invoice_Date+
Vendor_Invoice_Name+ Vendor_Invoice_Address_Line_1 +
Vendor_Invoice_Address_Line_2 +
Vendor_Invoice_Address_Line_3 + Vendor_State + Vendor_City +
Vendor_ Zip_Code + Vendor_Salesperson + PO_Number +
Vendor_Date_Shipped + Vendor_Shipped_Via +
Vendor_Required_Date + Vendor_Terms + 1{Item-Quantity +
Item_Description + Item_Unit_Price + Item_Amount} + Subtotal
Sales_Tax + Shipping/Handling + Invoice_Total_Due

The above example illustrates what a vendor invoice would usually contain and what is needed to be captured by the system. Note that Vendor_Invoice is made up of component data elements that in turn need to be defined in the DD. In addition, there is a repeating group of elements { Item-Quantity + Item_Description + Item_Unit_Price + Item_Amount } that represents each line item that is a component of the total invoice. Since there is no limit to the number of items that could make up one invoice, the upper limit of the iterations clause is left blank and therefore represents infinity. Figure 4.12 is a sample of how the physical invoice would appear.

It should be noted that many of the DD names have a qualifier of "Vendor" before the field name. This is done to ensure uniqueness in the DD as well as to document where the data element emanated from the DFD. To ensure that all data elements have been captured into the DD, we again apply functional decomposition, only this time we are searching for the functional primitive of the DD entry. We will call this functionally decomposed data element an Elementary Data Element. An Elementary Data Element is therefore an element that cannot be broken down any further. Let us functionally decompose Vendor_Invoice by looking to the right of the definition and picking up the data elements that have not already been defined in the DD. These elements are:

Vendor_Invoice_Number	=	1 { Numeric} 5
Vendor_Invoice_Date	=	8 { Numeric }8
Vendor_Invoice_Name	=	1 { Alphanumeric } 35
Vendor_Invoice_Address_Line_1	=	1 { Alphanumeric } 25
Vendor_Invoice_Address_Line_1	=	1 { Alphanumeric } 25
Vendor_Invoice_Address_Line_1	=	1 { Alphanumeric } 25
Vendor_State	=	** All States in USA, Self Defining
Vendor_City	=	1 { Alphanumeric } 30
Vendor_Zip	=	5 { Numeric } 5 + (4 {Numeric} 4)
Vendor_Salesperson	=	1 { Alphanumeric } 20
PO_Number	=	4 { Alphanumeric } 4
Vendor_Date_Shipped	=	8 { Numeric } 8
Vendor_Shipped_Via	=	1 { Alphanumeric } 10
Vendor_Required_Date	=	8 { Numeric } 8
Vendor_Terms	=	1 { Numeric } 3
Item_Quantity	=	1 { Numeric } 5
Item_Description	=	1 { Alphanumeric } 30
Item_Unit_Price	=	** Dollars Self-Defining
Item_Amount	=	** See Process Spec xxx
Subtotal	=	** See Process Spec yyy
Sales_Tax	=	1 { Numeric } 3 ** Assumed Percentage
Shipping/Handling	=	** Dollars Self-Defining
Invoice_Total_Due	=	** See Process Spec zzz

The following rules and notations apply:
1. A *self-defining definition* is allowed if the data definition is obvious to the firm or if it is defined in some general documentation (e.g., Standards and Reference Manual). In the case of Vendor_State, an alter-

native would be: Vendor_State = [AL/NY/NJ/CA..., etc.] for each state value.

2. Data elements that are derived as a result of a calculation cannot be defined in the DD but rather point to a process specification where they can be properly identified. This also provides consistency in that all calculations and algorithms can be found in the Process Specification section.

3. Typically values such as Numeric, Alphanumeric, and Alphabetic do not require further breakdown unless the firm allows for special characters. In that case, having the exact values defined is appropriate.

4. An *iteration definition*, where the minimum and maximum limit are the same (e.g., 8 { Numeric } 8), means that the data element is fixed (that is, must be 8 characters in length).

The significance of this example is that the DD itself, through a form of functional decomposition, creates new entries into the DD while finding the elementary data element. A good rule to follow is that any data element used in defining another data element must also be defined in the DD. The DD serves as the center for storing these entries and will eventually provide the data necessary to produce the stored data model. This model will be produced using logic data modeling (discussed in Chapter 5).

Precision Products
1456 Emerson St
Parsippany, NJ 07055-1254

INVOICE NO: 12345
DATE: February 25, 1997

To:

A. Langer & Assoc., Inc.
20 Waterview Blvd
Third Floor
Parsippany, NJ 07054

SALESPERSON	P.O. NUMBER	DATE SHIPPED	SHIPPED VIA	REQUIRED DATE	TERMS
John Smith	AC34	9/15/95	UPS	10/5/95	30 days

QUANTITY	DESCRIPTION	UNIT PRICE	AMOUNT
4	Towels	$ 10.00	$ 40.00
3	Shirts	$ 25.00	$ 75.00
			$ 0.00
			$ 0.00
			$ 0.00
			$ 0.00
			$ 0.00
		SUBTOTAL	$ 115.00
		SALES TAX	$ 0.00
		SHIPPING & HANDLING	$ 4.50
		TOTAL DUE	$ 119.50

Figure 4.12 Sample invoice form.

SQL Data Types

Relational database products define data elements using a construct called structured query language (SQL). SQL was originally created by IBM as a standard programming language to query databases. SQL quickly became the de facto standard in the computer industry, and while the generic data types used above are useful in understanding the pure definition of data elements, database analysts use SQL data types to define data elements. The principal SQL data types are as follows:

Alphanumeric or Character Data Elements

These elements can be defined in two ways: (1) as a fixed-length string; or (2) as a variable-length string. The word "string" means that there is a succession of alphanumeric values that are concatenated to form a value. For example, the string "LANGER" is really equivalent to five iterations of different alphanumeric characters that are connected, or concatenated, together. A fixed-length alphanumeric data type is denoted by CHAR(n), where n is the size, or qualifier, of the element. Fixed length means that the size of the data element must always be n. This correlates to the generic definition of $n\{alphanumeric\}n$, which states that the lower and upper limits of the iteration are the same. For example, if the data element INVOICE was defined as a fixed-length string of seven characters, its SQL definition is defined as CHAR(7).

Variable alphanumeric fields, on the other hand, relate to strings that can vary in size within a predefined string limit. This means that the size of the string can fall anywhere between one character and its maximum size. The SQL data type definition of a variable-length field is VARCHAR2 (n),[7] where n represents the maximum length of the string. If the data element "LAST_NAME" was defined as having up to 35 characters, its SQL data definition would be VARCHAR2(35). This SQL data definition is equivalent to $1\{alphanumeric\}35$.

Numbers or Numeric Data Elements

These elements can be defined in various ways. Let's first look at the representation of a whole number in SQL. Whole numbers are known mathematically as integers. SQL supports integers using the INTEGER(n) format, where n is the number of digits in the whole number. However, as is so often available with SQL definitions, there is an alternative way of specifying an integer using the NUMBER clause. Thus NUMBER(n) will also store a whole number value up to n positions in length. The equivalent representation using the generic format is $n\{number\}n$.

Real numbers, or those that contain decimal positions, cannot be defined using the INTEGER clause but can be defined using NUMBER. For example, a number that contains up to 5 whole numbers and 2 decimal places would be defined as NUMBER(7,2). Note that the first digit represents the total size of the field, that is, 5 whole digits plus 2 decimal positions, which equals 7 positions in total. The number "2" after the comma represents the number of decimal places after the integer portion of the number. The second position preceding the comma represents the number of places from the total digits that are assumed to be decimal positions. The word assumption is important here in that it means that an actual decimal point (.) is not stored in the data type. An

---

[7] There is an SQL data definition called VARCHAR, but most database products use the revised definition of VARCHAR2.

alternative notation is NUMERIC. NUMERIC, as opposed to NUMBER, can be used only to define real numbers. However, it uses the same format as the NUMBER datatype to define a real number: NUMERIC (7,2). Depicting real numbers using the generic format is possible but tricky. The generic specification would be (1{number}5) + 2{number}2. Note that the first part of the definition, the whole number portion, is defined within optional brackets. This is done to allow for the situation where the number has only a decimal value, such as ".25."

Special Data Types

SQL offers special notation that makes it easy to depict specialized data definitions, like date and time. Below are just some examples of the common special notation used:

DATE:	denotes a valid date by assigning a 4-digit year. This kind of notation is compliant with year-2000 standards. The validity of the value is handled internally by SQL.
TIME:	denotes a valid time using the format *hh/mm/ssss*, where *hh* is two digits of the hour; *mm* is two digits of the minute, and *ssss* are four digits of the second. This format can vary by SQL product.
TIMESTAMP:	denotes the concatenation of the Date and the Time SQL clauses. The combination of the two values provides a unique specification of the exact time, day, and year that something has occurred.
FLOAT:	denotes the storage of a value as a floating point number. The format is usually FLOAT (*n*), where *n* represents the size in digits.

The data element list below shows the definitions from Figure 4.12 in both the generic and SQL formats:

Data Element	Generic Format	SQL Format
Vendor_Invoice_Number	1 { Numeric} 5	Number (5)
Vendor_Invoice_Date	8 { Numeric }8	Date
Vendor_Invoice_Name	1 { Alphanumeric } 35	Varchar2 (35)
Vendor_Invoice_Address_Line_1	1 { Alphanumeric } 25	Varchar2 (25)
Vendor_Invoice_Address_Line_2	1 { Alphanumeric } 25	Varchar2 (25)
Vendor_Invoice_Address_Line_3	1 { Alphanumeric } 25	Varchar2 (25)
Vendor_State	** All States in USA, Self Defining	Char (2)[8]
Vendor_City	1 { Alphanumeric } 30	Varchar2 (30)
Vendor_Zip	5 { Numeric } 5 + (4 {Numeric} 4)	Varchar2 (9)[9]
Vendor_Salesperson	1 { Alphanumeric } 20	Varchar2 (20)
PO_Number	4 { Alphanumeric } 4	Char (4)
Vendor_Date_Shipped	8 { Numeric } 8	Date
Vendor_Shipped_Via	1 { Alphanumeric } 10	Varchar2 (10)
Vendor_Required_Date	8 { Numeric } 8	Date
Vendor_Terms	1 { Numeric } 3	Number (3)
Item_Quantity	1 { Numeric } 5	Number (5)
Item_Description	1 { Alphanumeric } 30	Varchar2 (30)

Process Specifications

Many analysts define a *process specification* as everything else about the process not already included in the other modeling tools. Indeed, it must contain

---

[8] The contents of the data element would be enforced by using a database constraint. A database constraint is provided by the database product and is used to enforce the contents of a particular data element or attribute.

[9] The contents of a nine-digit ZIP code can be handled in SQL by adding a constraint as explained in Footnote 8, or by breaking the element into two separate parts, or as two data elements.

the remaining information that normally consists of business rules and application logic. DeMarco suggested that every functional primitive DFD point to a "Minispec" which would contain that process's application logic.[10] We will follow this rule and expand on the importance of writing good application logic. There are, of course, different styles, and few textbooks that explain the importance to the analyst of understanding how these need to be developed and presented. Like other modeling tools, each process specification style has its good, bad and ugly. In Chapter 3, we briefly described reasons for developing good specifications and the challenges that can confront the analyst. In a later chapter, the art of designing and writing both business and technical specifications will be discussed in detail; here we are concerned simply with the acceptable formats that may be used for this purpose.

Pseudocode

The most detailed and regimented process specification is *pseudocode* or structured English. Its format requires the analysts to have a solid understanding of how to write algorithms. The format is very "COBOL-like" and was initially designed as a way of writing functional COBOL programming specifications. The rules governing pseudocode are as follows:

- use the Do While with an Enddo to show iteration;
- use If-Then-Else to show conditions and ensure each If has an End-If;
- be specific about initializing variables and other detail processing requirements.

Pseudocode is designed to give the analyst tremendous control over the design of the code. Take the following example:

There is a requirement to calculate a 5% bonus for employees who work on the 1st shift and a 10% bonus for workers on the 2nd or 3rd shift. Management is interested in a report listing the number of employees who receive a 10% bonus. The process also produces the bonus checks.

The pseudocode would be

```
Initialize 10% counter = 0
Open Employee Master File
Do While more records
        If Shift = "1" then
                Bonus = Gross_Pay * .05

Else
                If Shift = "2" or "3" then
                        Bonus = Gross_Pay * .10
                        Add 1 to Counter
                Else
                Error Condition
```

---

[10] Tom DeMarco, *Structured Analysis and System Specification*, Yourdon Press, pp. 85–86.

```
        Endif
                Endif
    Enddo
    Print Report of 10% Bonus Employees
    Print Bonus Checks
    End
```

The above algorithm gives the analyst great control over how the program should be designed. For example, note that the pseudocode requires that the programmer have an error condition should a situation occur where a record does not contain a 1st, 2nd or 3rd shift employee. This might occur should there be a new shift which was not communicated to the information systems department. Many programmers might have omitted the last "If" check as follows:

```
    Initialize 10% counter = 0
    Open Employee Master File
    DoWhile more records
            If Shift = "1" then
                    Bonus = Gross_Pay * .05
            Else
                    Bonus = Gross_Pay * .10
                    Add 1 to Counter
            Endif
    Enddo
    Print Report of 10% Bonus Employees
    Print Bonus Checks
    End
```

The above algorithm simply assumes that if the employee is not on the 1st shift then they must be either a 2nd or 3rd shift employee. Without this being specified by the analyst, the programmer may have omitted this critical logic which could have resulted in a 4th shift worker receiving a 10% bonus! As mentioned earlier, each style of process specification has its advantages and disadvantages, in other words, the good, the bad, and the ugly.

The Good

The analyst who uses this approach has practically written the program, and thus the programmer will have very little to do with regards to figuring out the logic design.

The Bad

The algorithm is very detailed and could take a long time for the analyst to develop. Many professionals raise an interesting point: do we need analysts to be writing process specifications to this level of detail? In addition, many programmers may be insulted and feel that an analyst does not possess the skill set to design such logic.

The Ugly

The analyst spends the time, the programmers are not supportive, and the logic is incorrect. The result here will be the "*I told you so*" remarks from programmers, and hostilities may grow over time.

Case

Case[11] is another method of communicating application logic. Although the technique does not require as much technical format as pseudocode, it still requires the analyst to provide a detailed structure to the algorithm. Using the same example as in the pseudocode discussion, we can see the differences in format:

```
Case 1st Shift
        Bonus = Gross_Pay * .05
Case 2nd or 3rd Shift
        Bonus = Gross_Pay * .10
        Add 1 to 10% Bonus Employees
Case Neither 1st, 2nd or 3rd Shift
        Error Routine
EndCase
Print Report of 10% Bonus Employees
Print Bonus Checks
End
```

The above format provides control, as it still allows the analyst to specify the need for error checking; however, the exact format and order of the logic are more in the hands of the programmer. Let's now see the good, the bad, and the ugly of this approach.

The Good

The analyst has provided a detailed description of the algorithm without having to know the format of logic in programming. Because of this advantage, Case takes less time than pseudocode.

The Bad

Although this may be difficult to imagine, the analyst may miss some of the possible conditions in the algorithm, such as forgetting a shift! This happens because the analyst is just listing conditions as opposed to writing a specification. Without formulating the logic as we did in pseudocode, the likelihood of forgetting or overlooking a condition check is increased.

---

[11]The Case method should not be confused with CASE (computer-aided software engineering) products, software used to automate and implement modeling tools and data repositories.

The Ugly

Case logic can be designed without concern for the sequence of the logic, that is, the actual progression of the logic as opposed to just the possibilities. Thus the logic can become more confusing because it lacks actual progressive structure. As stated previously, the possibility of missing a condition is greater because the analyst is not actually following the progression of the testing of each condition. There is thus a higher risk of the specification being incomplete.

Pre-Post Conditions

Pre-post is based on the belief that analysts should not be responsible for the details of the logic, but rather for the overall highlights of what is needed. Therefore, the pre-post method lacks detail and expects that the programmers will provide the necessary details when developing the application software. The method has two components: Pre-Conditions and Post-Conditions. Pre-conditions represent things that are assumed true or that must exist for the algorithm to work. For example, a pre-condition might specify that the user must input the value of the variable X. On the other hand, the post-condition must define the required outputs as well as the relationships between calculated output values and their mathematical components. Suppose the algorithm calculated an output value called Total_Amount. The post-condition would state that Total_Amount is produced by multiplying Quantity times Price. Below is the pre-post equivalent of the Bonus algorithm:

Pre-Condition 1:
        Access Employee Master file and where 1st shift = "1"
Post-Condition 1:
        Bonus is set to Gross_Pay * .05.
        Produce Bonus check.
Pre-Condition 2:
        Access Employee Master file and where 2nd shift = "2" or 3rd shift ="3"
Post-Condition 2:
        Bonus is set to Gross_Pay * .10
        Add 1 to 10% Bonus count.
        Produce Bonus check and Report of all employees who receive 10% bonuses.
Pre-Condition 3:
        Employee records does not contain a shift code equal to "1", "2", or "3"
Post-Condition 3:
        Error Message for employees without shifts = "1", "2", or "3"

As we can see, this specification does not show how the actual algorithm should be designed or written. It requires the programmer or development team to find these details and implement the appropriate logic to represent them. Therefore, the analyst has no real input into the way the application will be designed or the way it functions.

The Good

The analyst need not have technical knowledge to write an algorithm and need not spend an inordinate amount of time to develop what is deemed a programming responsibility. Therefore, less technically oriented analysts can be involved in specification development.

The Bad

There is no control over the design of the logic, and thus the potential for misunderstandings and errors is much greater. The analyst and the project are much more dependent on the talent of the development staff.

The Ugly

Perhaps we misunderstand the specification. Since the format of pre–post conditions is less specific, there is more room for ambiguity.

Matrix

A *matrix* or *table approach* shows the application logic in tabular form. Each row reflects a result of a condition, with each column representing the components of the condition to be tested. The best way to explain a matrix specification is to show an example (see Figure 4.13).

Bonus Percent	Shift to be tested
5 % Bonus	1st Shift
10% Bonus	2nd Shift
10% Bonus	3rd Shift

Figure 4.13 Sample matrix specification.

Although this is a simple example that uses the same algorithm as the other specification styles, it does show how a matrix can describe the requirements of an application without the use of sentences and pseudocode.

The Good

The analyst can use a matrix to show complex conditions in a tabular format. Many programmers prefer the tabular format because it is organized, easy to read, and often easy to maintain. Very often the matrix resembles the array and table formats used by many programming languages.

The Bad

It is difficult, if not impossible, to show a complete specification in matrices. The example in Figure 4.13 supports this, in that the remaining logic of the bonus application is not shown. Therefore, the analyst must incorporate one of the other specification styles to complete the specification.

The Ugly

Matrices are used to describe complex condition levels, where there are many "If" conditions to be tested. These complex conditions often require much more detailed analysis than shown in a matrix. The problem occurs when the analyst, feeling the matrix may suffice, does not provide enough detail. The result: the programmer may misunderstand conditions during development.

Conclusion

The same question must be asked again: what is a good specification? We will continue to explore this question. In this chapter we have examined the logic alternatives. Which logic method is best? It depends! We have seen from the examples that each method has its advantages and shortcomings. The best approach is to be able to use them all and to select the most appropriate one for the task at hand. To do this effectively means clearly recognizing both where each style provides a benefit for the part of the system you are working with, and who will be doing the development work. The table in Figure 4.14 attempts to put the advantages and shortcomings into perspective.

Pseudocode	Case	Pre–Post	Matrix
Complex and detailed algorithms that need significant clarification.	The application logic is detailed, but it is not necessary to develop the complete flow of the process.	Tremendous level of confidence in development staff to get the necessary application logic detail.	Large number of conditions ("If" statements) with an emphasis on lots of conditions before the answer is reached (i.e., complex "If" statements).
The analyst is also having difficulty with defining the logic.	There is more confidence in the programming staff.	The application logic is very simple and does not need further clarification.	No need for error-checking condition.
Should be used when the analyst is very concerned about the aptitude of the programming staff.	The analyst wants to define all error-handling conditions but not to design them.	Few conditions ("If" statements).	Little application logic that needs to be further explained.
The analyst is very sensitive to error handling.	There are a reasonable number of "If" statements.	No need for or limited error-handling requirements.	

Figure 4.14 Process specification comparisons.

State Transition Diagrams

State transition diagrams (STD) were designed to model events that are time-dependent in behavior. Another definition of the STD is that it models the application alternatives for event-driven activities. An event-driven activity is any activity that depends directly on the behavior of a pre-condition that makes that event either possible or attractive. Before going any further, let's use an example to explain this definition further:

> Mary leaves her office to go home for the day. Mary lives 20 minutes' walking distance from the office. When departing from the office building, she realizes that it is raining very hard. Typically, Mary would walk home; however, due to the rain, she needs to make a decision at that moment about how she will go home. Therefore, an event has occurred during the application of Mary walking home which may change her decision and thus change the execution of this application.

As shown above, we have defined an event that, depending on the conditions during its execution, may have different results. To complete the example, we must examine or define what Mary's alternatives for getting home.

The matrix in Figure 4.15 shows us the alternative activities that Mary can choose. Two of them require a certain amount of money. All of the alternatives have positive and negative potentials that cannot be determined until executed; therefore, the decision to go with an alternative may depend on a calculation of probability. We sometimes call this a calculated risk or our "gut" feeling. Is it not true that Mary will not know whether she will be able to find a taxi until she tries? However, if Mary sees a lot of traffic in the street and not many taxis, she may determine that it is not such a good idea to take a taxi.

Alternative	Pre-Condition	Positive Result	Negative Result
1. Walk Home	None	Mary gets home and does not spend money	Mary gets very wet
2. Take Subway train	Must have $1.50 for Subway	Mary gets home without getting too wet.	Mary spends money and must be careful for her safety when going into the Subway
3. Take a Taxi	Must have $15.00 for the Taxi ride	Mary gets home faster and without getting wet.	It's expensive and it may be difficult to find a Taxi. There could also be a lot of traffic, resulting in delays.

Figure 4.15 Mary's event alternatives.

Much of the duplication of the scenario above falls into the study of Artificial Intelligence (AI) software. Therefore, AI modeling may require the use of STDs. The word "state" in STD means that an event must be in a given pre-condition before we can consider moving to another condition. In our example, Mary is in a state called "Going Home From the Office." Walking, taking a train or taking a taxi are alternative ways of getting home. Once Mary is home she has entered into a new state called "Home." We can now derive that walking, taking a train or taking a taxi are conditions that can effect a change in state, in this example leaving the office and getting home. Figure 4.16 shows the STD for going home.

Figure 4.16 State transition diagram for going home.

This STD simply reflects that two states exist and that there is a condition that causes the application to move to the "Home" state. When using STDs, the analyst should:

    1.   identify all states that exist in the system (in other words, all possible permutations of events must be defined),

2.   ensure that there is at least one condition to enter every state,

3.   ensure that there is at least one condition to leave every state.

The reasons for using STD differ greatly from those for a DFD. A DFD should be used when modeling finite, sequential processes that have a definitive beginning and end. We saw this situation in the previous examples in this chapter. The STD, on the other hand, is needed when the system effectively never ends, that is, when it simply moves from one state to another. Therefore, the question is never whether we are at the beginning or end of the process, but rather the current state of the system. Another example, one similar to that used by Yourdon in *Modern Structured Analysis*, is the Bank Teller state diagram shown in Figure 4.17.

Although you may assume that "Enter Valid Card" is the start state, an experienced analyst would know better. At any time, the automated teller is in a particular state of operation (unless it has abnormally terminated). The "Enter Valid Card" state is in the "sleep" state. It will remain in this mode until someone creates the condition to cause a change, which is actually to input a valid card. Notice that every state can be reached and every state can be left. This rule establishes perhaps the most significant difference between the DFD and STD. Therefore, a DFD should be used for finite processes, and an STD should be used when there is ongoing processing, moving from one status to another.

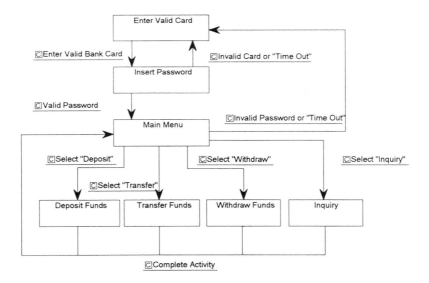

Figure 4.17 Bank Teller state transition diagram.

Let us now show a more complex example which emphasizes how the STD can uncover conditions that are not obvious or were never experienced by the user. Take the matrix of states for a thermostat shown in Figure 4.18.

Current State	Condition to cause a change in State	New State
Furnace Off	Temperature drops below 60 degrees	Furnace On
Furnace On	Temperature exceeds 70 degrees	Furnace Off
Air On	Temperature drops below 65 degrees	Air Off
Air Off	Temperature exceeds 75 degrees	Air On

Figure 4.18 Thermostat states.

Figure 4.19 depicts the STD for the above states and conditions.

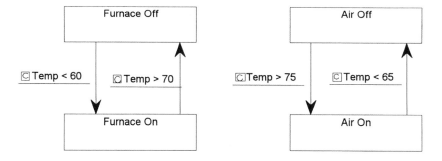

Figure 4.19 State transition diagram based on the user-defined states.

Upon review, we notice that there are really two systems and that they do not interface with each other. Why? Suppose, for example, that the temperature went above 70 and that the system therefore went into the Furnace Off state, but that the temperature nevertheless continued to increase unexpectedly. Users expect that whenever the Furnace Off state is reached, it must be winter. In the event of a winter heat wave, everyone would get very hot. We have therefore discovered that we must have a condition to put the air on even if a heat wave had never occurred before in winter. The same situation exists for the Air Off where we expect the temperature to rise instead of falling. We will thus add two new conditions (see Figure 4.20).

Current State	Condition to cause a change in State	New State
Furnace Off	Temperature exceeds 75 degrees	Air On
Air Off	Temperature drops below 65 degrees	Furnace On

Figure 4.20 Additional possible states of the thermostat.

The STD is then modified to show how the Furnace and Air subsystems interface (see Figure 4.22).

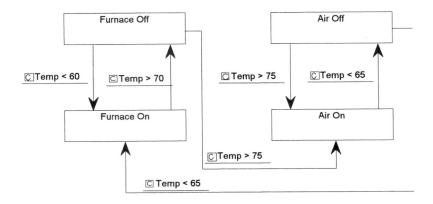

Figure 4.21 Modified state transition diagram based on modified events.

Using STDs to discover missing processes (that would otherwise be omitted or added later) is very important. This advantage is why STDs are considered very effective in Artificial Intelligence and Object Oriented analysis, where the analyst is constantly modeling event-driven, never ending processes. We will see further application of STDs in Chapter 9: Object-Oriented Techniques.

Entity Relational Diagrams

The model that depicts the relationships among the stored data is known as an *entity relational diagram* (ERD). The ERD is the most widely used of all modeling tools and is really the only method to reflect the system's stored data.

An *entity* in database design is an object of interest about which data can be collected. In a retail database application, customers, products, and suppliers might be entities. An entity can subsume a number of attributes: product attributes might be color, size, and price; customer attributes might include name, address, and credit rating.[12]

The first step to understanding an entity is to establish its roots. Since DFDs have been used to model the processes, their data stores (which may represent data files) will act as the initial entities prior to implementing logic data modeling. Logic data modeling and its interface with the DFD will be

---

[12] Microsoft Press, *Computer Dictionary*, 2nd ed, p. 149.

discussed in Chapter 5, thus the scope of this section will be limited to the attributes and functions of the ERD itself.

It is believed, for purposes of data modeling, that an entity can be simply defined as a logical file which will reflect the data elements or fields that are components of each occurrence or record in the entity. The ERD, therefore, shows how multiple entities will interact with each other. We call this interaction the "relationship." In most instances, a relationship between two or more entities can exist only if they have at least one common data element among them. Sometimes we must force a relationship by placing a common data element between entities, just so they can communicate with each other. An ERD typically shows each entity and its connections as follows:

Figure 4.22 Entity relational diagram showing the relationship between the Orders and Customers entities.

The above example shows two entities: Orders and Customers. They have a relationship because both entities contain a common data element called Customer#. Customer# is depicted as "Key Data" in the Customers entity because it must be unique for every occurrence of a customer record. It is notated as "PK1" because it is defined as a Primary Key, meaning that Customer# uniquely identifies a particular customer. In Orders, we see that Customer# is a primary key but it is concatenated with Order#. By *concatenation* we mean that the two elements are combined to form a primary key. Nevertheless, Customer# still has its separate identity. The line that joins the entities is known as the relationship identifier. It is modeled using the "Crow's Foot" method, meaning that the many relationship is shown as a crow's foot, depicted in Figure 4.23 going to the Order entity. The double vertical lines near the Customer entity signify "One and only One." What does this really mean? The proper relationship is stated:

> "One and only one customer can have one to many orders."

It means that customers must have placed at least one order, but can also have placed more than one. "One and only One" really indicates that when a Customer is found in the Order entity, the Customer must also exist in the Customer entity. In addition, although a Customer may exist multiple times in the Order entity, it can exist in the Customer master entity only once. This relationship is also know as the association between entities and effectively identifies the common data elements and the constraints associated with their relationship. This kind of relationship between entities can be difficult to grasp, especially without benefit of a practical application. Chapter 5 will provide a step-by-step approach to developing an ERD using the process of logical data modeling.

Problems and Exercises

1. What is a functional primitive?
2. What are the advantages and disadvantages of a data flow diagram? What is meant by "leveling up"?
3. What is a PFD? Describe its relationship to a DFD.
4. What is the purpose of the data dictionary?
5. Define each of the following data dictionary notation symbols: =, +, [ ], /, ( ), { }, **
6. What is an elementary data element? How does it compare with a functional primitive?
7. Define the functions of a process specification. How does the process specification interface with the DFD and the DD?
8. Compare the advantages and disadvantages of each of the following process specification formats:
   - Pseudocode
   - Case
   - Pre–Post Condition
   - Matrix
9. What is an event-driven system? How does the Program Manager in Windows applications represent the behavior of an event driven system?
10. When using an STD, what three basic things must be defined ?
11. What is an Entity? How does it relate to a Data Store of a DFD?
12. Explain the concept of an Entity Relational Diagram.
13. What establishes a relationship between two entities?
14. Define the term "association."

Mini-Project #1

An application is required that will calculate employee bonuses as follows:

1. There are three (3) working shifts. The bonuses are based on shift:
    - 1st Shift: 5% bonus
    - 2nd Shift: 10% bonus
    - 3rd Shift: 10% bonus
2. The bonus is calculated by multiplying the percentage by the annual gross pay of the employee.
3. The employee records are resident on the employee master file, which resides on a hard disk.
4. Bonus checks are produced for all employees.
5. There is a report produced that lists the number of employees who received a 10% bonus.

Assignment

Draw the PFD.

Mini-Project #2

You have been asked to automate the Accounts Payable process. During your interviews with users you identify four major events as follows:

I. Purchase Order Flow

1. The Marketing Department sends a purchase order (P.O.) form for books to the Accounts Payable System (APS).
2. APS assigns a P.O. # and sends the P.O.-White copy to the Vendor and files the P.O.- Pink copy in a file cabinet in P.O.#.sequence.

II. Invoice Receipt

1. A vendor sends an invoice for payment for books purchased by APS.
2. APS sends invoice to Marketing Department for authorization.
3. Marketing either returns invoice to APS approved or back to the vendor if not
4. authorized.
5. If the invoice is returned to APS it is matched up against the original P.O.-Pink. The PO and vendor invoice are then combined into a packet and prepared for the voucher process.

III. Voucher Initiation

1. APS receives the packet for vouchering. It begins this process by assigning a voucher number.
2. The Chief Accountant must approve vouchers > $5,000.
3. APS prepares another packet from the approved vouchers. This packet includes the P.O.-Pink, authorized invoice and approved voucher..

IV. Check Preparation

1. Typist receives the approved voucher packet and retrieves a numbered blank
2. check to pay the vendor..
3. Typist types a two-part check (blue,green) using data from the approved voucher and enters invoice number on the check stub.
4. APS files the approved packet with the Check-green in the permanent paid file.
5. The check is either picked up or mailed directly to the vendor.

Assignment

1. Provide the DFDs for the four events. Each event should be shown as a single DFD on a separate piece of paper.
2. Level each event to its functional primitives.
3. Develop the Process Specifications for each functional primitive DFD.
4. Create a PFD.

Mini-Project #3

Based on the mini-project from Chapter 2, the following information was obtained from Mr. Smith during the actual interview:

1. The hiring department forwards a copy of a new hire's employment letter.
2. The copy of the hire letter is manually placed in a pending file, which has a date folder for every day of the month. Therefore, Mr. Smith's department puts the letter in the folder for the actual day the new employee is supposed to report for work.
3. When the employee shows up, he/she must have the original hire letter.
4. The original and copy are matched. If there is no letter in the file, the hiring department is contacted for a copy.
5. The new employee is given a "New Employee Application" form. The form has two sides. The first side requires information about the individual; the second side requests insurance-related information.
6. The employee is given an employee ID card and is sent to work.

7. The application form and letter are filed in the employee master cabinet.
8. A copy of side two of the application form is forwarded to the insurance company. The copy of the form is filed in an insurance pending file, using the same concept for follow-up as the new-hire pending file system.
9. The insurance company sends a confirmation of coverage to the department. At that time, the pending file copy is destroyed.
10. Based on the employee level, insurance applications are followed up with a call to the insurance company.

Assignment

Based on the above facts, create the DFDs that depict the system. Level the DFDs until they are at a functional primitive level.

Mini-Project #4

The following is the information obtained during an interview with the ABC Agency:

People or potential renters call the ABC Agency and ask them if apartments are available for rent. All callers have their information recorded and stored in an information folder. The agency examines the file and determines whether their database has any potential matches on the properties requested. People also call the agency to inform them that they have an apartment for rent. Fifteen days before rent is due, the agency sends invoices to renters. Sixty days before the lease is up, the agency sends a notice for renewal to the renter.

Assignment

1. Draw the DFDs.
2. Level DFDs to functional primitive.
3. Provide process specifications for each functional primitive DFD. Use at least three different process specification "styles."

5
Logic Data Modeling Tools

Logic data modeling is a set of procedures that examines an entity to ensure that its component attributes (data elements) should reside in that entity, rather than being stored in another or new entity. Therefore, LDM focuses solely on the stored data model. The LDM process is somewhat controversial and subject to various opinions; however, listed below are the common steps used by many professionals in the industry:

1. identify major entities
2. select primary and alternate keys
3. determine key business rules
4. apply normalization to 3rd normal form
5. combine user views
6. integrate with existing models (legacy interfaces)
7. determine domains and triggering operations
8. de-normalize carefully

Normalization Defined

Perhaps the most important aspect of logical data modeling is Normalization. Normalization, at a high level, is generally defined as the elimination of redundancies from an entity. Although this is an accurate definition, it does not fully convey the true impact of what normalization is trying to accomplish, and more important, what it means not to apply it to your model.

We can see from the above list that normalization is only one step in the LDM process, albeit the most critical. I have found, however, that there is an advantage to understanding normalization first, before trying to understand the entire LDM process.

Before we explain this any further it is necessary to define the three forms of normalization.[13] These forms are known as 1st normal form, 2nd normal form and 3rd normal form. Normal form is typically abbreviated "NF." Each normal form should be dependent on the completion of the previous form,

---

[13] Although there are 5 published normal forms, most industry leaders have accepted that normal forms 4 and 5 are difficult to implement and typically unnecessary. Therefore, this book omits forms 4 and 5.

therefore, normalization should be applied in order. Below are the rules that satisfy each normal form:

1st NF:	No repeating elements or repeating groups
2nd NF:	No partial dependencies on a concatenated key
3rd NF:	No dependencies on non-key attributes

Normalization Approaches

If DFDs have been completed, all data stores that represent data files become the initial major entities or the first step in the LDM. Therefore, if process models are done first, the selection of major entities is easier. If process models are not used then the analyst must hope that a legacy system exists from which the data can be converted and then tested for compliance with normalization. If no legacy system exists, you will need to examine forms and try to determine what constitutes an entity.[14] The following example assumes that a DFD exists and shows that the process creates a data store called "Orders." This data store represents the storage of all orders sent by customers for the various items that the company sells. Figure 5.1 is a sample of a customer order and the data elements that exist on the form.

---

[14] There are several techniques that analysts have used, but they are beyond the scope of this book.

Precision Products
1456 Emerson St
Parsippany, NJ 07055-1254

ORDER

ORDER NO: 12345
DATE: March 4, 1997

To:

A. Langer & Assoc.. Inc.
20 Waterview Blvd
Third Floor
Parsippany, NJ 07054

P.O. NUMBER	DATE SHIPPED	SHIPPED VIA	REQUIRED DATE	TERMS
AC34	9/15/95	UPS	10/5/95	30 days

QUANTITY	ITEM ID	ITEM NAME	UNIT PRICE	AMOUNT
4	31	Towels	$ 10.00	$ 40.00
3	27	Shirts	$ 25.00	$ 75.00
				$ 0.00
				$ 0.00
				$ 0.00
				$ 0.00
				$ 0.00
		SUBTOTAL		$ 115.00
		SALES TAX		$ 0.00
		SHIPPING & HANDLING		$ 4.50
		TOTAL DUE		$ 119.50

Figure 5.1 Sample customer order form.

We begin this normalization example assuming that steps 1, 2 and 3 of the LDM are complete (Identifying Major Entities, Selecting the Primary and Alternate Keys, and Identifying Key Business Rules, respectively). Our major entity is the data store "Orders" and its Primary Key is "Order#." There are no Alternate Keys (a concept discussed later). The first aspect to point out is that the data store from the DFD becomes an entity in the LDM process (see Figure 5.2).

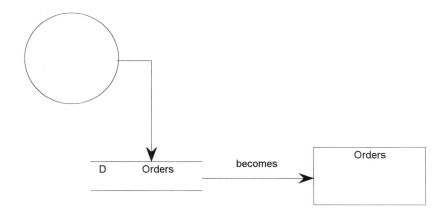

Figure 5.2 This diagram shows the transition of a data store into an entity.

To show how normalization works, Figure 5.3 depicts the Orders entity with its primary key Order# inside the box. The non-keyed attributes (data elements are often called *attributes* of an entity when performing LDM) are shown as dependent cells. These cells or attributes basically belong to or "depend on" the entity and do not affect the outcome of the normalization process. However, a dependent attribute may become a key attribute as a result of normalization. We will see this in the example shown in Figure 5.3.

The form shows that a repeating body of elements exists in the area of items ordered. That is, many items can be associated with a single order. We call this a repeating group, and it is shown within the box in Figure 5.3. Looking at this entity, we must first ask ourselves: are we in 1st NF? The answer is clearly *no* because of the existence of a repeating element or group. By showing the box surrounding the repeating body, we are, in effect, exposing the fact that there is a primary key being treated as a non-key attribute. In other words, there really is another entity embedded within the Orders entity. *Whenever a normal form is violated, the solution is to create a new entity.* If it is a 1st NF failure, the new entity will always have a concatenated primary key composed of the primary key from the original entity joined with a new key from the repeating group. This new key must be the attribute in the group that controls the others. All other attributes will be removed from the original entity and become part of the new one, as shown in Figure 5.4.

Figure 5.3 The Orders entity and its associated attributes.

Figure 5.4 now shows a new entity: Order Items which has a concatenated primary key composed of the Order# from the original entity and the Item ID which is the identifier of each item that is contained within an order. Note that all the non-key (dependent) attributes now become part of the new entity. First NF now allows the system to store as many items associated with an order as required. The original file would have required an artificial occurrence to be included in each record. This would result in (1) order records that waste space because the order had fewer items than the maximum, and (2) the need to create a new order if the number of items exceeds the maximum allotted per order in the file.

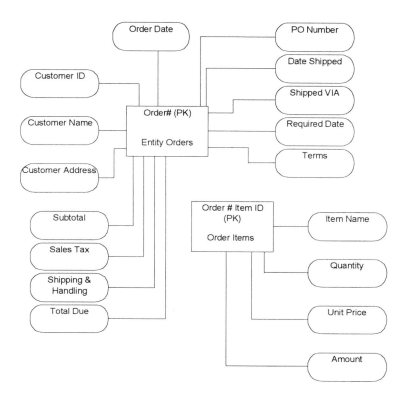

Figure 5.4 This diagram shows the entities in 1st NF.

Our entities are now said to be in 1st NF. Don't rejoice yet—we must now check 2nd NF. Second NF applies only to entities that have concatenated primary keys. Therefore, any entity that is in 1st NF and does *not* have a concatenated primary key must be in 2nd NF, simply by definition. As a result, the Orders entity must be in 2nd NF. The issue becomes the Order Items entity. To check for 2nd NF compliance, the analyst needs to ensure that every non-key attribute is totally dependent on all parts of the concatenated primary key. When we run this test on Item Name, we see that it depends only on the Item ID and has no dependency on Order#. It is, therefore, considered a 2nd NF violation. Once again, a new entity must be created. The primary key of this new entity will always be the key attribute for which elements had a partial dependency. In this case, it is Item ID. All non-key attributes dependent only on Item ID will become part of the new entity, which we will call "Items." Note that non-key attributes "Quantity" and "Amount" stay with the Order Items entity because they are dependent on both the order and item keys. To be clearer, the quantity of an item ordered will be different for each order (or the same by coincidence). The result now is three entities as shown in Figure 5.5.

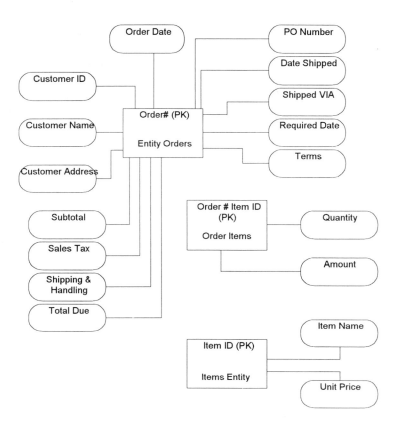

Figure 5.5 This diagram shows the entities in 2nd NF.

We are now in 2nd NF. Once again, don't rejoice too early—we must test for 3rd NF. Third NF tests the relationship between non-key attributes to determine if one is dependent on another, that is, if a non-key attribute is dependent on another non-key attribute. If this occurs, then the controlling non-key attribute is really a primary key and should be part of a new entity. If we look at the Order entity, we will find that both Customer Name and Customer Address[15] are really dependent on the non-key attribute Customer ID. Therefore, it fails 3rd NF, and a new entity is formed with the controlling attribute, now a key. The new entity is Customers (see Figure 5.6).

---

[15] Customer Address would normally be comprised of more components, namely more than one address line, city, state, and zip, but it has been left out of this example for the sake of simplicity.

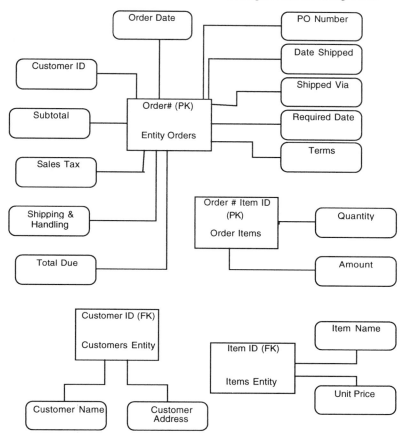

Figure 5.6 This diagram shows the entities in the first phase of 3rd NF.

Note that the Customer ID also remains as a non-key attribute in Orders. All 3rd NF failures require this to happen. The non-key attribute Customer ID is called a *foreign key* and enables the Customer entity and Order entity to have a relationship.

We may ask ourselves if we have now reached 3rd normal form. The answer is still no! Although not intuitively obvious, there are still non-key attributes that are dependent on non-key attributes. These are, however, slightly different from the Customer ID case. For example, if you look at the Order Items entity, there is a non-key attribute called Amount. Amount represents the total of each item included in an order. Amount is a calculation, namely Quantity * Unit Price. Attributes that are calculations are said to be dependent and are known as a *derived* value. One can see that Amount is indirectly dependent on Quantity in the entity Order Items. When non-key attributes are deemed derived and thus redundant because their values can be calculated at any time, they are removed from the entity.[16] The same problem also exists in the entity Orders. Subtotal and Total Due are also derived and therefore must be removed from the logical model. Our 3rd NF LDM is now modified as shown in Figure 5.7.

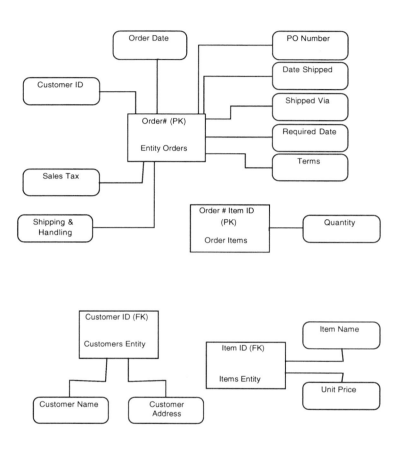

Figure 5.7 This diagram shows the entities in the second phase of 3rd NF.

At this point we believe that 3rd NF has been reached and we should now produce the Entity Relational Diagram (ERD), which will show the relation-

---

[16] Although derived attributes are removed from the logical model during normalization, they may be put back into the entity in the physical model. The physical model is the entity in actual database format. These attributes are put back due to performance problems in physical database products. We call this *de-normalization*, which will be discussed later in the chapter.

ships (connections) of one entity with others. The ERD is fairly simple to draw, and the analyst should start by putting each entity into the accepted ERD format (see Figure 5.8).

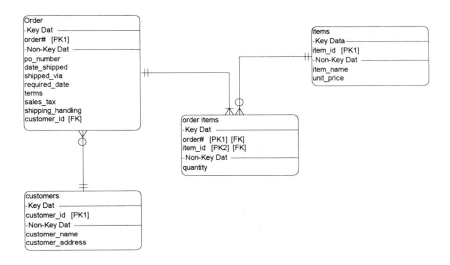

Figure 5.8 The entities in ERD model.

The ERD in Figure 5.8 depicts the relationships of all the entities. Let's see what it tells the analyst:

- The Order entity has a "one and only one to one to many" relationship with the Order Items entity. That is, there must be at least one item associated with an Order, or the order cannot exist.
- The Items entity has a "one and only one to zero to many" relationship with the Order Items entity. The difference between this relationship and the one established with Orders, is that here an Item does not have to be associated with any order. This would be the case for a new item that has not yet been ordered by any customer.
- The Order Items entity has a primary key that is comprised of the concatenation of order# and item_id, which are the primary keys of Order and Items, respectively. The Order Item entity is said to be an "associative" entity, in that it exists as the result of a many-to-many relationship between Order and Items. Specifically, one or many orders could be associated with one or many items. A many-to-many relationship not only violates normalization, but creates significant problems in efficient SQL[17] coding. Therefore, associative entities are

---

[17] SQL stands for Structured Query Language. SQL is the standard query language used in relational database products. SQL was invented by IBM in the early 1980s.

created to avoid these relationships. First NF failures often result in associative entities. It should also be noted that the primary keys of Order Items are shown with an "(FK)" symbol. This model, which was developed using Popkin's System Architect CASE tools, shows all primary keys that originate in a foreign entity with a "(FK)" notation. Although this is not an industry standard, software products vary in their depiction of derived primary keys.

- Customers has a "one and only one to zero-to-many" relationship with the Order entity. Note that a Customer may not have ever made an order. In addition, this model shows customer_id in the Order entity as a non-key attribute pointing to the primary key of Customers. This is the standard definition of a foreign key pointer.

What Normalization Does Not Do

Although we have reached 3rd NF and completed the ERD, there is a problem. The problem is serious and exists in the case of a change in Unit Price. Should the Unit Price change, there is no way to calculate the historical costs of previous order items. Remember that we eliminated Amount because it was a derived element. This poses an interesting problem in that it appears that normalization has a serious flaw—or does it ? Before making this evaluation, let's first determine the solution to this problem. Does replacing Amount in the Item entity solve the problem? Although we could "back into" the old price by dividing the Amount by Quantity, it would not represent a true solution to the problem. Looking closer, we will ultimately determine that the real problem is a missing attribute: Order Item Unit Price or the price at the time of the order. Order Item Unit Price is dependent on both the Order and the Item and is therefore wholly dependent on the entity Order Items. It becomes a non-key attribute of that entity, which means our ERD must be modified. It is important to note that Order Item Unit Price is not a derived element. It is only related to Unit Price from the Item entity at the time of the order[18]; thereafter they are separate elements. Because of this phenomenon, the analyst has actually discovered a new data element during normalization. To be consistent with the rules, this new data element must be added to the ERD and the Data Dictionary (see Figure 5.9).

---

[18] The Order Item Unit Price would retrieve the Unit Price during data entry of the order and would therefore be controlled via the application program that governs the entry of orders.

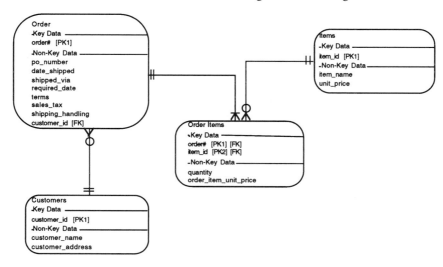

Figure 5.9 ERD with the addition of order_item_unit_price.

The question now is: what does all this mean? To put the above problem and solution into perspective is actually quite simple: normalization will not work completely unless all attributes are included during the process. While normalization itself will not uncover missing elements, the good news is that the normalization process and the ensuing ERD did uncover the problem! If the analyst stands to learn anything from this example, it is that normalization does not ensure that the model is complete nor is it a panacea for the art of data modeling. It is simply another tool that the analyst can use to reach the logical equivalent, albeit a very important one.

The Supertype/Subtype Model

A troublesome database issue occurs in the LDM when there are records within an entity that can take on different characteristics or have many "types" of data elements. By "type" we mean that a portion of the data elements in a specific record can vary depending on the characteristic or identification of the record within that entity. Another way of describing this issue is that a portion of the elements contained within a given record can be different from other records of the same entity depending on the *type* of row it represents, or as it is defined as a "subtype" of the record. A subtype, therefore, is the portion of the record that deviates from the standard or "supertype" part of the record. The "supertype" portion is always the same among all the records in the entity. In other words, the "supertype" represents the global part of the attributes in an entity. A diagram of this phenomenon can best explain this concept:

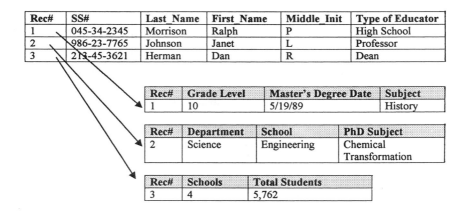

Rec#	SS#	Last_Name	First_Name	Middle_Init	Type of Educator
1	045-34-2345	Morrison	Ralph	P	High School
2	986-23-7765	Johnson	Janet	L	Professor
3	213-45-3621	Herman	Dan	R	Dean

Rec#	Grade Level	Master's Degree Date	Subject
1	10	5/19/89	History

Rec#	Department	School	PhD Subject
2	Science	Engineering	Chemical Transformation

Rec#	Schools	Total Students
3	4	5,762

Figure 5.10 Supertype/subtype relationship.

The significant difference between a subtype and just a type identifier (using a foreign key) is the existence of at least one nonkey attribute that follows just that subtype part of the record. Thus, the main reason to design a supertype/subtype database is the existence of multiple permutations of different elements that exist in just certain types of records. Keeping all the permutations of elements within a record format can be problematic. First, it can waste storage, especially if each subtype has a significant number of unique elements. Second, it can create massive performance issues, particularly as it relates to the querying of data. Using the above example, we show two potential ways to store the data. The first (Figure 5.11) represents a simple solution with all the permutations existing in the record. The "type" of record is identified using a foreign key pointer to an entity called "Educator Type."

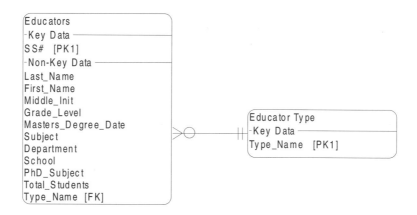

Figure 5.11 Educator ERD using one entity with foreign key identifier.

This solution, while having only one main entity, wastes space because all elements are not used in any one "type" of record. The user must be aware of the meanings of the type identifier and remember which elements exist for each type of educator. This method of logic data modeling violates the concepts of normalization, and entrusts the integrity of values of elements in an entity to either an application program's control, or to the memory of the user. None of these choices are particularly dependable or have proven to be a reliable method of data dependency.

On the other hand, Figure 5.12 provides a different solution using the supertype/subtype construct.

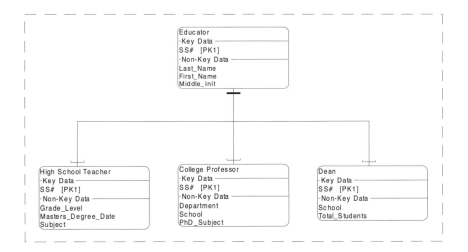

Figure 5.12 Supertype/subtype entity construct.

This construct depicts each type of educator as a separate entity, linked via a special notation in the relational model, known as the supertype/subtype relation. The relationship is mutually exclusive, meaning that any global supertype can have only one of the three subtypes for any one supertype occurrence. Thus, the relationship between any row of a supertype must be one-to-one with a subtype. The supertype/subtype model creates a separate subtype entity to carry only its related elements that are unique to its subtype.

There are two major benefits to this alternative structure. First, the construct saves storage, in that only elements that exist in a subtype are stored in each entity. Second, the subtype information can be directly addressed without first accessing its supertype. This is because each permutation subtype entity contains the same primary key as the parent. Having this capability is significant because a user can automatically obtain the unique information from any subtype without having to search the entire database, as would be the case with one entity holding all the elements (as in Figure 5.11). The benefits from this construct are particularly advantageous when the number of rows among the subtypes varies significantly. Suppose, for example, there are 5 million educators in the database. The Educator database would therefore contain 5 million rows. Four million of the educators are high-school teachers, and as such, the High School subtype entity has 4 million records. Nine hundred thousand educators are professors and the remaining 100,000 educators are deans. Therefore, the Professor database and Dean database have 900,000 and 100,000 records, respectively. In the supertype/subtype configuration applications could access the sample of each type without searching through every record. This improves not only performance, but also access speed, in that each entity is separate and would not interfere with access to the other.

The supertype/subtype construct is not limited to mutual exclusivity; it can support multiple subtype permutations. For example, suppose an educator could be a high-school teacher, college professor, and a dean at the same time,

Figure 5.13 Supertype/subtype model without mutual exclusivity.

or any combination from among the three types. The model would be modified to show separate one-to-one relationships as opposed to the "T" relationship depicted in Figure 5.13.

Supertype/subtypes can cascade, that is, can continue to occur within the subtypes. Take the following example in Figure 5.14.

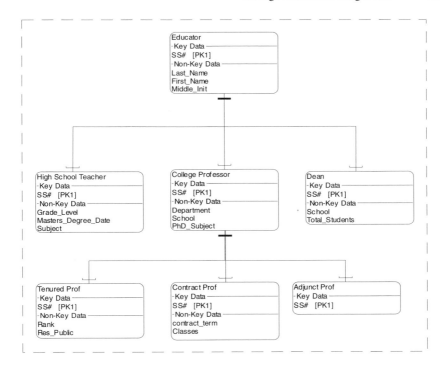

Figure 5.14 Cascading subtypes.

The above example reflects how subtypes can continue to cascade. Notice that the same primary key continues to link the one-to-one relationships of the entities. In addition, Figure 5.14 also exposes another interesting aspect of the supertype/subtype model relating to a subtype that has no non-key attributes. Such is the case with the subtype entity *Adjunct Prof*. In this situation, the empty entity serves only to identify the existence of the subtype, but has no other distinct elements that are attributed to its occurrence. The use of *Adjunct Prof*, therefore, was created only because the other two subtypes (*Tenured Prof* and *Contract Prof*) had unique elements and were used as subtypes. This example serves only to show that the supertype/subtype model is not perfectly balanced, and often has components that are necessary due to other factors that benefited the model.

Cascading subtypes do not need to be of the same relationship. In other words, the subtype educator could have been exclusive to a cascade that is mutually exclusive as follows in Figure 5.15.

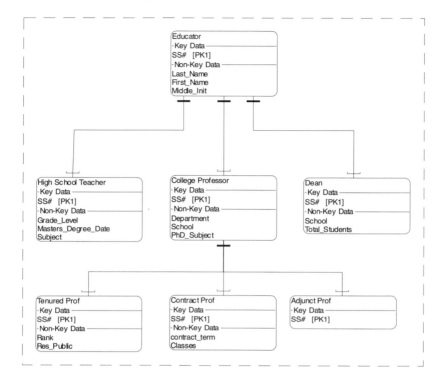

Figure 5.15 Cascading subtypes with alternating exclusivities.

Note that the example shows the subtype identifier Professor Types is a validation entity in 3rd normal form.

Supertypes and subtypes must also be normalized following the same rules that govern any entity decomposition. For example, the subtype Educator Types contains elements that are not fully normalized. For example, Grade_Level and Subject in the subtype entity High School Teacher can be validated using a look-up table. Department, School, and PhD_Subject can also be validated. The resulting fully normalized ERD is shown below in Figure 5.17.

Combining User Views

Normalization has concentrated our analysis on the challenges of moving and placing attributes in the correct entity. In each of the normalization examples, a violation of an NF has always resulted in the creation of a new entity. However, experienced analysts must deal with combining user views. In many aspects this has the opposite result of normalization in that entities will most likely be combined. Combining or joining entities typically occurs when users

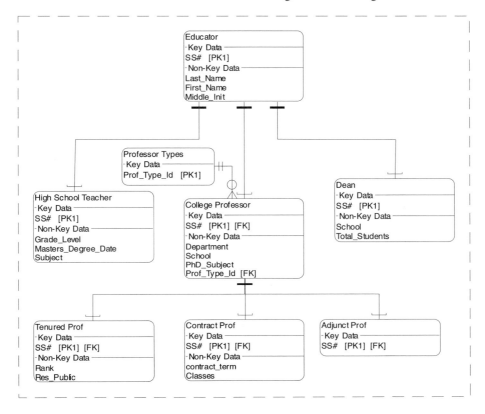

Figure 5.16 Supertype/subtype with subtype identifier element.

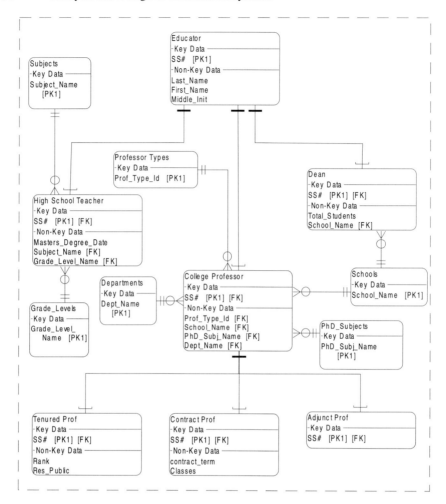

Figure 5.17 Fully normalized supertype/subtype ERD.

have separate views of the same data. A better way to comprehend this concept is to remember the lesson of the logical equivalent. Although this lesson focused on processes, we can try to redirect its point to the stored data model. First we must ask, can data elements that have been physically defined differently really be logically the same (or equivalent)? The answer is yes, and it occurs regularly during the analysis process. Let us now use an example to help illustrate this idea:

The Analyst met with Charles on the 15th floor. During the interview, a data store called Clients was created. The Clients data store was made up of the following data elements shown in Figure 5.18.

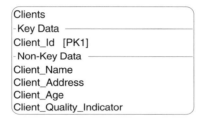

Figure 5.18 The data store for Clients.

After the meeting, the Analyst then went to the 19th floor and visited with Mary of another department. During this interview a data store called Customers was created with the data elements listed in Figure 5.19.

```
Customers
- Key Data
Customer_Id  [PK1]
- Non-Key Data
Customer_Name
Customer_Address
Customer_Buyer_Indicator
Customer_Credit_Rating
```

Figure 5.19 The data store for Customers.

In reality, these two entities are both part of the same object. Whether the entity name is Client or Customer, these entities must be combined. The difficulty here is the combining of the identical elements versus those that need to be added to complete the full view of the entity. Charles and Mary, unbeknownst to each other, had similar but different views of the same thing. Their names for the objects were also different. By applying the concept of the logical equivalent, we determined that only one entity should remain (see Figure 5.20).

```
Customers
─ Key Data ────────────────
Customer_Id  [PK1]
─ Non-Key Data ────────────
Customer_Name
Customer_Address
Customer_Buyer_Indicator
Customer_Credit_Rating
Customer_Age
Customer_Quality_Indicator
```

Figure 5.20 The combined data store for Clients and Customers.

Finding that two or more entities are really identifying the same object may be difficult, especially when their names are not as similar as the ones used in the above example. It is therefore even more important that the analyst ensure the logical meaning of entities and their component elements. Note that we chose to call the combined entity "Customers" and added to it the unique elements not already stored. However, combining these user views raises a new and ugly issue: Why Customer, not Client? Charles and his staff may not care about the internal name of the entity, but may find the name Customer used in screens and reports to be unacceptable. What do we do? The answer is to provide what is called an Alias entry into the Data Dictionary. This will allow both names to point to the same element and allow each to be used in different screen programs and reports. The use of an Alias is not new, as it has existed as a feature in many programming languages such as COBOL for years. Its usefulness continues, and both Charles and Mary should remain happy. (But don't tell Charles that the internal name is Customer!) Combining user views will always boost performance of the database, as it reduces the number of entities and the related links to make the connection.

Integration with Existing Models: Linking Databases

We have discussed the challenges of dealing with Legacy Systems. Most firms are approaching the replacement of legacy systems by phasing business area components into completely re-developed systems. As each business area is completed, there needs to be a "Legacy Link" with data files that connect business area components. This strategy allows a gradual porting of the entire system. The problem with the "Legacy Link" is that the normalized databases must interface and in many cases be dependent upon non-normalized files. This effectively upsets the integrity of the new component and may permanently damage the stored data in the new model. The linking of legacy applications is only one example of this problem. Often, subsidiary companies or locations must depend on data being controlled by less dependable master files. Therefore, linking databases may force analysts to rethink how to preserve integrity while still maintaining the physical link to other corporate data components. Let us use the following example to show how this problem arises:

> The Analyst is designing a subsystem that utilizes the company's employee master file. The subsystem needs this information to allocate employees to projects. Project information is never purged, and therefore the employee project file will contain employees who may no longer be active. Unfortunately, the company master deletes all terminated employees. The employee master must be used in order to ensure that new employees are picked up. The subsystem cannot modify any information on the company master. The ERD in Figure 5.21 depicts these relationships:

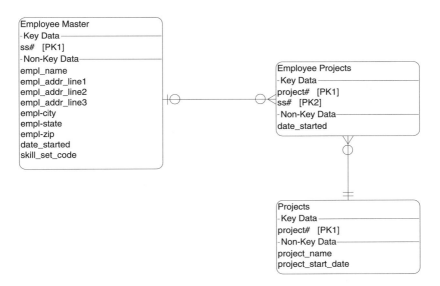

Figure 5.21 ERD showing an association between Employees and Projects.

Note that the Employee Project entity has a one or zero relationship with the Employee Master entity. This simply means that there could be an employee that exists in the Employee Project entity that does not exist in the Employee Master. Not only does this violate normalization rules, it has a serious integrity problem. For example, if we wanted to print a report about the project and each participating employee, all employees who do not exist in the Employee Master will print blanks, since there is no corresponding name information in the master file. Is there an alternative that could provide integrity and normalization? The answer is yes. The subsystem needs to access the Company employee master and merge the file with an Employee Master subsystem version. The merge conversion would compare the two files and update or add new information and employees. It would not, however, delete terminated employees. Although this is an extra step, it maintains integrity, normalization, and most of all, the requirement not to modify the original Employee Master. The ERD would be modified as shown in Figure 5.22.

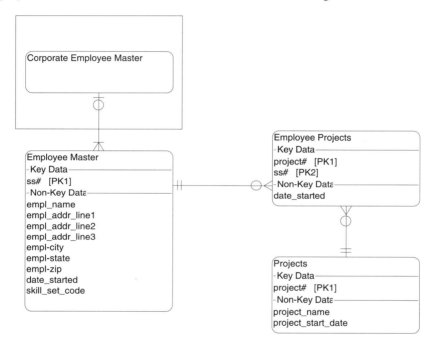

Figure 5.22 ERD reflecting a legacy link to the Corporate Employee Master file.

The Corporate Employee Master and its relation to Employee Master is shown only for informational purposes. The Corporate Employee Master in effect becomes more of an application requirement rather than a permanent part of the ERD. It is important to understand that this solution may require the analyst to produce a list of existing projects in which terminated employees are needed. The first conversion from the Corporate Employee Master will not contain these terminated employees, and they will therefore have to be added directly to the subsystem Employee Master.

Business Rules

The growth of the relational model has created a mechanism for storing certain application logic at the database level. Business rules are application logic that enforces the integrity of the business, that is, that maintains the rules as set forth by the users. Such rules could include: If Last_Name is entered, the First_Name must also be entered. This "rule" simply means that a valid name must contain both the first and last name of the individual being entered into the database. These business rules were traditionally part of the application program code. This meant that every program that would need to enforce a rule would need to encapsulate the same logic within each application program. What followed historically was a maintenance nightmare which required programmers to remember where the logic had been used, especially when changes to the code were required. In addition, there was always the issue of re-coding the same logic without error, so it meant greater testing time. Although there were and are techniques for storing common code in global libraries for applications to incorporate into the code, the procedures tended to be archaic and awkward to support. The establishment of SQL as a robust and end-user query tool also posed a new problem. Business rules coded in applications can enforce them only if the program is executed. Because SQL allows users to create and execute query sessions, they can easily avoid an applications enforcement of a business rule. This therefore created a serious integrity problem in the implementation of database products. Although the tendency in the industry has been to separate data from applications, we will see here that the industry is moving back towards combining data and applications again. It is important not to view this as a return to the old way, but rather as a more intelligent and structured way to combine data with its permanent logic. The word permanent is crucial: certain logic is really an inherent part of the relationship that elements have with other elements. Having business rules stored as part of the data, then, allows anyone to use the information without violating the permanent relationship rules as set forth by the business. It means that SQL users can query all they want or even create and modify data without losing the controls necessary to support integrity.

Business rules are implemented at the database level via stored procedures. Stored procedures are implemented by each database manufacturer, and although they are similar, they are not the same as business rules. Therefore, moving stored procedures from one database to another is not trivial. Why do we care? In Chapter 12, we will discuss the challenges facing corporate CIOs, in particular, creating company-wide distributed networks. These networks are being built around the concept of client/server computing and may often require communication among many different database vendor systems. If business rules are to be implemented at the database level, the compatibility and transportability of such code becomes a challenge. This issue will be discussed in greater detail throughout the later chapters of this book.

Business-rule implementations fall into three categories: keys, domains, and triggers. Key business rules are concerned with the behavior of a primary key in an entity. They include the rules that can affect the insertion, deletion, and updating of primary and foreign keys. For example, if an order is deleted, all order items must also be deleted automatically. Many people call this feature *referential integrity*. Domains represent the constraints related to an attribute's range of values. If an attribute (key or non-key) can have a range of values from 1 to 10, we say that range is the domain value of the attribute. This is, of course, very important information to be included and enforced at the database level through a stored procedure. The third and most powerful business rule is triggers.

Triggering Operations

Triggers are defined as stored procedures that, when activated, "trigger" one or a set of other procedures to be executed. Triggers usually act on other entities, although in many databases such as Oracle, triggers are becoming powerful programming tools to provide significant capabilities at the database level. In many ways they represent their own programming languages and allow embedded SQL code to be used in the stored procedure. Stored procedures resemble BAT files in DOS and are actually implemented as an option in many RDBMS packages. Below is an example of an Oracle 8 trigger:

```
/* Within B.D. only users who are president or director may mark   */
/* company as confidential .              */

if user_type not in ('P', 'D') then
 :new.cmpConfidential := 'N';
 end if;

end if;

/* Ensure user has right to make a company executive private.   */
if exec_com = 'N' then
 :new.cmpexec_private := 'N';
 end if;
```

This trigger is designed to allow a company's information to be marked as confidential only by the President. This means that the president of the company can enter information that only he or she can see. The second part of the trigger is set to allow certain executives to mark their contacts with companies as private. Here we see two sets of application logic that will execute via Oracle triggers. In addition, it will be enforced by the database regardless of how the information is accessed.

Too much power can be a problem, however, and it can cause difficulties with triggers. Why? Because triggers can initiate activity among database files, designers must be careful that they do not cause significant performance problems. For example, let's say a trigger is written which accesses 15 database files. If this trigger is initiated during a critical processing time in the firm, major problems with productivity could result. Once again, the good and the bad!

The subject of business rules is broad but very specific to the actual product implementation style. Since analysts should remain focused on the logical model, it is important for them to define the necessary key business rules, domains and triggers required by the system. It should not be their responsibility to implement them for a specific Relational Database Management Software (RDBMS) product.

Problems and Exercises

1. What is logic data modeling trying to accomplish?
2. Define Normalization. What are the three normal forms?
3. What does normalization *not* do?
4. What is meant by the term "derived" data element?
5. Describe the concept of combining user views. What are the political ramifications of doing this in many organizations?
6. What are legacy links? Describe how they can be used to enforce data integrity.
7. Name and define the three types of business rules.
8. Why are stored procedures in some ways a contradiction to the rule that data and processes need to be separated?
9. What are the disadvantages of database triggers?
10. What is meant by denormalization? Is this a responsibility of the analyst?
11. Define a supertype/subtype. When should this entity construct by used?

Mini-Project #1

The Physician Master File from a DFD contains the following data elements:

Data Element	Description
Social Security #	Primary Key
Physician ID	Alternate Key
Last_Name	Last Name
First_Name	First Name
Mid_Init	Middle Initial
Hospital_Resident_ID	Hospital Identification
Hospital_Resident_Name	Name of Hospital
Hospital_Addr_Line1	Hospital Address
Hospital_Addr_Line2	Hospital Address
Hospital_Addr_Line3	Hospital Address
Hospital_State	Hospital's State
Hospital_City	Hospital's City
Hospital_Zip	Hospital's Zip Code
Specialty_Type	The Physician's specialty
Specialty_Name	Description of specialty
Specialty_College	College where received degree
Specialty_Degree	Degree Name
Date_Graduated	Graduation Date for specialty
DOB	
Physician's Date of Birth	
Year_First_Practiced	First year in practice
Year's_Pract_Exp	Practice Experience Years
Annual_Earnings	Annual Income

Assumptions

1. A physician can be associated with many hospitals, but must be associated with at least one.
2. A physician can have many specialties, or have no specialty.

Assignment

Normalize to 3rd normal form.

Mini-Project #2

1. Check the appropriate column that best identifies the use of each named item as to whether it describes an element or whether it is an element.

Item Examples:	Used to Describe	May be Described
Blue	X	
Temperature of a plain in Spain		X

20 Degrees celsius		
Color		
The White House		
1600 Pennsylvania Avenue		
Continental drift		
1.5 inches		
Hourly wage		
$80		
Difficulty of this exercise		
5th Grade school level		
Ed Sullivan		
Duration of study		
45 days		
Appointment date		
01/01/2004		
Physical location of a university campus		
Odds of winning the publishers clearinghouse sweepstakes		
1/100,000 of 1 percent (or 0.00001% or one in ten million)		

2. For the following list of named entity types, provide a natural and unique identifier that provides significant information. Where no natural unique indentifier exists, create a new one and describe it

Example: Checking Account	Bank ID + Check Account Number

Hospital Patient	
Your Residence	
Box of Cereal	
Bottle of Vintage Wine	
Carton of Milk	
The Wall Street Journal	
Textbook	
Beach Boys Music CD	
Pair of Nike Sneakers	
Rolex Wristwatch	
Airline Flight to London	

Exercise provided by Greg Vimont.

Mini-Project #3

Crow's-Foot Exercise

1.   (a) What is the total number of possible pairings of crow's-foot indicators?_____
    How many mirror image pairs exist in these possible combinations (like matching bookends)? _____
    (b) How many unique pairs exist? _____ And if you didn't count the reversed version of each unique pairing, how many are there? _____

Hint: Use this table diagram of crow's-foot indicators to plot all of the possible instances.

	O|	||	O<	|<
|O	|O O|			
||				
>O				
>|				

2. Draw the crow's-foot cardinality for the following situation:

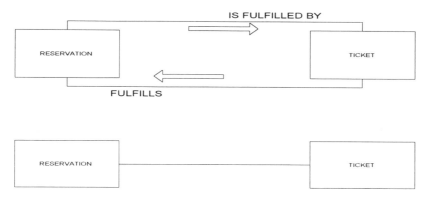

A1 Travel takes reservations from clients and provides them with travel arrangements on common carriers throughout the world. For some reservations, tickets are never issued. Reservations can be made and tickets can be issued for them at a later time. Sometimes, when reservations are made one or more tickets are issued simultaneously. A ticket may fulfill only a single reservation. Tickets, once issued, are never reissued to fulfill anything other than the original reservation.

(3) Draw the crow's-foot cardinality for the following situation:

The Party Palace is a catering facility that hosts many types of social engagements. One type of event is the dinner party. Guests and their respective dates are normally issued seating cards with table assignments. Every guest will have a seating assignment. Not every guest will have a date. Dates may not be unaccompanied, and they must accompany only one guest.

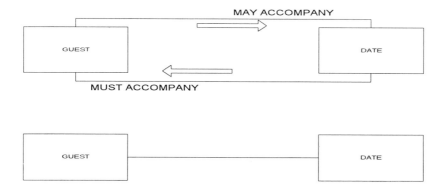

4. Based on the following business case, draw an entity relation diagram. You need only to name the entities; no keys or attributes are required.

> (a) In the operation of its business, *Top-Flight Limo Service* records information about drivers who chauffeur the company's patrons. Drivers must own and drive their own cars. A driver may own more than one vehicle. *Top-Flight Limo* tracks driver traffic citations during the time of their employment with the company. Drivers begin employment with a clean slate.

> (b) In the ERD that you have created, what is the functional significance of "optional" vs. "required" as it is applied to business rules in implementing a database and populating it with data?

Exercise provided by Greg Vimont.

6
Graphical User Interface Tools

Another important component that analysts must address is the design of the user interface. Increasingly over recent years, this interface has become graphically driven as opposed to being character-based.[19] Thus, the acronym GUI for "graphical user interface," has been adopted by the industry. The GUI interface is made up of icons and other symbols that represent functions that the user can implement.

The history of GUI can be traced as far back as the early Xerox systems. Apple was the first company, through its introduction of the Macintosh computer, to effectively commercialize the concept of graphical applications using a mouse. When Microsoft Windows was introduced in the late 1980s, the use of GUI got another major boost. While there are no industry-mandated rules for GUI design, the dominance of the Microsoft Windows product line has resulted in some de facto design standards.

Character-based screens, on the other hand, are often associated with mainframe applications of the 1960s and 1970s; however, many such applications still exist today and continue to be found on mid-range and personal computers. While character-based applications remain important, they are diminishing over time, especially as a result of the popularity of Web-based applications that depend on icons and graphical images. Therefore, this chapter will focus on designing the user interface with graphically driven screens.

---

[19] Character-based screens are those that are composed of only words and captions. Selection of screen options is accomplished through the entering of a code, as opposed to through an object typically called an icon. Character-based screens also do not contain built-in screen features such as drop-down menus, radio buttons, and check boxes.

GUI and Styles of Manipulation

A GUI is the primary mechanism that enables the user to interact with a collection of elements, called "screen objects," that are visible to the user and used by him/her to perform tasks. To accomplish these tasks, users perform various types of operations on these objects. Operations are executed using one of the two types of GUI manipulation: direct and indirect.

The term "direct manipulation" was first used by Ben Shneiderman in 1982 to describe a particular style of human interaction with a screen. Direct manipulation portrays the system as an extension of the real world where users can relate to objects and icons that remind them of real-world symbols. Direct manipulation allows the user to access and modify these symbols so that they can be used to activate tasks. Thus, selecting an icon to perform a task, such as hitting the "save" icon in a word processing program, is an example of a direct manipulation. Direct manipulation relates to the concept of WYSIWYG (what you see is what you get) and must therefore result in an immediate reaction or resultant event.

Indirect manipulation, on the other hand, represents a task that effectively executes another. Thus, selecting an icon that provides a list of other selections can be considered an indirect method for executing what is really desired. An indirect manipulation can be thought of as an easy way to select alternative direct methods. Most GUI designs use a combination of both manipulation methods.

Advantages of GUI Systems

Overall, GUI represents a simplified interface that promises to:

- reduce the need for users to remember how applications work;
- enhance the human ability to process information through a computer interface; and
- reduce the learning time to master a computer application.

Listed below are a number of specific examples of how GUI systems help users.

1. Symbols are recognized faster than text because their shapes and colors are more easily classifiable.

| Different shapes | Text looks similar | Different shapes in similar circles. |

2. Symbols can be easily learned. A graphical, pictorial representation has been found to aid learning.
3. Visual or spatial representations of information have been found to be easier to retain and manipulate.
4. Greater simplicity of graphics makes remembering easier.
5. Actions and visual skills developed before languages in humans. Human beings have a powerful image memory.
6. Spatial relationships are usually more quickly understood than verbal representations.
7. Concrete thinking is enhanced when objects are displayed directly in the high-level task domain. Abstract thinking is minimized.
8. Concrete thinking reduces errors.
9. Immediate feedback develops quicker reflexes. If the path of action is going in the wrong direction, then prompts to correct the path occur sooner.
10. Ability to reverse unwanted or reconsidered actions increases user control, confidence, and system mastery.
11. Icons possess more universality than text and are more easily comprehended worldwide.
12. Moving from a command language to direct manipulation is relatively easy. The reverse is not the case.

Disadvantages of GUI Systems

Some users have found the GUI to be more difficult to work with in some cases, particularly with respect to applications that require only simple data input. Furthermore, as graphical systems become more sophisticated, interfaces will become increasingly more complex. This idea will be explored in Chapter 11, Internet/Intranet and Web Analysis. The following is a list of perceived GUI disadvantages.

1. Design complexity. Layers upon layers of options are packed into an interface.
2. When a user confronts the interface in an application for the first time, the sequence of necessary steps does not always seem intuitive.
3. Lack of thoroughly researched guidelines. Increased GUI complexity unleashes too many variables that must be controlled in order to establish meaningful cause-and-effect relationships.
4. Inconsistencies in technique and terminology occur because of copyright and legal constraints and product differentiation pressures.
5. The working domain is always in the present. Usually, icons don't have past or future tense. When users click on a button, the button takes action immediately. However, there is no reason that delay options could not be implemented.

6. Symbolic representations may not be as familiar as words or numbers.
7. There may be a limit to a human's capability to engage a more complex interface.
8. GUI interfaces are slower to act than character-based applications. There is also more application overhead.
9. Symbols cannot be clearly produced across different hardware technologies. Some are not equally legible or recognizable.
10. Inefficient for touch typists. Moving a mouse is a much slower motor movement than typing.
11. The screen can easily become more cluttered, resulting in the user having more responsibility to do screen housekeeping.
12. Requires more computer processing power.

Conclusion

Regardless of the relative pluses and minuses of GUI, the reality is that today's systems increasingly require it, and Web applications demand it. Different interface styles have different capacities. Some concepts and tasks are better suited than others for pure graphical presentation. Therefore, it is the design of the interface and not its interaction style that is the most reliable success factor. The success of a graphical system depends on the skills of its analysts and designers in following established principles of usability.

Where to Begin

Screens can be designed using a number of approaches. Under the best circumstances, the analyst should first complete data flow and process flow diagramming, creating the data dictionary, and producing process specifications. Taking these steps is an important precursor to screen design, allowing the analyst to begin mapping elements needed for screens to the data elements that exist in the data dictionary. The process specifications are also critical because they usually contain the business rules that often govern the way the elements behave during the user interface. Furthermore, the process of designing screens may even lead to process specification updates because of new requirements that get formulated during the development and approval of screen functionality. We must remember that in GUI applications, most functions are initiated through a screen program. Process flow diagrams may be extremely useful to screen design because they follow the user's sequential needs. Thus, mapping screen requirements to each process can be a useful step in beginning design. It should be understood, however, that screens and processes do not have a one-to-one relationship. While such a relationship may exist, it is totally incidental. Take the following example:

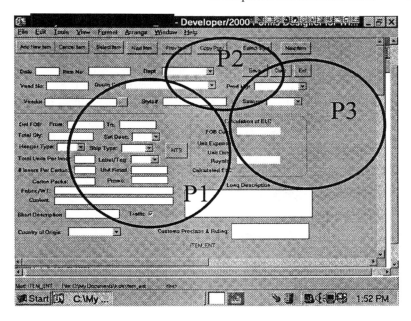

Figure 6.1 Order item entry screen.

The screen of Figure 6.1 depicts three actual processes. Figure 6.2 shows the corresponding processes as they are represented in a PFD.

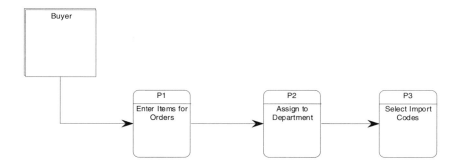

Figure 6.2 Process flow of order entry screen.

Another, alternative, approach to designing screens is to start with the ERD. In this case, every data element in the ERD is mapped to a specific processing point in the system. This processing point is then correlated to a screen. Unfortunately, this approach has many limitations. First, not every data element in the ERD may be required to appear on a screen. Second, there are many fields that are results of calculations that must be displayed, but are not elements in the database (remember that 3rd normal form will eliminate derived elements). Figure 6.3 depicts a screen that has been mapped to an ERD. The actual data element names are linked to the screen fields. Notice, however, that the screen fields labeled "Duty" and "Expenses" are not mapped because they must be computed each time the screen program is executed. Thus, these elements are 3rd NF failures because they are derived.

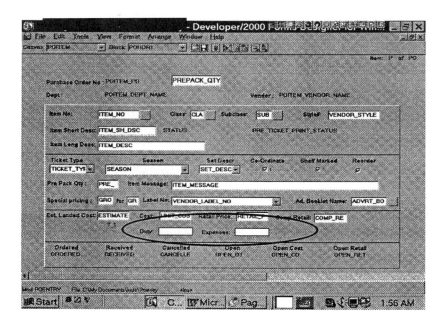

Figure 6.3 GUI screen showing corresponding data element reference.

Yet another common method is to use the screens from the legacy system as a starting point. Most software development projects are not done from scratch, meaning that there is an existing system in place. Under this procedure, the analyst obtains copies of every screen in the existing system. The screens are then modified with new GUI functionality that is needed by the new system. While this sounds very straightforward, character-based screens often do not map easily to their GUI counterparts. The analyst must be especially careful not to attempt to simply duplicate the screens in the legacy software. Figure 6.4 depicts a character-based legacy screen. Note that there can be up to four Contract/POs as shown in the upper right-hand corner. The user is required to enter each Contract/PO on a separate screen.

	Bill of Lading Container	Screen 1 of 4

B/L:_____ SCAC: _____ VESSEL: _____ Total: _____
                        VOYAGE: _____ CTN: _____

PO Information

Contract/PO: _____   Tot Unit: _____
Item: _____   GWT: _____
Style: _____   CBM: _____
Stat: _____   O/F Chrg: _____
Orig Country: _____   Con Rate: _____

Activities

Activity	Descr	Date	Location

Figure 6.4 Character-based user screen.

On the other hand, the replacement GUI screen below takes advantage of the view bar that allows for scrolling in a window. Therefore, the GUI version requires only one physical screen, as opposed to four.

Still another method of designing screens is to hold separate user interviews, with the sole focus of determining the types of screens that are needed. This process, which can be effectively done using JAD sessions, is a way of reconciling the screens against the process specifications, data dictionary, and flow diagrams (DFDs and PFDs). Often, analysts may try to develop prototype screens based on their knowledge and understanding of the requirements from the structured tools. This can at least provide users with something to critique. Screens can be quickly drawn using a number of prototype packages, although almost every development tool, such as Oracle/2000, Visual Basic, and Powerbuilder, have easy-to-use screen painter features. A screen painter is a graphic tool within a development product that allows you to design a screen quickly for prototype use. The main advantage here is that the screen painter interfaces with features that allow the prototype to be converted to a production version of the screen. The production version or compile feature of the product can

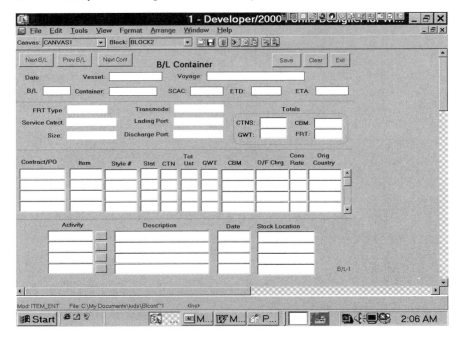

Figure 6.5 GUI replication screen of character-based system.

typically be used by programmers after the prototype screen is passed to them for development.

Screen design is a very iterative process. It usually starts with just a drawing of the screen in pencil. The analyst then prototypes the screen for presentation. At this point, the users may need to have the screens "linked" so that they can get a sense of how the screens integrate as a product. Screen linking can be accomplished by using Microsoft's Powerpoint; still others have actual linking capabilities in their prototype feature. In any event, users need to get a sense of how the screens work. After one or two iterations of review, the analyst should then provide development with the source screens so that they can be implemented. As screens are completed, they should again be shown to users for their approval.

Components of the GUI

There are a number of parts that can go with the design of a user screen: (1) operating system; (2) application; and (3) interapplication.

An operating system component relates to the de facto universal Microsoft or Apple menus and icons that interface with the operating system itself. Examples of these controls are the Application Window Menu Bar, sizing control icons, and the Microsoft Application bar. These controls are summarized below and shown on the sample application screen in Figure 6.6:

Border: Also known as a "frame," a border defines the boundaries of a window view and distinguishes it from other windows.

Title Bar: This is the top line of the window and explains the purpose or name of the window function.

Work Area: This is the portion of the screen inside the borders of the window where the user performs tasks.

System Menu Button: This button is located at the left corner of the title bar and is also called the "control menu" or the "window menu." This button is used as an aid to keyboard users and lists options for manipulating the window. This includes commands such as *Restore, Minimize, Maximize,* and, *Close.*

Title Bar Icon: This icon is located in the left corner of the title bar and is used to retrieve a pull-down menu of commands that apply to the object in the window.

Window Sizing Buttons: These buttons are located on the right corner of the title bar and are used to manipulate the size of the active window.

Menu Bar: This is used to organize and provide access to actions that are listed horizontally across the top of the screen and below the title bar.

Status Bar: Also known as a "message bar," the status bar provides information to the user about the state or status of the information or object inside the window.

Scroll Bars: These appear when all displayed information cannot be presented within the current window boundaries. The vertical scroll bar at the right of a window controls the up-and-down scrolling, while the horizontal scroll bar controls right-to-left movement.

Split Box/Split Bar: This is a window that is split into two or more pieces, or panes. Split boxes can be manipulated using the split bar, which is located above the vertical scroll bar.

Control Bar: This represents an array of choices and commands that need to be viewed in an accessible area of the screen and are maintained in the display area. Examples include button bars, color or pattern palettes, toolbars, rulers, and ribbons.

Size Grip: This a handle in a window that permits the window to be resized. The resizing is accomplished by dragging the grip and moving the window to the desired size. The grip is located in the lower right corner of the window. It is identified by 3 angled parallel lines.

What's This? The question mark indicates to the system that the user wishes to ask a question about the object being pointed to.

The application screen component consists of the specific data elements that are needed by the screen application program. One can visualize that the application component interfaces with the data elements in the ERD. The application component is the most free-flowing and involves the most design issues. There are a limited number of application screen tools such as buttons, check boxes, and drop-down selections. The specific component controls within an application screen are depicted below:

 Radio Button: This is used when there are two or more mutually exclusive options. A dot in the circle indicates that the option has been selected.

 Command or Push Button: This initiates an option. Command buttons typically contain a label on the button that identifies the nature of the option.

Check Box: This used when you have one or more options that are independent of each other. A checked box indicates that the option is selected.

 Scroll Bar: A scroll bar scrolls the screen either horizontally or vertically. The purpose of the scroll bar is to allow users to input or view more information than is available on the normal screen view.

 List Box: These are used to display several choices. There are two types of list boxes. Single selection list boxes force the user to choose one selection. Multiple selection list boxes allow the user to make several selections. Multiple selections is a useful option if the user is choosing several items that will be acted upon the same way.

Combo Box: This is used when you want to provide the user with the ability to either select from a list or enter a value. A good example is the "Save As" feature in Windows, where a user can either leave the default value or change the name by overwriting it. Combo boxes are also useful for ensuring that the insert of a foreign key points to a valid parent value (see the Chapter 5 section titled "Business Rules").

Text or Edit Box: This is used simply to enter or edit data. Text boxes are used frequently for screens that require data entry and for display of data. Data that is only displayed is often shown as gray without a black outline. Thus, just the text appears on the screen.

Figure 6.6 GUI screen features.

Interapplication features are defined as those that are "called" by the current screen program. Pop-up menus and pop-up screens are examples of interapplication functionality. The analyst must be able to design general types of pop-up menus that may be used by multiple screens. These were traditionally called "subprograms" or "subroutines" in legacy applications. The more robust implementation of subprograms that can be dynamically linked to screen programs is a significant advantage in the GUI paradigm. Examples of these types of GUI interfaces are shown in Figures 6.7 through 6.10.

1. Icon Window Control for the Application [Primary] Window.
2. Icon Window Control for the Secondary [Database] Window.
3. Application Window Title Bar
4. Secondary Window Title Bar.
5. Sizing Control Icons for Application [Primary] Window.
6. Sizing Control Icons for Application [Secondary] Window.
7. Command Buttons [Open, Design, New].
8. Sizing Grip for Application Window.
9. Microsoft Office Application Bar for NT [Operating System] Window.
10. Horizontal Scroll Bar for Application Window.
11. Notice the Tab Card Dialog Box that houses the Database Options.
12. Tool Bar for Query Datasheet [Unavailable because no table is open].
13. Open Application running in the background.
14. Open Application running in the foreground – Current Active Application.
15. Windows NT Title

Figure 6.7 GUI sample screen.

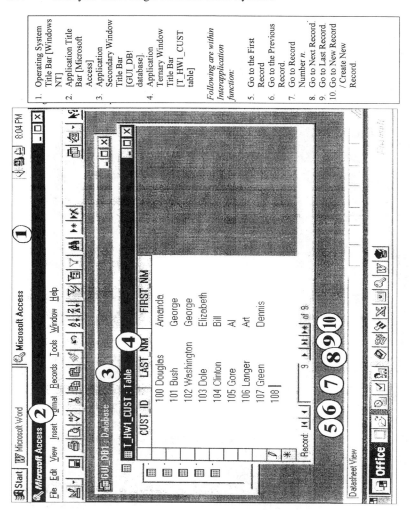

1. Operating System Title Bar [Windows NT]
2. Application Title Bar [Microsoft Access]
3. Application Secondary Window Title Bar [GUI_DB! database].
4. Application Ternary Window Title Bar [T_HW1_CUST table]

Following are within Interapplication function:

5. Go to the First Record
6. Go to the Previous Record.
7. Go to Record Number n.
8. Go to Next Record.
9. Go to Last Record.
10. Go to New Record / Create New Record.

Figure 6.8 GUI sample screen.

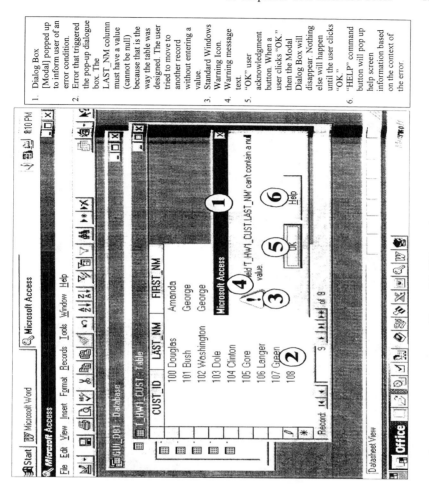

1. Dialog Box [Modal] popped up to inform user of an error condition.

2. Error that triggered the pop-up dialogue box. The LAST_NM column must have a value (cannot be null) because that is the way the table was designed. The user tried to move to another record without entering a value.

3. Standard Windows Warning Icon.

4. Warning message text.

5. "OK" user acknowledgment button. When a user clicks "OK," then the Modal Dialog Box will disappear. Nothing else will happen until the user clicks "OK."

6. "HELP" command button will pop up help screen information based on the context of the error.

Figure 6.9 GUI sample screen.

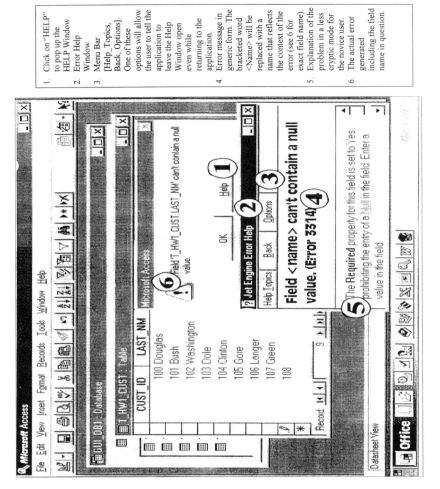

Figure 6.10 GUI sample screen.

1. Click on "HELP" to pop up the HELP Window.

2. Error Help Window

3. Menu Bar [Help_Topics, Back, Options]. One of these options will allow the user to tell the application to leave the Help Window open even while returning to the application.

4. Error message in generic form. The bracketed word <Name> will be replaced with a name that reflects the context of the error (see 6 for exact field name).

5. Explanation of the problem in a less cryptic mode for the novice user.

6. The actual error generated including the field name in question.

Problems and Exercises

1. Define what is meant by a GUI.
2. Explain the differences and similarities between character-based screens and GUI-based screens.
3. Describe the differences between direct manipulation and indirect manipulation.
4. Provide 10 advantages of GUI systems and 10 disadvantages. Explain your support for each pro and con.
5. How do GUI screens interface with a PDF? a DFD?
6. How do GUI screens interface with the ERD?
7. Explain how derived data elements exist between screens and the ERD.
8. List and explain five unique components of a GUI screen.
9. What is the functional difference between a check box and a radio button?
10. Explain the relationship among a derived data element, the ERD, and the process specification.

7
Design Specification Tools

Chapter 2 discussed specification formats that can be used to communicate information to both users and technical development personnel. Chapter 3 focused on the specific tools to create the logical equivalent. A diagram was used to show how an architect created a drawing for the user and a blueprint for the builder. This example was expanded to relate to the analyst:

Designing the System

| Prototype | Analyst | DFD |

Figure 7.1 Analyst interfaces.

In this chapter, we will focus on the process specification portions of the system, both from a user and a development perspective. The process specification is a component of every modeling tool.

Business Specifications

The ultimate purpose of the *business specification* is to confirm with the user the requirements of the system. In the picture above, this confirmation is shown in the form of a prototype. Although this is the best way to confirm requirements with a user, there is always a need to have certain logic and flow documented in the form of a business specification. Chapter 3 presented the business specification below and defined it as a summary of the overall requirements of the system.

Client: **XYZ Corporation**	Date: 9/5/94
Application: **Operations Database**	Supersedes:

Subject:
    Contact Management
	Author:
	    A. Langer

Process:
    Overview -- Business Spec
	Page:
	                    1 of 2

Overview

The contact management process will allow users to add, modify, or delete specific contacts. Contacts will be linked to various tables including Company. A contact refers to a person who is related to XYZ for business reasons. It can be a client, a vendor, a consultant, a person involved in a negotiation, etc.

Contact General Information:

The database must allow for the centralization of all the contacts handled by all the departments in XYZ. The database and screens will be focused on the following information component groupings:

Basic Information

This is the minimum data requirement and includes such elements as Name, Title, Organization, Phone, Fax, Address, Country, etc.

Contact Profile Information

Further qualification and related elements. Relations include:

- department
- type of client
- nature of client (primary, technical)
- interest of prospect
- importance of client
- memberships (FTUG)
- FT employee

This is a business specification that reflects the overall requirements in prose format. Its focus is to provide the user who is not technical with a document that he or she can authorize. This business specification should then point to detailed programming logic.

Figure 7.2 Sample business specification.

The business specification was written in a prose format so users could be comfortable with its meaning and intent, so that they could approve it. Although an overview like the one above is helpful, it is often incomplete and may not actually provide sufficient information for the user to approve. In order to provide more detail, the analyst should include the following components with many business specifications given to a user.

Functional Overview Sections

Functional overviews effectively take the business view a notch down in detail. A function can be considered a subset portion of the whole specification. For example, suppose a business specification was designed to handle order processing. Order processing would be considered the overall business specification goal; however, a subset function of the overall project could be picking order items from the warehouse. The subset description of the process is similar to the general overview and simply puts the subset functionality into perspective using prose format. After each subset functional overview is completed, the user should have enough information to understand the requirements of the system. It is important that the analyst make every attempt to keep the general and functional overviews as short as possible yet accurate and complete. This may sound contradictory; however, users typically do not like to read long documents summarizing all the detailed events of a system. Although Figure 7.3 looks like an overview, it is focused solely on a subprocess called Discounts.

Company: XYZ	Date: 9/27/95
Application: Discounting	Supersedes:
Subject: Discounting Plan	Author: A. Langer
Process: Functional Business Spec	Page: 2 of 2

Year-End Reconciliation

The XYZ discount is guaranteed at the starting discount level. Therefore, should the bookstore not meet last year's order level, the discount cannot be lowered during the year. The only time the discount can be lowered is at the end of the year. At year-end, a process runs which reevaluates all the customers based on the current year's and last year's sales. This procedure is used only to create the new level for next year.

> *Although Figure 7.3 looks like an overview, it is focused solely on a subprocess called Discounts*

Screens & Reports

The order entry screen and all customer inquiry screens need to display the current Book and Bible discount for these customers. The amount used to determine the discount should be available on a customer inquiry screen as well as a report. The current system displays the month-to-date, current quarter, and current year's sales, as well as last year's sales. Total net sales and returns are listed, as well as net sales and returns of the discount items.

Chain Stores

Another major difference between this plan and others is that for chain stores, all sales for each branch store are added together, and they all receive the discount based on the total net sales for the chain. There can be situations where one of the branches does not qualify to receive the discount, but their sales are still added into the total for the chain.

If two stores become a chain mid-year, their individual annual net sales are added together, and their discount is increased if applicable.

Figure 7.3 A functional business specification summarizing the requirements for a discount component of the entire business specification.

Functional Flow Diagrams

Wherever possible it is important to use graphical representations to verify the accuracy of a specification. A high level data flow is suggested to allow the user to see a graphical representation of the overall requirement (see Figure 7.4). Analysts should be encouraged to educate users so that they understand simple modeling concepts and tools.

Screens and Reports

The business specification should also include sample screens and reports. The level of detail of the screens and reports will vary depending on the prototype tools being used and the available time frame that the analyst has to get user sign-off on the requirements. CASE can be used where screen and report inter-face are available (see Figure 7.5). Analysts should avoid CASE products that contain drawing capabilities as opposed to true screen and report generators. Today's programming tools typically have prototype capabilities. The advan-tage here is that part of the development work is being accomplished during analysis and design. Using actual development tools during analysis and design is yet another form of Rapid Application Development (RAD).

Therefore a good business specification should include the following com-ponent documents:

Business specification overview	Business specification for each functional subsystem	High-level data flow diagrams	Screen prototypes	Report prototypes

Company: **XYZ**	Date: **5/27/94**
Application: **Discounting**	Supersedes:
Subject: **Discounting Plan**	Author: **A. Langer**
Process: **Data Flow Diagram**	Page: **1 of 1**

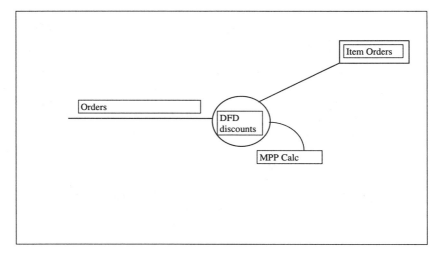

Figure 7.4 High Level DFD. Although a DFD, it is designed at a very simple level to allow a user to confirm flow.

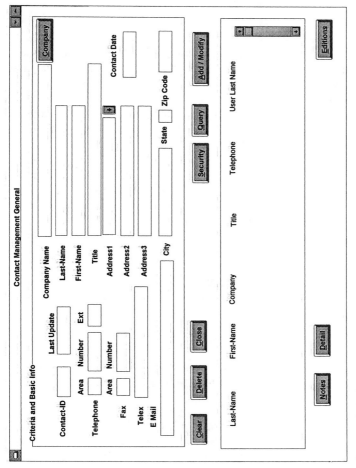

Figure 7.5 CASE screen design. The above screen was created in System Architect and contains connectivity to physical application products such as Powerbuilder.

Programming and Technical Specifications

Once the business specifications are completed and agreed upon by the users, the information must be mapped into a programming or technical specification. These specifications effectively provide all of the algorithms that are required by the functional primitive DFDs and STDs. That is, each functional primitive must point to a technical programming specification. This programming specification will define all algorithms which affect the process. The programming specification must also, however, point back to its original functional business specification as shown in Figure 7.6.

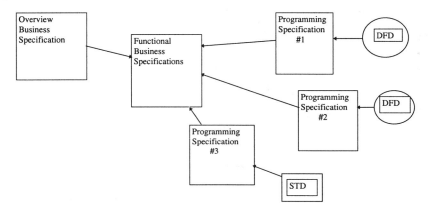

Figure 7.6 Relationship of specifications with DFDs and STDs.

Another way of explaining the relationship is to say that an overview business specification can have many functional business specifications. Functional business specifications can have many programming specifications and each programming specification should be associated with one or many functional primitive DFDs or STDs. The example of a technical/programming specification contained in Figure 7.7 initially appeared as Figure 3.11 of Chapter 3.

The programming specification in Figure 7.7 utilizes the pseudocode method discussed in Chapter 4 and provides the necessary information for a programmer to develop the application. Many IS professionals often feel the need for programmers to understand the business specification. If the program specifications are developed using the methods recommended herein, then there is no such requirement placed on the programming team. Good programming specifications stand alone, like a good blueprint that will allow a contractor to build a house without ever being part of the development and confirmation phases with the buyer. Programmers who can focus on the engineering issues rather than user requirements will be much more productive. Therefore, IS professionals who share both roles, that is, those with the title

"Pro-grammer/Analyst," will always be susceptible to doing both system requirements and engineering development simultaneously. Doing both "as you go" poses a real danger in that the individual has to continually change hats without really separating the tasks. In addition, when the two tasks are combined it typically results in a longer development life cycle and one that has less quality because neither task is ever really completed. Furthermore, the skill sets of analysts tend to conflict with those of programmers. For example, analysts should enjoy interacting with users and need to develop skills that allow them to gather the information they need. Programmers, on the other hand, often are not comfortable with user interaction and are more focused on their technical knowledge of software and hardware products.

Client: XYZ Company	Date: 9/15/99
Application: Contact Management	Supersedes: 9/5/99
Subject: Program Specification Detail	Author: A. Langer
Spec-ID FTCM01 - Add/Modify Screen Processing	Page: 1 of 1

Process Flow Description:
 The user will input information in the top form. At a minimum, at least the Last Name or Contact ID will be entered. The system must check a Security indicator prior to allowing a user to modify a Contact. The Security will be by Department or Everyone. Therefore, if the Modify button is selected and the user is restricted by a different department, Display:
  " Access Denied, not eligible to modify, Department Restriction"

 If Security authorized, the Add/Modify Button will activate the following business rules:

  If Contact-ID (cntid) not blank
   Find match and replace entered data into record
   If no match display "Invalid Contact-ID" and refresh cursor

  If Contact-ID (cntid) Blank and Last-Name (cntlname) Blank then
    Display " Contact-ID or Last-Name must be entered"
    Place Cursor at Contact-ID (cntid) entry.

> This area actually states the algorithm required by the program. It is in a format called Pseudocode" meaning "false code."   This type of logic resembles Cobol format. (see Chapter 4)

   If Contact-ID (cntid) Blank and Last-Name (cntlname) + First-Name (cntfname) is Duplicate
   Display Window to show matches so that user can determine if contact already in system
   If user selects the Add Anyway button
        assume new contact with same name and assign new Contact-ID (cntid)
    else
        upon selection bring in existing data and close window.
  Else
   Create new record with all new information fields and assign Contact-ID (cntid)

 If Company button activated
  Prompt user for Company-ID (cmpcd) and/or Company-Name (cmpna)
  If duplicate
        link foreign-key pointer to matched company
   else
        add Company-Name (cntcmpna) to Contact Table only
        Display "You must use Company Screen to Link, Company Master File Not Updated"

Figure 7.7 Technical/Programming Specification.

Screen Specifications

Another method of creating specifications, particularly when data flow diagrams and process diagrams are not used, is to create them directly from the screens themselves. This is usually accomplished by having two levels of screen processing specifications. The first type of specification is used to describe the functionality of the screen, especially as it relates to its execution options. The second type of specification relates to how the data elements on the screen are to be processed. By process we mean the business rules that govern how the data element is treated by the screen program. For example, a data element in one screen program may be used only in display mode and not allow its value to be modified. Yet in another screen, the very same data element may require modification.

Therefore, a screen specification has three components: (1) the screen itself; (2) screen processing specifications; and (3) data element specifications. There should be one data element specification for every data element that appears on a screen. Good specifications will even use the same data element definition across multiple screen specifications just to ensure that there are no elements that are left undefined in any screen definition documentation.

Figure 7.8 shows a screen designed using Oracle Developer 2000. Figure 7.9 depicts the screen processing requirements. Specifically, the screen processing specifications provide a description of the purpose and functionality of the screen, as well as stating how each function button is to be handled by the program. Figure 7.10 is an example of a screen data element definition in which Vendor_No is used to fetch and display Vendor, which is the vendor's name. Note that the form is designed to state specific information necessary for a programmer to complete development, including the domain of values of the data element, its definition in terms of processing, and whether the value can be added, deleted, or modified from the database.

Screens and Derived Elements

In Chapter 5, the handling of derived data elements in normalization was defined as a type of 3rd normal form failure. That is, derived data elements, commonly known as calculated fields, were eliminated as a stored attribute in an entity. However, screens often need to calculate and display these derived elements. For example, the screen in Figure 7.8 has a field called "ELC" standing for "Estimated Landing Cost." This element is calculated, both for the season and for year-to-date. The calculations for "ELC Season" and "ELC YTD" are defined in their corresponding Screen Data Element Definition forms as shown in Figures 7.11 and 7.12 respectively. Thus, every data element in the data dictionary that appears on a screen must have a corresponding

Screen Data Element Definition form, regardless of whether it is a stored attribute in an entity or a derived element that requires dynamic calculation.

Figure 7.8 GUI screen using Oracle Developer/2000.

Venden01

Client:	Date: 2/28/99
Application: **Vendor Expense Allocation**	Supersedes: 12/28//98

Process:
          Screen Processing
	Author:
	          A. Langer

Description & Source:
This screen allows for the entry of expenses and other pertinent information about vendors. The screen can also be executed in edit mode and allows users to browse sequentially by Vendor. The screen allows for up to three (3) expense allocations. The expense allocation is used to calculate the ELC (see Item-1)

ANALYSIS OF SCREEN FUNCTIONS

Button Function:	Process Definition:
Select Vendor	Locates a particular vendor to add or edit information.
Next Vend	Displays next sequential Vendor stored in the database
Previous Item	Displays previous Vendor in database
Save	Saves contents of screen to database
Clear	Clears screen values (only in Add New Item mode)
Exit	Cancel execution of screen program and display calling screen

Copyright A. Langer 1994-1997

Figure 7.9 Screen processing requirements.

Form: Vendd01

Client:	Date: 12/28/99
Application: **Vendor Expense Allocation**	Supersedes:

Process:
    Screen data Element Definition
	Author:
	    A. Langer

Data Element:
    Vendor
	SQL Data Type and Qualifier
	    Varchar18

Description:
This element represents the Vendor Name. Vendors can be created only from Unisys. Therefore, they may be assigned to only for further editing with respect to expenses and other imports-specific information. The changes do not update the Unisys system.

ANALYSIS OF DATA ELEMENT

Values:
Value is assigned from advanced selection button.

Definition:
Search/Select from table. New Vendor may not be added. Entry required.

✓	Data Element Action	Table Action	Name / Value
✓	ADDED	Assign from Vendor Table	Vendor_No
	DELETED		
✓	MODIFIED	Assign from Vendor table:	Vendor_No

Copyright A. Langer 1994-2000
Form xxxd01

Figure 7.10 Screen data element definition.

Form: Vendd11

Client:	Date: 12/28/99
Application: **Vendor Expense Allocation**	Supersedes:
Process: Screen data Element Definition	Author: A. Langer
Data Element: ELC Season	SQL Data Type and Qualifier Number 15,2

Description:
This element represents the calculated Estimated Landing Costs Season-to-Date.

ANALYSIS OF DATA ELEMENT

Values:
Must be a calculated from all ELC from Vendor items season to date.

Definition:
Calculated field IMP_ELC_SN. Add all Item ELCs for Vendor for season. See Item-Ent.

✓	Data Element Action	Table Action		Name / Value
	ADDED		Add	
	DELETED		Delete	
	MODIFIED		Modify:	

Copyright A. Langer 1994-99
Form xxxd01

Figure 7.11 Screen data element definition for ELC season calculation.

Form: Vendd11a

Client:	Date: 2/27/99
Application: Vendor Expense Allocation	Supersedes: 12/28/98

Process:
      Screen data Element Definition
	Author:
	      A. Langer

Data Element:
      ELC Year
	SQL Data Type and Qualifier
	      Number 15,2

Description:
This element represents the calculated Estimated Landing Costs Year-to-Date.

ANALYSIS OF DATA ELEMENT

Values:
Must be a calculated from all
ELC from Vendor items year to
date.

Definition:
Calculated field IMP_ELC_YR. Add all Item ELCs for Vendor for
year. See Item-Ent.

✔	Data Element Action	Table Action	Name / Value
	ADDED	Add	
	DELETED	Delete	
	MODIFIED	Modify	

Copyright A. Langer 1994-99
Form xxxd01

Figure 7.12 Screen data element definition for ELC YTD calculation.

Problems and Exercises

1. What is the purpose of business specifications?
2. How do functional overview sections relate to the entire business specification?
3. What is the use of a functional flow diagram? Which modeling tool is used?
4. What are the five most common components of the business specification?

5. How does the business specification relate to the programming specification?
6. How does the programming specification interface with DFDs and STDs?
7. Define the three components of a screen specification.
8. Explain the purpose of a "Screen Data Element Definition."
9. What is the purpose of having "Screen Processing" instructions?

Mini-Project

The process specifications and GUI screens are part of the requirements of a contact management system. Based on this specification, design the ERD in 3rd normal form.

Client:	Date: 9/5/99
Application: **Operations Database**	Supersedes:
Subject: **Contact Management**	Author: **A. Langer**
Process: **Overview - Business Spec**	Page: **1 of 2**

Overview

The Contact Management Process will allow users to add, modify, or delete specific contacts. Contacts will be linked to various tables including Company. A Contact refers to a person who is related to the business. It can be a Client, a Vendor, a consultant, a person involved in a negotiation, etc.

Contact General Information:

The Database must allow for the centralization of all the contacts handled by all departments.
The database and screens will be focused on the following information component groupings:

Basic Information

This is the minimum data requirement and includes such elements as Name, Title, Organization, Phone, Fax, Address, Country.

Contact Profile Information

Further qualification and related elements. Relations include:

- department
- type of client
- nature of client (primary, technical)
- interest of prospect
- importance of client
- memberships (FTUG)
- FT employee

Copyright A. Langer & Assoc, Inc 1999   \contbs.doc

Client:	Date: 9/5/99
Application: **Operations Database**	Supersedes:

Subject:
    Contact Management
	Author:
	    A. Langer

Process:
    Overview – Business Spec
	Page:
	    2 of 2

Mailing Information
Mailing selections to produce labels include:

- Selected Mailing Groupings via Query
- Source of Lead
- The Region
- Description of the salutation for the contact

Log Information:
This will include general information in the form of comments and a related date of entry.

Contact-Specific Information:

In addition to the groupings listed above, there is specific information required:

Market Observation/Business Development Information:
This involves activity of a visit and requires linkage to the main contact database. Elements needed are:
- Objective of Visit
- Date of Visit
- Place of Visit
- Visit Report

Press Information:
This includes:
- related contact publication
- areas of expertise
- circulation

Copyright A. Langer & Assoc, Inc 1999   \contbs2.doc

Client:	Date: 9/5/99
Application: Contact Management	**Supersedes:**
Subject: Specification Detail	**Author: A. Langer**
ID FTCMSDR	**Page: 1 of 1**

REQUIREMENTS INDEX	SPEC-ID
Add / Modify Button	FTCM01
Query Button	FTCM02
Delete Button	FTCM03
Clear Button	FTCM04
Detail Button and Screen	FTCM05
Notes Button	FTCM06

ftcmSDR.doc rev. 8/22/99   Copyright © A. Langer & Assoc., Inc 1999

Client:	Date: 9/15/99
Application: Contact Management	**Supersedes: 9/5/99**
Subject: Program Specification Detail	**Author: A. Langer**
Spec-ID FTCM01 - Add/Modify Screen Processing	**Page: 1 of 1**

Process Flow Description:
The user will input information in the top form. At a minimum, at least the Last Name or Contact ID will
be entered. The system must check a Security indicator prior to allowing a user to modify a Contact.
The Security will be by Department or Everyone. Therefore, if the Modify button is selected and the user
is restricted by a different department, Display:
　　　"Access Denied, not eligible to modify, Department Restriction"

If Security authorized, the Add/Modify Button will activate the following business rules:

　　　If Contact-ID (cntid) not blank
　　　　　　Find match and replace entered data into record
　　　　　　If no match display "Invalid Contact-ID" and refresh cursor

　　　If Contact-ID (cntid) Blank and Last-Name (cntlname) Blank then
　　　　　　Display " Contact-ID or Last-Name must be entered"
　　　　　　Place Cursor at Contact-ID (cntid) entry.

　　　If Contact-ID (cntid) Blank and Last-Name (cntlname) + First-Name (cntfname) is Duplicate
　　　　　　Display Window to show matches so that user can determine whether contact already in
　　　　　　system
　　　　　　If user selects the Add Anyway button
　　　　　　　　　assume new contact with same name and assign new Contact-ID (cntid)
　　　　　　else
　　　　　　　　　upon selection bring in existing data and close window.
　　　Else
　　　　　　Create new record with all new information fields and assign Contact-ID (cntid)

　　　If Company button activated
　　　　　　Prompt user for Company-ID (cmpcd) and/or Company-Name (cmpna)
　　　　　　If duplicate
　　　　　　　　　link foreign-key pointer to matched company
　　　　　　else
　　　　　　　　　add Company-Name (cntcmpna) to Contact Table only
　　　　　　　　　Display "You must use Company Screen to Link, Company Master File Not
　　　　　　　　　Updated"

Client:	Date 9/15/99
Application: Contact Management	Supersedes: : 9/5/99
Subject: Program Specification Detail	Author: A. Langer
Spec-ID FTCM02 - Query	Page: 1 of 1

Process Flow Description:

The user will have the ability to select the Query Button after entering information in upper portion of the screen. The Query button will activate a search on the Contact database for matches based on entered information.

      If Matches (Based on Access Authorization, if not authorized, display in gray without Company Name):
            Display matched records (see screen format)
      else
            Display "No Matches Found"

      If Matches and User enables Edition buttons
            select appropriate option for labels or ASCII File creation on matched query records

      If user highlights specific match and double clicks
            Display General and Detail and allow user to activate Modify to make changes

Client	Date 9/15/99
Application: Contact Management	**Supersedes: :** 9/5/99
Subject: Program Specification Detail	**Author: A. Langer**
Spec-ID FTCM03 - Delete	**Page:** 1 of 1

Process Flow Description:

The user will have the ability to select the Delete Button in order to delete a Contact. Only certain users will have authorization to perform this function. Therefore, this process must interface with a security table.

To preserve referential integrity on Company, the user must be prompted to delete the Company based on the following rules:

> If Company Name in Contact database (meaning that Company database was not updated)
> > delete Contact record only (no foreign key pointer)
>
> else
>
> > do not delete related Company in Company database

Client	Date 9/15/99
Application: Contact Management	Supersedes: : 9/5/99
Subject: Program Specification Detail	Author: A. Langer
Spec-ID FTCM05 -Detail	Page: 1 of 1

Process Flow Description:

The user will have the ability to select the Detail Button in order to activate the Contact Management Detail Screen (see sample). The following rules apply:

1. Basic Information = Basic Information from General Screen. This data cannot be modified from Detail Screen.

2. Mailing Information includes pick lists for Sources, Leads, and Regions

3. Press Information includes pick list for Expertise

4. Contact Profile includes Departments, CTC types, CTC nature, Interest Level, and Importance Level

5. Activating the Cancel Button at any time will cancel any new input/modifications and link back to the General Screen.

6. Activating the OK button will save all Detail Screen Data to record and return to General Screen.

Client	Date 9/15/99
Application: Contact Management	Supersedes: : 9/5/99
Subject: Program Specification Detail	Author: A. Langer
Spec-ID FTCM05 -Detail	Page: 1 of 1

Process Flow Description:

The user will have the ability to select the Detail Button in order to activate the Contact Management Detail Screen (see sample). The following rules apply:

1. Basic Information = Basic Information from General Screen. This data cannot be modified from Detail Screen.

2. Mailing Information includes pick lists for Sources, Leads, and Regions

3. Press Information includes pick list for Expertise

4. Contact Profile includes Departments, CTC types, CTC nature, Interest Level, and Importance Level

5. Activating the Cancel Button at any time will cancel any new input/modifications and link back to the General Screen.

6. Activating the OK button will save all Detail Screen Data to record and return to General Screen.

Client:	Date: 9/5/99
Application: Contact Management	**Supersedes:**
Subject: Program Specification Detail	**Author: A. Langer**
Spec-ID FTCM06 -Notes	**Page:** **1 of 1**

Process Flow Description:

The user will have the ability to select the Notes Button in order to enter free-form about the Contact.

1.The System should record the date of each note when entered.

2. There is no limit to the number of Notes.

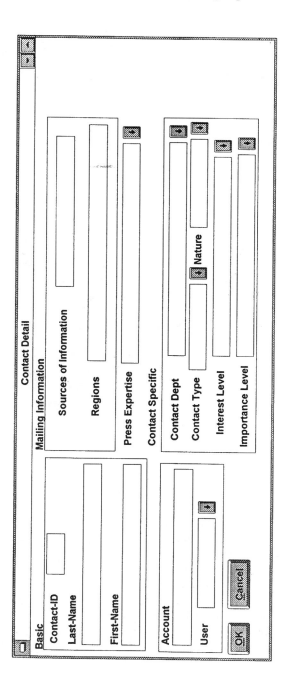

8
CASE and Automated Techniques

CASE Defined

We have mentioned CASE (Computer-Aided Software Engineering) in previous chapters. Although its meanings can vary, CASE is traditionally defined as "a comprehensive label for software designed to use computers in all phases of computer development, from planning and modeling through coding and documentation. CASE represents a working environment consisting of programs and other development tools that help managers, systems analysts, programmers, and others automate the design and implementation of programs and procedures for business, engineering, and scientific computer systems."[20] CASE became popular during the late 1970s as a way of automating and integrating modeling tools. It also allows for the creation and maintenance of data repositories which provide organizations with a tool to establish a central place to store all of their data elements. Figure 8.1 shows the common components of most integrated CASE products.

Data Repository Inputs

The design of CASE is based on inputs which create entries into the data repository. A data repository can be defined as a "robust data dictionary." A data dictionary essentially provides the definition of the data element itself. A data repository, on the other hand, stores information relating to the data element's behavior. This can include the element's stored procedures, descriptions, and documentation about how and where it is used. Therefore, the data dictionary can actually be considered a subset of the data repository. Inputs to the data repository are typically the modeling tools discussed in Chapter 4: DFDs, ERDs, STDs, and process specifications as well as the object oriented analysis discussed in Chapter 9. These input capabilities can be summarized as follows.

---

[20] Microsoft Press, *Computer Dictionary*, 2nd ed., p. 66.

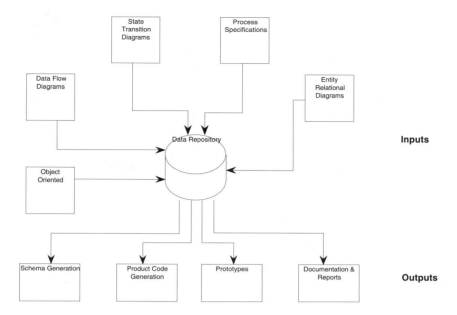

Figure 8.1 Components of CASE.

Data Flow Diagrams (DFD)

Every named data flow will automatically require an entry into the data repository. This named flow may consist of other elements and therefore require functional decomposition down to the elementary data element level. Unique data elements that are components of data stores will also generate entries into the data repository. Figures 8.2. and 8.3 show these interfaces in the Popkin System Architect CASE product.

Figure 8.2 CASE flow elements. The above diagram shows how a data flow is defined by its elementary data elements.

Figure 8.3 CASE data flow definition. The above diagram shows how the data components of the Vendor_Invoice flow define each data element in the repository.

Entity Relational Diagrams (ERD)

The ERD interfaces with the data repository by mapping an element to particular tables (entities), that is, each unique data element within an entity points to a data repository definition (see Figure 8.4).

Figure 8.4 CASE entity attributes. This figure reflects how the Orders entity is defined by its component data attributes. These attributes then point to their respective data elements in the data repository.

State Transition Diagram (STD)

The STD interfaces with the data repository via the "conditions that cause a change in state." These condition arrows map to the data repository and allow component elements to be defined as shown in Figure 8.5.

Figure 8.5 CASE STD data element definition. The above diagram shows how the condition-arrow "Enter Valid Bank Card" in an STD points to its component data attributes. These attributes are then defined as data elements in the data repository.

Process Specifications

Process Specifications are typically defined via the functional primitive process of the DFD or a particular state in an STD. The example in Figure 8.6 reflects how this is done using a DFD. Once the process specification is defined, data elements embedded in the application logic are mapped to the data repository.

The OO paradigm is also supported by CASE where objects can store both attributes and methods and point data element definitions into the data repository (Figure 8.7).

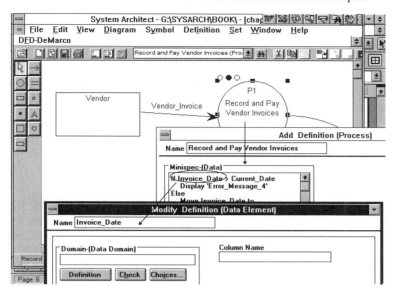

Figure 8.6 CASE process specification. The process specification above in System Architect is mapped to a process in a DFD called "Record and Pay Vendor Invoices." The algorithm of the process is defined and any elements used in the process specification must point to its data element definition in the data repository.

Figure 8.7 CASE object. This figure diagrams the creation of an object/class which points to an attribute of an object that then points to the data repository definition of the element itself.

Data Repository Outputs

CASE outputs provide links to physical products and services. Its capabilities therefore allow for the storage of various design-specific features that can automatically produce output that can then be used by other products. The rest of this section describes the features in each of the areas shown in Figure 8.1: schema generation; product code generation; prototypes; and documentation and reports.

Schema Generation

The schema generation facility in CASE allows various interfaces with physical database products. These schemas include support for most of the popular database products such as Oracle, Sybase, Informix, Microsoft's SQL_Server, and DB2. A *schema* is defined as the description of the data elements in the format necessary for a particular RDBMS product. Most of the databases just mentioned support SQL (Structured Query Language) data type identifiers as shown in Figure 8.8.

Figure 8.8 CASE schema generation. This diagram shows the Orders entity and how definitions specific for Oracle schema generation can be stored.

Product Code Generation

Product Code Generation relates to storing specific information needed by programming products such as Powerbuilder and C++ (see Figure 8.9). This information, similar to the process in schema generation, allows the analyst to export information directly into the intended product. The ability to store multiple product definitions also provides a central capability to provide information about a data element for different product languages. This translates to providing a mechanism to support multiple development environments and languages without the need to have the definition given only in the programming language code.

Figure 8.9 CASE program interface. This is an example of how CASE can store data element information for the Powerbuilder programming product.

Prototypes

Prototypes are usually screens and reports that are produced so that users can get a visual view of the system. Prototypes do not actually work; they are like cars with no engines. CASE prototypes can range in capabilities from simple views of the way a screen or report will look to an actual demonstration of the application's functional capabilities. These demonstration capabilities can provide a way of linking screens with the data repository to show the "look and feel" of the application to the user. In addition, certain CASE products allow screen and report information to be directly ported into a development language (see Figure 8.10).

Figure 8.10 CASE screen painter. The above diagram shows the screen painter properties of System Architect. The data elements contained in the screen are mapped to the data repository and therefore contain their appropriate definitions.

Documentation and Reports

CASE provides both documentation and reports to reflect the information stored in the data repository. The information can range from a simple data element report to more sophisticated comparison information (e.g., missing data element descriptions), as Figure 8.11 illustrates.

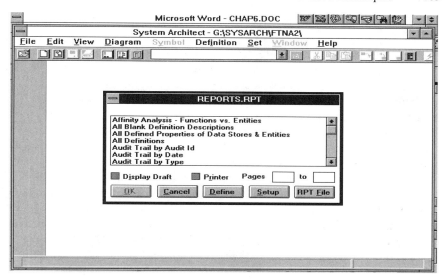

Figure 8.11 CASE report writer. The above screen shows the report menu from System Architect.

The data repository of CASE is therefore the central component of the product and serves to store all related information of a particular data element. A data element in the data repository does not necessarily need to belong to any entity, schema, prototype or program product, but rather it may be an independent piece of information. However, CASE provides an easier way to make a data element associated with an entity, schema, prototype, and so on, without losing this independence. The integration facility of CASE allows analysts to modify the definitions of a data element and have that change propagated throughout the data repository.

Why Does CASE Fail?

Unfortunately, many of the implementations of CASE during the 1980s were not successful. Information systems professionals began to shy away from its use. The reasons for this are very straightforward:

- Organizations were not properly trained how to use structured tools.
- CASE products did not comply with GUI (Graphic User Interface) and therefore were not robust.[21]

---

[21] The term robust or robustness is defined as the ability of a program to function, or to continue functioning well, in unexpected situations. Microsoft Press, *Computer Dictionary*, 2nd ed., p. 342.

- CASE products were methodology driven, and therefore required the organization to commit to a particular approach. Such approaches did not typically conform to the organization's culture.
- There were limited third party product interfaces to enable efficient transfer from logical models to physical products and databases.

Perhaps the CASE transition was bound to occur in a slow and methodical manner. Many organizations could not afford to buy the popular CASE products then that included Knowledgeware, Excellerator and IEF (Information Engineering Facility). Those who did buy them still feel scarred, and even today CASE is considered a bad word in some circles.

A key factor in the success of CASE is understanding where and when to use it in the software implementation cycle. To determine this point, the table in Figure 8.3 is a replication of the table of the Tiers of Analysis and Software Application Development developed in Chapter 1. This table can also be used to *compare* or *map* the analyst's proficiency level to that of the software development process being used.

Tier	Analyst Proficiency
6	Internet/Intranet – Web-based transaction processing, media, and graphics
5	Client/Server – breaking down objects to their client and server applications
4	Object orientation – selection of objects and classes
3	CASE – automation and productivity of Tier 2
2	Structured Tools – DFD, PFD, ERD, STD, process specification, data repository
1	User Interface – interviewing skills, JAD, RAD

Figure 8.12 Analyst Proficiency Skills Correlation.

The table shows that CASE should not be considered until tier 3, that is, until an analyst is proficient with the user interface and the structured tools. CASE can then be used as a way of automating the analysis process. By automating portions of the analysis functions, organizations can thus become more productive when modeling systems.

Why CASE Should Succeed

Using CASE is the only means of creating and maintaining any central storage of information for enterprise level systems. Today, the CASE products are far more robust, contain the GUI interface and allow for the handling of multiple analysis methodologies. Analysts can therefore create data repositories as they see fit for their organizations. In addition, there are many database and development third party products that can be linked to CASE. Many companies like Oracle now produce their own CASE products (Oracle Designer/2000) that are focused on creating even more interfaces between data repositories and the Oracle RDBMS. Frankly, an IS organization that does not consider CASE cannot provide the long-term support for many of the features and capabilities required by the applications of the future. These applications will be based on the OO paradigm and client/server computing. Perhaps the most significant advantage to CASE is in the area of maintenance. Definitions of quality software have included the word "maintenance" for decades: systems that are difficult to maintain will not be considered quality systems. When there is a central repository of data as well as defined processes, the maintenance of both databases and applications becomes easier and more productive. The data repository also allows both analysts and developers to use CASE as a means of training and documenting existing systems. Having new programmers use an automated tool to see the contents of each entity and how the data is used in an application provides IS organizations with greater flexibility and productivity for future enhancements.

Open Systems Requirements and Client/Server

Perhaps the most significant support for today's use of CASE is Open Systems architecture. Open systems architecture can be defined as a set of standards for both hardware and software that allows portability of applications and databases. Open systems architecture includes such operating systems as UNIX, LINUX, Windows and Windows NT, DOS and Netware. These operating systems support the standards in application software that allow such software to run across one another's operating systems. Although this concept is not fully transparent, application developers have enjoyed more portability of their code than ever before. The software industry will continue to support open systems, especially through the use of OO technology. Essentially, without CASE it is impossible to support the open systems model. In order for an IS organization to be compliant with open systems, it must have the ability to store data elements free from specific hardware and software products, that is, it must not be proprietary.

Client/server even further strengthens the need to use CASE. Built on the basis of open systems and OO, client/server establishes the need for additional standards in the area of object interfaces across LANs and WANs. The use of the Internet as a key component of the future for IS processing is also constructed on the basis of OO and client/server concepts. The analysis proficiency skills tiers (Figure 8.12) showed us that CASE is a prerequisite for OO and client/server. Chapter 9 will demonstrate that OO is constructed via the structured tools and that client/server is developed after determining the appropriate objects and classes. None of these links can be accomplished without a central point of control, evaluation and reconciliation, all of which CASE provides to us.

We mentioned above that client/server established new needs for standards for communicating among and WANs. Much of this interface is called *middleware*. Middleware contains the necessary APIs (application program interface), protocols, metadata, gateways and object messaging necessary to provide communication across client/server networks. The driving force behind middleware is that today's applications must communicate with other applications and databases without knowing one another's hardware and software configurations. This means that the middleware must contain information for the client or server about what data is being sent or received respectively. For example, without knowing the receiving application's programming language, middleware must provide the details of the layout of data being sent. This data layout is defined in the metadata (data about the data) facility of the middleware. The components of open systems and client/server architecture are shown below in the client/server three tier architecture depicted in Figure 8.13.

Our discussions of CASE can be mapped to every tier of the client/server architecture. CASE thus provides the underlying facility to record information and data to build such systems.

Types of CASE Tools

The CASE components which comprise analysis and design capabilities are typically known as Upper-CASE. Many CASE products may provide only the input side that has been shown. CASE products that also provide for output to the physical product side are known as *Lower*-CASE. Once again, there are CASE products that do not provide the analysis tools but rather only a data repository to create outputs. These CASE products are also known as *Code Generators*. CASE products that do both the input analysis and output generation are known as *I-CASE* or *Integrated CASE*. I-CASE tools will continue to become more popular as open systems and client/server architectures become more widely used.

CASE tools should also support multiple data repositories. This means that some repositories can be either mutually exclusive or dependent as children in a tree structure. *Mutually exclusive* repositories simply mean that there are multiple libraries of data elements that have no relationship with each other. This situation can occur in organizations that have different business lines or subsidiaries that are in different businesses. Mutually exclusive libraries should be created only if the analyst is sure that there is no need for an enterprise model.

Tree structure libraries are used more often. The tree of repositories allows an organization to have a central parent repository with all common data elements of the enterprise. *Child libraries* inherit the global definitions. Locally

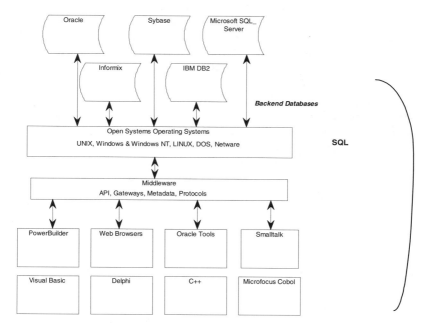

Figure 8.13 Client/server three tier architecture.

defined data elements will become only global if they are needed by at least two entities in the organization. Another use of the tree structure repositories is *work-in-process*. Specifically this means that new projects may create potentially new data elements to be added to the global data repository. This allows the IS organization to properly control any new entries into the global data repository until the project is completed or the data element candidate is approved by the appropriate people in the organization. In any event, good CASE products allow for this versatility, and it is recommended that analysts utilize such capabilities.

Reverse Engineering

Analysts will often be confronted with a system that is not in any existing CASE product. The issue then becomes the chicken-and-egg paradox: how do I create a data repository if the product already exists? Advanced CASE products typically contain a module that allows for *reverse engineering*. "Reverse Engineering is the process of analyzing existing application programs and database code to create higher-level representations of the code. It is sometimes called *design recovery*." [22] For example, reverse engineering features would allow for the input of an existing Oracle table into the CASE product. This input would result in the creation of a logical ERD and the creation of all the data elements into the data repository. In addition foreign key links, triggering operations and other stored procedures would automatically populate the appropriate repository areas. Reverse engineering therefore allows analysts to "start somewhere" and eventually to get the organization into forward engineering, that is, building physical products and databases directly from the CASE tool.

Problems and Exercises

1. Define the applications of a CASE tool.
2. What are the benefits of the input facilities of CASE? Of the output facilities?
3. Explain the concept of a data repository. How does it relate to the dictionary?
4. What is schema generation? Why is this important for forward engineering?
5. How does the data repository assist in the development of screen prototypes?
6. What is I-CASE? Explain.
7. What are the most important issues to ensure the success of CASE?
8. What are the five analysis proficiencies?
9. How does CASE relate to the implementation of object and client/server system?
10. What is a three tiered architecture?
11. Why is reverse engineering so prevalent in most IS organizations?

---

[22] Jeffrey Whitten, Lonnie Bently, Victor Barlow, *Systems Analysis & Design Methods*, 3rd ed., p. 181.

9
Object-Oriented Techniques

What Is Object-Oriented Analysis?

Object-oriented analysis has become a key issue in today's analysis paradigm. It is without question the most important element of creating what may be called the "complete" requirement of a system. Unfortunately, the industry is in a state of controversy about the approaches and tools that should be used to create object systems. This chapter will focus on developing the requirements for object systems and the challenges of converting legacy systems. Therefore, many of the terms will be defined based on their fundamental capabilities and how they can be used by a practicing analyst (as opposed to a theorist!).

Object orientation (OO) is based on the concept that every requirement ultimately must belong to an object. It is therefore critical that we first define what is meant by an object. In the context of OO analysis, an *object* is any cohesive whole made up of two essential components: data and processes.

Classic and even structured analysis approaches were traditionally based on the examination of a series of events. We translated these events from the physical world by first interviewing users and then developing what was introduced as the concept of the logical equivalent. Although we are by no means abandoning this necessity, the OO paradigm requires that these events belong to an identifiable object. Let us expand on this difference using the object shown in Figure 9.1, an object we commonly call a "car."

Figure 9.1 A car is an example of a physical object.

The car shown in Figure 9.1 may represent a certain make and model, but it also contains common components that are contained in all cars (e.g., an engine). If we were to look upon the car as a business entity of an organization, we might find that the three systems shown in Figure 9.2 were developed over the years.

Figure 9.2 This diagram reflects the three systems developed to support the car object.

Figure 9.2 shows us that the three systems were built over a period of 11 years. Each system was designed to provide service to a group of users responsible for particular tasks. The diagram shows that the requirements for System 1 were based on the engine and front-end of the car. The users for this project had no interest in or need for any other portions of the car. System 2, on the other hand, focused on the lower center and rear of the car. Notice, however, that System 2 and System 1 have an overlap. This means that there are parts and procedures common to both systems. Finally, System 3 reflects the upper center and rear of the car and has an overlap with System 2. It is also important to note that there are components of the car that have not yet been defined, probably because no user has had a need for them. We can look at the car as an object and Systems 1 to 3 as the software which has so far been defined about that object. Our observations should also tell us that the entire object is not defined and more important, that there is probable overlap of data and functionality among the systems that have been developed. This case exemplifies the history of most development systems. It should be clear that the users who stated their requirements never had any understanding that their own situation belonged to a larger composite object. Users tend to establish requirements based on their own job functions and their own experiences in those functions. Therefore, the analyst who interviews users about their events is exposed to a number of risks:

- Users tend to identify only what they have experienced, rather than speculating about other events that could occur. We know that such events can take place, although they have not yet occurred (you should recall the discussion of using STDs as a modeling tool to identify unforeseen possibilities). Consider, for example, an analysis situation in which $50,000 must be approved by the firm's Controller. This event might show only the approval, not the rejection. The user's response is that the Controller, while examining the invoices, has never rejected one and therefore no rejection procedure exists. You might ask why. Well, in this case the Controller was not reviewing the invoices for rejection but rather holding them until he/she was confident that the company's cash flow could support the issuance of these invoices. Obviously, the Controller could decide to reject an invoice. In such a case, the software would require a change to accommodate this new procedure. From a software perspective we call this a system enhancement, and it would result in a modification to the existing system.
- Other parts of the company may be affected by the Controller's review of the invoices. Furthermore, are we sure that no one else has automated this process before? One might think such prior automation could never be overlooked, especially in a small company, but when users have different names for the same thing (remember Customer and Client!) it is very likely that such things will occur. Certainly in our example there were two situations where different systems overlapped in functionality.
- There will be conflicts between the systems with respect to differences in data and process definitions. Worst of all, these discrepancies may not be discovered until years after the system is delivered.

The above example shows us that requirements obtained from individual events require another level of reconciliation to ensure they are complete. Requirements are said to be "complete" when they define the whole object. The more incomplete they are, the more modifications will be required later. The more modifications in a system, the higher the likelihood that data and processes across applications may conflict with each other. Ultimately this results in a less dependable, lower quality system. Most of all, event analysis alone is prone to missing events that users have never experienced. This situation is represented in the car example by the portions of the car not included in any of the three systems. System functions and components may also be missed because users are absent or unavailable at the time of the interviews, or because no one felt the need to automate a certain aspect of the object. In either case, the situation should be clear. We need to establish objects prior to doing event analysis. The question is how?

Before we discuss the procedures for identifying an object, it is worth looking at the significant differences between the object approach and earlier approaches. This particular example was first discussed with a colleague,

Eugene O'Rourke, on the generations of systems and how they compare to the object methodology:

The first major systems were developed in the 1960s and were called Batch, meaning that they typically operated on a transaction basis. Transactions were collected and then used to update a master file. Batch systems were very useful in the financial industries, including banks. We might remember having to wait until the morning after a banking transaction to see our account balance because a batch process updated the master account files overnight. These systems were built based on event interviewing, where programmer/analysts met with users and designed the system. Most of these business systems were developed and maintained using COBOL.

In the early 1970s, the new buzz word was "on-line, real-time" meaning that many processes could now update data immediately or on a "real-time" basis. Although systems were modified to provide these services, it is important to understand that they were not reengineered. That is, the existing systems, which were based on event interviews, were modified, and in many cases portions were left untouched.

In the late 1980s and early 1990s the hot term became "client/server." These systems, which will be discussed later, are based on sophisticated distributed systems concepts. Information and processes are distributed among many Local and Wide Area Networks. Many of these client/server systems are re-constructions of the on-line real-time systems which in turn were developed from the 1960s batch systems. The point here is that we have been applying new technology to systems that were designed over 30 years ago without considering the obsolescence of the design.

Through these three generations of systems, the analyst has essentially been on the outside looking in (see Figure 9.3). The completeness of the analysis was dependent upon—and effectively dictated by—the way the inside users defined their business needs.

Object-orientation, on the other hand, requires that the analyst have a view from the inside looking out. What we mean here is that the analyst first needs to define the generic aspects of the object and then map the user views to the particular components that exist within the object itself. Figure 9.4 shows a conceptual view of the generic components that could be part of a bank.

Figure 9.4 shows the essential functions of the bank. The analyst is on the inside of the organization when interviewing users and therefore will have the ability to map a particular requirement to one or more of its essential functions. In this approach, any user requirement must fit into at least one of the essential components.. If a user has a requirement that is not part of an essential component, then it must be either qualified as missing (and thus added as an essential component) or rejected as inappropriate.

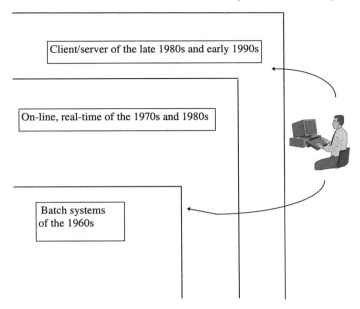

Figure 9.3 Requirements are often developed by analysts from an outside view. The specifications are therefore dependent on the completeness of the user's view.

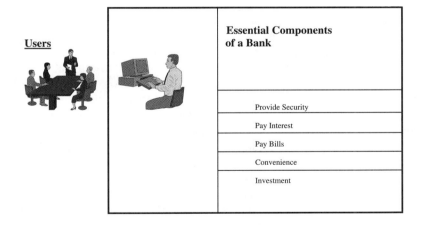

Figure 9.4 Using the object approach, the analyst interviews users from the inside looking out.

The process of taking user requirements and placing each of their functions into the appropriate essential component can be called mapping. The importance of mapping is that functions of requirements are logically placed where they generically belong, rather than according to how they are physically implemented. For example, suppose Joseph, who works for a bank, needed to provide information to a customer about the bank's investment offerings. Joseph would need to access investment information from the system. If OO methods were used to design the system, all information about banking investments would be grouped together generically. Doing it this way allows authorized personnel to access investment information regardless of what they do in the bank. If event analysis alone was used, Joseph would probably have his own subsystem that defines his particular requirements for accessing investment information. The problem here is twofold: first, the subsystem does not contain all of the functions relating to investments. Should Joseph need additional information, he may need an enhancement or need to use someone else's system at the bank. Second, Joseph's subsystem may define functions that have already been defined elsewhere in another subsystem. The advantage of OO is that it centralizes all of the functions of an essential component and allows these functions to be "reused" by all processes that require its information. The computer industry calls this capability Reusable Objects.

Identifying Objects and Classes

The most important challenge of successfully implementing OO is the ability to understand and select Objects. We have already used an example which identified a car as an object. This example is what can be called the tangible object, or as the industry calls them "physical objects." Unfortunately, there is another type of object called an "abstract" or intangible object. An intangible object is one that you cannot touch or as Grady Booch describes: "something that may be apprehended intellectually...Something towards which thought or action is directed."[23] An example of an intangible object is the security component of the essentials of the bank. In many instances OO analysis will begin with identifying tangible objects which will in turn make it easier to discover the intangible ones.

Earlier in the book, we saw that systems are comprised of two components: Data and Processes. Chapter 4 showed how the trend of many database products is toward combining data and processes via stored procedures called triggers. Object orientation is somewhat consistent with this trend in that all objects contain their own data and processes, called *attributes* and *services*, respectively. Attributes are effectively a list of data elements that are permanent components of the object. For example, a steering wheel is a data element

---

[23] Grady Booch , *Object Solutions: Managing the Object-Oriented Project*, Addison Wesley Publishing Co., p. 305.

that is a permanent attribute of the object "Car." The services (or operations), on the other hand, define all of the processes that are permanently part of or "owned" by the object. "Starting the Car" is a service that is defined within the object Car. This service contains the algorithms necessary to start a car. Services are defined and invoked through a method. A method is a process specification for an operation (service).[24] For example, "Driving the Car" could be a method for the Car object. The "Driving the Car" method would invoke a service called "Starting the Car" as well as other services until the entire method requirement is satisfied. Although a service and method can have a one-to-one relationship, it is more likely that a service will be a subset or one of the operations that make up a method.

Objects have the ability to inherit attributes and methods from other objects when they are placed within the same class. A *class* is a group of objects that have similar attributes and methods and typically have been put together to perform a specific task. To further understand these concepts, we will establish the object for "Car" and place it in a class of objects that focuses on the use of transmissions in cars (see Figure 9.5).

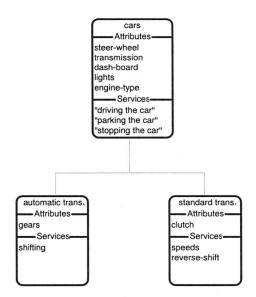

Figure 9.5 Class Car Transmissions.

---

[24] James Martin and James Odell, *Object-Oriented Methods*, Prentice-Hall, p. 158.

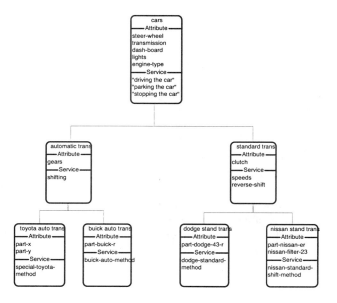

Figure 9.6 Class-Car Transmission types.

Figure 9.5 represents an object class called Car Transmissions. It has three component objects: cars, automatic trans, and standard trans. The car object is said to be the parent object. Automatic trans and standard trans are object types. Both automatic trans and standard trans will inherit all attributes and services from their parent object, Cars. Inheritance in object technology means that the children effectively contain all of the capabilities of their parents. Inheritance is implemented as a tree structure[25]; however, instead of information flowing upward (as is the case in tree structures), the data flows downward to the lowest level children. Therefore, an object inheritance diagram is said to be an inverted tree. Because the lowest level of the tree inherits from every one of its parents, only the lowest level object need be executed, that is, executing the lowest level will automatically allow the application to inherit all of the parent information and applications as needed. We call the lowest level objects concrete, while all others in the class are called abstract. Objects within classes can change simply by the addition of a new object. Let us assume that there is

---

[25] A data structure containing zero or more nodes that are linked together in a hierarchical fashion. The topmost node is called the root. The root can have zero or more child nodes, connected by links; the root is the parent node to its children. Each child node can in turn have zero or more children of its own. Microsoft Press, *Computer Dictionary*, 2nd ed., p. 397.

another level added to our example The new level contains objects for the specific types of automatic and standard transmissions (see Figure 9.6).

The above class has been modified to include a new concrete layer. Therefore, the automatic trans object and standard trans object are now abstract. The new four concrete objects not only inherit from their respective parent objects, but also from their common grandparent, cars. It is also important to recognize that classes can inherit from other classes. Therefore, the same example could show each object as a class: that is, cars would represent a class of car objects and automatic trans another class of objects. Therefore, the class automatic trans would inherit from the cars class in the same manner described above. We call this *class inheritance*.

We mentioned before the capability of OO objects to be reusable (Reusable Objects). This is very significant in that it allows a defined object to become part of another class, while still keeping its own original identity and independence. Figure 9.7 demonstrates how Cars can be reused in another class.

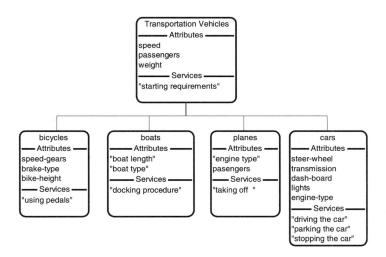

Figure 9.7 Class: Transportation Vehicles

Notice that the object Car is now part of another class called Transportation Vehicles. However, Car, instead of being an abstract object within its class, has become concrete and thus inherits from its parent, Transportation Vehicles. The object Cars has methods that may execute differently depending on the class it is in. Therefore, Cars in the Transportation Vehicle class might interpret a request for "driving the car" as it relates to general transportation vehicles. Specifically, it might invoke a service that shows how to maneuver a car while it is moving. On the other hand, Cars in the Transmission class might interpret the same message coming from one of its children objects as meaning how the transmission shifts when a person is driving. This phenomenon is called *polymorphism*. Polymorphism allows an object to change its behavior within the same methods under different circumstances. What is more important is that polymorphism is dynamic in behavior, so its changes in operation are determined when the object is executed or during run time.

Because objects can be reused, keeping the same version current in every copy of the same object in different classes is important. Fortunately, objects are typically stored in dynamic link libraries (DLL). The significance of a DLL is that it always stores the current version of an object. Because objects are linked dynamically before each execution, you are ensured that the current version is always the one used. The DLL facility therefore avoids the maintenance nightmares of remembering which applications contain the same subprograms. Legacy systems often need to relink every copy of the subprogram in each module where a change occurs. This problem continues to haunt the COBOL application community.

Another important feature in object systems is *instantiation* and *persistence*. Instantiation allows multiple executions of the same class to occur independent of another execution. This means that multiple copies of the same class are executing concurrently. The significance of these executions is that they are mutually exclusive and can be executing different concrete objects within that class. Because of this capability, we say that objects can have multiple *instances* within each executing copy of a class to which it belongs. Sometimes, although class executions are finished, a component object continues to operate or *persist*. Persistence is therefore an object that continues to operate after the class or operation that invoked it has finished. The system must keep track of each of these object instances.

The abilities of objects and classes to have inheritance, polymorphic behavior, instantiation and persistence are just some of the new mechanisms that developers can take advantage of when building OO systems.[26] Because of this, the analyst must not only understand the OO methodology, but must also apply new approaches and tools that will allow an appropriate schematic to be produced for system developers.

---

[26] This book is not intended to provide all of the specific technical capabilities and definitions that comprise the OO paradigm, but rather its effects on the analyst's approach. Not all of the OO issues are analyst responsibilities, and many of them are product-specific. Because OO is still very controversial, OO products are not consistent in their use of OO facilities. For example, C++ allows multiple inheritance, meaning that a child can have many parent objects. This is inconsistent with the definition of a class as a tree structure, since children in tree structures can have only one parent.

Object Modeling

In Chapter 4, we discussed the capabilities of a state transition diagram (STD) and defined it as a tool useful for modeling event driven and time dependent systems. A state very closely resembles an object/class and therefore can be used with little modification to depict the flow and relationships of objects. There are many techniques available such as Rumbaugh's Object Modeling Technique (OMT) and Jacobson's Object-Oriented Software Engineering (OOSE) that can also be applied. However, be careful, as many of the methodologies are very complex and can be overwhelming for the average analyst to use in actual practice.

The major difference between an object and a state is that an object is responsible for its own data (which we call an attribute in OO). An object's attributes are said to be *encapsulated* behind its methods, that is, a user cannot ask for data directly. The concept of encapsulation is that access to an object is allowed only for a purpose rather than for obtaining specific data elements. It is the responsibility of the method and its component services to determine the appropriate attributes that are required to service the request of the object. For this reason, object relationships must include a cardinality definition similar to that found in the ERD. An object diagram, regardless of whose methodology is used, is essentially a hybrid of an STD and an ERD. The STD represents the object's methods and the criteria for moving from one object to another. The ERD, on the other hand, defines the relationship of the attributes between the stored data models. The result is best shown using the order processing example contained in Figure 9.8.

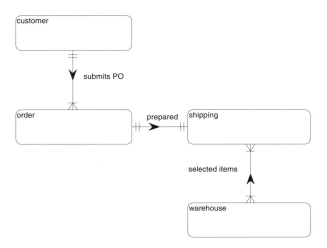

Figure 9.8 An object/class diagram.

The object diagram in Figure 9.8 reflects that a customer object submits a purchase order for items to the order object. The relationship between customer and order reflects both STD and ERD characteristics. The "submits purchase order" specifies the condition to change the state of or move to the order object. The direction arrow also tells us that the order object cannot send a purchase order to the customer object. The crow's-foot cardinality shows us that a customer object must have at least one order to create a relationship with the order object. After an order is processed, it is prepared for shipment. Notice that each order has one related shipment object; however multiple warehouse items can be part of a shipment. The objects depicted above can also represent classes suggesting that they are comprised of many component objects. These component objects might in turn be further decomposed into other primitive objects. This is consistent with the concept of the logical equivalent and with functional decomposition (see Figure 9.9).

It is important that the analyst specify whether classes or objects are depicted in the modeling diagrams. It is not advisable to mix classes and objects at the same level. Obviously the class levels can be effective for user verification, but objects will be inevitably required for final analysis and engineering.

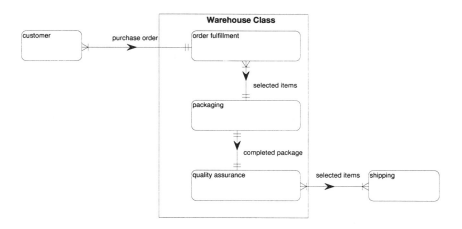

Figure 9.9 The component objects of the Warehouse class.

Relationship to Structured Analysis

Many analysts make the assumption that the structured tools discussed in Chapter 3 are not required in OO analysis. This simply is not true, as we have shown in the previous examples. To further emphasize the need to continue using structured techniques, we need to understand the underlying benefit of the OO paradigm and how structured tools are necessary to map to the creation of objects and classes. It is easy to say: "find all the objects in the essential components"; actually to have a process to do so is another story. Before providing an approach to determine objects, let us first understand the problem.

Application Coupling

Coupling can be defined as the measurement of an application's dependency on another. Simply put, does a change in an application program necessitate a change to another application program? Many known system malfunctions have resulted from highly coupled systems. The problem, as you might have anticipated, relates back to the analysis function, where decisions could be made as to what services should be joined to form one single application program. Coupling is never something that we want to do, but no system can be made up of just one program. Therefore, coupling is a reality and one that analysts must focus on. Let us elaborate on the coupling problem through the example depicted in Figure 9.10.

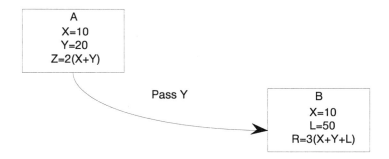

Figure 9.10 Application coupling.

The two programs A and B are coupled via the passing of the variable Y. Y is subsequently used in B to calculate R. Should the variable Y change in A, it will not necessitate a change in B. This is considered good coupling. However, let us now examine X. We see that X is defined in both A and B. Although the value of X does not cause a problem in the current versions of A and B, a subsequent change of X will cause a programmer to remember to change the value in B. This is a maintenance nightmare. In large enterprise level systems, analysts and programmers cannot "remember" where all of these couples have occurred, especially when the original developers are no longer with the

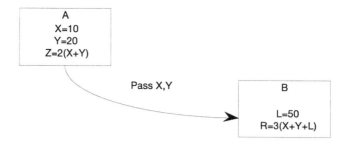

Figure 9.11 Application coupling using variables X and Y.

organization. The solution to this problem is also to pass X from program A (see Figure 9.11).

We now see that both X and Y are passed and programs A and B are said to have *low coupling*. In addition, program A is said to be more cohesive.

Application Cohesion

Cohesion is the measurement of how independent a program is on its own processing. That is, a cohesive program contains all of the necessary data and logic to complete its applications without being directly affected by another program; a change in another program should not require a change to a cohesive one. Furthermore, a cohesive program should not cause a change to be made in another program. Therefore, cohesive programs are independent programs that react to messages to determine what they need to do; however they remain self-contained. When program A also passed X it became more cohesive because a change in X no longer required a change to be made to another program. In addition B is more cohesive because it gets the change of X automatically from A. Systems that are designed more cohesively are said to be more maintainable. Their codes can also be reused or retrofitted into other applications as components because they are wholly independent. A cohesive program can be compared to an interchangeable standard part of a car. For example, if a car requires a standard 14-inch tire, typically any tire that meets the specification can be used. The tire, therefore, is not married to the particular car, but rather is a cohesive component for many cars.

Cohesion is in many ways is the opposite of coupling. The higher the cohesion, the lower the coupling. Analysts must understand that an extreme of either cohesion or coupling cannot exist. This is shown in the graph in Figure 9.12.

100% Coupling ←――――――――――•――――•――― 100% Cohesion ――――――――――→
                                                50%   75%

Figure 9.12 Coupling and cohesion relationships.

The graph shows that we can never reach 100% cohesion; that would mean there is only one program in the entire system, a situation that is unlikely. However, it is possible to have a system where a 75% cohesion ratio is obtained.

We now need to relate this discussion to OO. Obviously OO is based very much on the concept of cohesion. Objects are independent reusable modules that control their own attributes and services. Object coupling is based entirely on message processing via inheritance or collaboration.[27] Therefore, once an object is identified, the analyst must define all of its processes in a cohesive manner. Once the cohesive processes are defined, the required attributes of the object are then added to the object. Figure 9.13 contains a table showing how processes can be combined to create the best cohesion:

Tier	Method	Method Description
1	By function	Processes are combined into one object/class based on being a component of the same function. Examples include: Accounts Receivable, Sales, and Goods Returned are all part of the same function. A sale creates a receivable and goods returned decreases the sale and the receivable.
2	By data	Processes are combined based on their use of the same data and data files. Processes that tend to use the same data are more cohesive.
3	By generic operation	Processes are combined based on their generic performance. Examples could be "editing" or "printing."
4	By lines of code	Processes are created after an existing one reaches a maximum number of lines in the actual program source code.

Figure 9.13 Methods of selecting cohesive objects.

The tiers above are based on best to worst, where the by function method is the most desirable and by lines of code method the least desirable. Tiers 1 and 2 will render the best object cohesiveness. This can be seen with the example in Figure 9.14.

---

[27] *Collaboration* is the interaction between objects and classes where inheritance is not used. Inheritance can operate only in hierarchical structures; however, many object and class configurations can simply "talk" to one another through messaging systems.

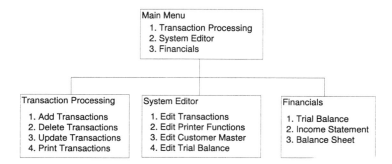

Figure 9.14 Applications with varying types of object cohesion.

Figure 9.14 depicts a four-screen system that includes four objects, that is, each screen is a separate object. The Transaction Processing object has been designed using tier 2, By Same Data since it deals only with the Transaction File. The object is cohesive because it does not depend on or affect another module in its processing. It provides all of the methods required for transaction data.

The Financials object is an example of tier 1, the by function method since a Balance Sheet is dependent on the Income Statement and the Income Statement is dependent on the Trial Balance. The object therefore is self-contained within all the functions necessary to produce financial information (in this example).

The System Editor, on the other hand, being an example of tier 3, shows that it handles all of the editing (verification of the quality of data) for the system. Although there appears to be some benefit to having similar code in one object, we can see that it affects many different components. It is therefore considered a highly coupled object and not necessarily the easiest to maintain.

We can conclude that tiers 1 and 2 provide analysts with the most attractive way for determining an object's attributes and services. Tiers 3 and 4, although practiced, do not provide any real benefits in OO and should be avoided as much as possible. The question now is what technique do we follow to start providing the services and attributes necessary when developing logical objects?

The structured tools discussed in Chapter 4 provide us with the essential capabilities to work with OO analysis and design. The STD can be used to determine the initial objects and the conditions of how one object couples or relates to another. Once the STD is prepared it can be matured into the object model discussed earlier in this chapter. The object model can be decomposed to its lowest level; the attributes and services of each object must then be defined. All of the DFD functional primitives can now be mapped to their respec-

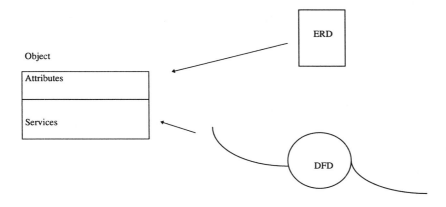

Figure 9.15 The relationships between an object and the ERD and DFD.

tive objects as services within their methods. It is also a way of determining whether an object is missing (should there be a DFD that does not have a related object). The analyst should try to combine each DFD using the tier 1, by function approach. This can sometimes be very difficult depending on the size of the system. If the tier 1 approach is too difficult, the analyst should try tier 2 by combining DFDs based on their similar data stores. This is a very effective approach; since tier 1 implies tier 2,[28] it is a very productive way to determine how processes should be mapped to their appropriate objects. This does not suggest that the analyst should not try tier 1 first.

The next activity is to determine the object's attributes or data elements. The ERD serves as the link between an attribute in an object and its actual storage in a database. It is important to note that the attribute setting in an object may have no resemblance to its setting in the logical and physical data entity. The data entity is focused on the efficient storage of the elements and its integrity, whereas the attribute data in an object is based on its cohesiveness with the object's services.

The mapping of the object to the DFD and ERD can be best shown graphically, as in Figure 9.15.

---

[28] We have found that application programs that have been determined using tier 1 will always imply tier 2. That is, applications that are combined based on function typically use the same data. Although the converse is not necessarily true, we believe it is an excellent approach to backing-in to the functions when they are not intuitively obvious.

Thus, the functional primitive DFDs and the ERD resulting from the normalization process provide the vehicles for providing an object's attributes and services.

Object-Oriented Databases

There is a movement in the industry to replace the traditional relational database management systems (RDBMS) with the object-oriented database management system (OODBMS). Object databases differ greatly from the relational model in that the object's attributes and services are stored together. Therefore, the concept of columns and rows of normalized data becomes extinct. The proponents of OODBMS see a major advantage in that object databases could also keep graphical and multimedia information about the object, something that relational databases cannot do. The answer will come in time, but it is expected that the relational model will continue to be used for some time. However, most RDBMS products will become more object-oriented. This means they will use the relational engine but employ more OO capabilities, that is, build a relational hybrid model. In either case, analysts should continue to focus on the logical aspects of capturing the requirements. Changes in the OO methodologies are expected to continue over the next few years.

Problems and Exercises

1. What is an object?
2. Describe the relationship between a method and a service.
3. What is a class?
4. How does the object paradigm change the approach of the analyst?
5. Describe the two types of objects and provide examples of each type.
6. What are essential functions?
7. What is an object type and how is it used to develop specific types of classes?
8. What is meant by object and class inheritance?
9. How does inheritance relate to the concept of polymorphism?
10. What are the association differences between an ERD and an object diagram?
11. How does functional decomposition operate with respect to classes and objects?
12. What is coupling and cohesion ? What is their relationship with each other?

13. How does the concept of cohesion relate the structured approach to the object model?
14. What four methods can be used to design a cohesive object?
15. What are object databases?

10
Client/Server and Network Analysis

Client/Server and Object-Oriented Analysis

Client/server provides another level of sophistication in the implementation of systems. The concept of client/server is based on distributed processing, where programs and data are placed in the most efficient places. Client/server systems are typically installed on *local area networks* (*LANs*) or *wide area networks* (*WANs*). LANs can be defined as multiple computers linked together to share processing and data. WANs are linked LANs. For the purposes of this book, we will restrict our discussion about client/server within the concepts of application development. Our focus will therefore be the development of client/server application software.

Before you can design effective client/server applications, the organization should commit to the object paradigm. Based on an OO implementation, client/server essentially requires one more step: the determination of what portions of an object or class should be moved to client-only activities, server-only activities, or both.

Definition of Client/Server Applications

We have already stated that client/server is a form of distributed processing. Client/server applications have three components: a client, a server, and a network. Setting aside the implications of the network for a moment, let us understand what clients and servers do. Although client/server applications tend to be seen as either permanent client or permanent server programs, we will see that this is not true in the object paradigm.

A *server* is something that provides information to a requester. There are many client/server configurations that have permanent hardware servers. These hardware servers typically contain databases and application programs that provide services to requesting network computers (as well as other LANs). This configuration is called *back-end* processing. On the other hand, we have network computers that request the information from servers. We call these computers *clients* and categorize this type of processing as *front-end*. When we expand these definitions to applications only, we look at the behavior of an object or class and categorize it as client (requesting services), server (providing services), or both (providing and requesting services).

Understanding how objects become either permanent servers or clients is fairly straightforward. For example, the Cars object in the Car Transmission Types class is categorized as a server. If this were the only use of cars, then it would be called a *dedicated* server object. On the same basis, the Cars object in the Transportation Vehicles class is categorized as a client object. In turn, if it were the only use of the object in a class, it would be defined as a *permanent* client. However, because it exists in more than one class and is polymorphic, the Cars object is really both a client and a server, depending on the placement and behavior of the object. Therefore, when we talk about an object's client/server behavior we must first understand the "instance" it is in and the class it is operating within.

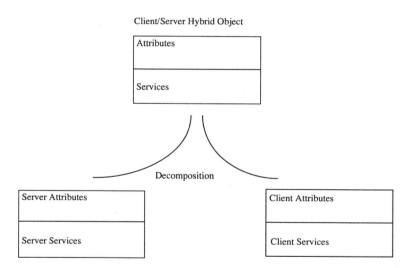

Figure 10.1 Decomposition of client/server objects to dedicated client and server objects.

The difficulty in client/server is in the further separation of attributes and services for purposes of performance across a network. This means that the server services and attributes components of the Cars object might need to be separated from the client ones and permanently placed on a physical server machine.

The client services and attributes will be then be stored on a different physical client machine(s). To put this point into perspective, an object may be further functionally decomposed based on processing categorization. Therefore, the analyst must be involved in the design of the network and must understand how the processing will be distributed across the network. Client/server analysis should employ Rapid Application Development (RAD)[29] because both analysis and design are needed during the requirements phase of the system. Once the analyst understands the layout of the network, then further decomposition must be done to produce hybrid objects. These hybrid objects break out into dedicated server and object functions as shown in Figure 10.1.

Moving to client/server is much easier if OO has been completed. Getting the analysis team involved in network design early in the process is much more difficult. The role of the analyst in client/server will continue to expand as the distribution of objects in these environments continues to grow and mature.

Network Analysis

The Role of the Analyst in Network Design

With the advent of the client/server three-tier architecture, analysts should play a role in deciding how applications will operate over a network. The importance of this role has only been further expanded with the advent of Internet/Intranet and Web processing.

This means that application analysis and design is part of the process of establishing how programs will operate over a wide variety of network topologies. Thus, the purpose of this chapter is to introduce some of the salient components of network design and to show how design ties in with application requirements analysis. While this section does not describe all possible components, listed below are some of the key pieces of what analysts need to define.

Network Server

Network servers are computers that provide data and applications to a number of workstations. There are, as described in Chapter 8, a number of different combinations of software and data that can reside on a particular server. In a three-tier architecture, there is a database server that provides data to many

---

[29] RAD is defined as "an approach to building computer systems which combines the Computer-Assisted Software Engineering (CASE) tools and techniques, user-driven prototyping, and stringent project delivery time limits into a potent, tested, reliable formula for top-notch quality and improvement." James Kerr, Richard Hunter, *Inside RAD*, McGraw-Hill, Inc., p. 3.

application servers. In this context, analysts need to provide information to network designers that identifies:

- the size of the databases
- users' data access requirements
- users' required response time objectives
- users' downtime limitations.

The issue of the size of the databases relates to the number of data elements within each entity. Furthermore, the expected number of records in each entity ultimately allows an analyst to predict the actual size of the data using the following formula by entity:

$$(\text{Estimated number of records} \times \text{length of each record})$$

For example, if an employee master file has 100 employees, and each row or record is a total of 205 bytes,[30] then the appropriate physical database size is:

$$100 \times 205 = 20,500 \text{ bytes}$$

The entity of the database is defined as follows:

```
Employee Master
Physical Display
SS#              NUMBER(9)  [PK1]
Employee_ID      CHAR(5)
Last_Name        VARCHAR2(35)
First_Name       VARCHAR2(35)
M_Init           CHAR(1)
Address_Line1    VARCHAR2(30)
Address_Line2    VARCHAR2(30)
Address_Line3    VARCHAR2(30)
State            CHAR(2)
City             VARCHAR2(15)
Zip_Head         CHAR(5)
Zip_Foot         CHAR(4)
Title            VARCHAR2(4)
```

Understanding the data requirements allows analysts to provide valuable information to network designers regarding the amount of data storage or disk size needed.

---

[30] A byte of data is one storage unit or character of information.

Access requirements refers to the applications that users are allowed to use. This provides network designers with information that they need to "configure" a user's profile on the network. User profiles dictate to which databases and applications users have access rights. In addition, these rights can be restricted with respect to read-only, insert/update, or delete. Access requirements also relates to where data and applications should reside on the network. For instance, suppose an accounting organization needs access to most of its accounting software in a specific location. Network designers might elect to design a topology that provides a dedicated server to the accounting department. This dedicated LAN might contain the applications needed by accounting. This design might create better application performance for the accounting department, which in this case might represent the significant users of the accounting system. This does not suggest that other users do not have access to these programs, but rather that the placement and design of the network can be affected by the users and their location. What is critical to acknowledge is that the analyst is the best individual to perform this task, given that he/she is involved with users already and have the requisite skills to gather the information.

User-required response time objectives must be understood in order to complete an appropriate network design. Indeed, response time is the most crucial component in the user's view. Response times that exceed six seconds are often seen as unacceptable to users; however, they can vary based on application and industry. For example, there are many stock market activities that require strict response time limitations. Thus, during the interview process, analysts need to be aware of the importance of examining response time limitations. In fact, all screen designs should contain an area that addresses response time requirements. It should be recognized that response time performance is not limited to the network. The design of the application and how it is organized by the program development department is equally critical. Unfortunately, many GUI-based applications cannot overcome performance response time problems solely through their design. Response time design must be augmented by careful client/server design of the network; therefore, the analyst, programmer, and network architect must jointly participate in the design of the hardware infrastructure.

User downtime limitations relate to the length of time that the system can be inoperable before there are serious consequences to the organization. The method of addressing this problem is handled in two areas: (1) hardware architecture, and (2) software design.

The hardware solution to downtime problems is known as "no single point of failure." This means that all critical parts of the network hardware are examined, and replication of hardware is implemented wherever downtime issues become critical. One can think of "no single point of failure" as a train track scheme, in which a train can be put on an alternative track if there is a blockage on its normal track. Advanced long-distance telephone systems have used this concept for decades, and current network communications systems usually employ a third-party frame-relay system, which provides the same protection.

Thus, "no single point of failure" is a kind of insurance policy against disaster. The amount of network redundancy needed is directly related to the time and critical nature of the application.

Software design can also provide protection against downtime problems. Redundant databases or distributed database design can offer protection against lost data, and quicken data restoration. A good example is Microsoft's Exchange server. Many systems today are integrating e-mail with telephony. Thus Exchange becomes a vital component in keeping both e-mail and telephones working, with the latter being the most critical component. The restoration of e-mail and telephone data from tape backup could take many hours, and in some cases as long as a day. The way to address this problem is to have the Exchange server broken down into multiple servers so that no single server can bring down the entire system. The Exchange database has the ability to operate among multiple servers, so that the actual number of servers could be determined by the user's defined downtime limitation and the time required for tape restoration. To ensure that certain key users always have e-mail, duplicate or alias accounts can be put on each subset Exchange server. Ultimately, the restoration requirements of data can dramatically change the network infrastructure, as in this case from one Exchange e-mail server to multiple servers working together.

In terms of application redundancy, multiple application servers can be installed under the auspices of the client/server middle tier. Application redundancy is probably the easiest of the redundancies to implement, setting aside the actual cost for hardware and communication.

Network Workstations

Network workstations can essentially be defined as the desktop of the user. Today, most desktop workstations consist of a microcomputer using the Microsoft Windows environment. While this is the most common desktop operating system, it is not the only possible workstation configuration. Apple workstations are still common in businesses that use desktop publishing and video. Apple workstations may indeed expand with the proliferation of Web-based applications that require video and high-performance graphics. Furthermore, UNIX- and LINUX-based systems are very relevant and still utilize a "dumb" terminal interface. However, using X-Windows software, both UNIX and LINUX can provide GUI interfaces on a terminal interface as well.

More important than the brand is the configuration of the workstation itself, and whether multiple-type interfaces are required. This means that a workstation may need to be configured to interface with a number of different host computers. Each interface may require unique software. For example, a UNIX interface might require a non-GUI dumb terminal interface as opposed to a GUI Windows-based application.

Perhaps the most complex issue of workstation software analysis is deciding what software should reside on the "client" itself. I discussed the client/server model in Chapter 5. In the client/server section, the decomposition of what software should actually reside on each tier was discussed. The analyst must work cooperatively with network engineers to determine how software will be configured. The ultimate question is who influences whom? Specifically, should the decision about the size and configuration of a network workstation be made before software is designed? or vice versa? It is a case of which comes first—the chicken or the egg? The decision about what software resides on the workstation should emanate from the software requirements. This means that execution expectations, reusability needs, and ease of maintenance all play a major role in network design. This suggests then that workstation configuration should not be finalized without input from analysts who have performed application requirements analysis.

Another important aspect of workstation software analysis is the interfaces with "office" software products. "Office" software typically includes off-the-shelf products such as Microsoft's Word, Excel, and Powerpoint. Users often require software that makes use of these products and thus requires direct product interfaces. Another popular implementation is the connectivity between electronic mail (e-mail) and applications. The usual bridge relates to the contact management features of Microsoft's Outlook Exchange database and its integration with application products. For example, Exchange has a built-in customer database feature that integrates with e-mail. Users can create lists of contacts, and relevant information such as phone number and address in Exchange. The information can also be seamlessly integrated with e-mail, providing users with a useful contact and e-mail system. Often, application products, such as accounts payable and accounts receivable software also keep lists of contacts. The Exchange database can be integrated with the application to form one central database. This dramatically reduces data entry time and eliminates redundancy. The effects of this integration are dramatic for analysts. First, there is the decision about whether or not to do the integration. Second, there are the specifications of what portion of the application can and should be integrated. In this situation, analysts must be able to understand the Exchange database configuration and to apply good database design to integrating its entities with those of the application. Third, the analyst needs to work with network engineers to determine where the applications should reside, on the workstation or the server.

The Middle Tier

The middle tier of the client/server three-tier architecture is usually reserved for application software. The question and challenge for the analyst is, Which software? Typically, the middle tier is called the *application server level* because this tier holds the production software. The middle tier contains applica-

Figure 10.2 Three-tier client/server network with application servers.

tions, because at this level better response can be provided by simply adding another application server. When additional application servers are added, the number of workstations per server is decreased, thus making for less resource competition and better performance. Take the following example. Figure 10.2 depicts an existing three-tier architecture that contains one database back-end server, three application servers, and 12 workstations. The application servers are each handling four workstations.

Figure 10.3 shows the same network with an additional application server that makes for one fewer workstation per server. Thus, the additional application server means a more efficient network, because each server has one workstation fewer to support. This example, of course, shows the support of workstations symmetrically. Whether each workstation would be designed in this manner depends on many other variables, such as location and user work habits. This example also assumes that every server contains the same application software, which in many situations will not be the case.

There is ongoing debate about which application products should reside on the workstation and which on the middle tier. Generally, there are advantages and disadvantages on both sides. Keeping the office software on the workstation increases performance but creates a fatter and more expensive client. Keeping application products on the middle tier, on the other hand, makes them easier to administer, and creates thinner and cheaper clients, but can cause network traffic conflicts. These decisions should be made jointly, since neither the analyst nor the network engineer can make the call alone. Making

Figure 10.3 Three-tier client/server network additional application servers.

collective decisions also resolves the chicken-and-egg problem; when professionals work jointly, they can have both chickens and eggs simultaneously!

Problems and Exercises

1. What is client/server?
2. How do objects relate to client/server design?
3. Why is there a need for a hybrid object in client/server design?
4. Describe the relationship between client/server and network analysis.
5. What are the four components of analysis of network servers?
6. How do issues of user interface affect the design of network servers?
7. If a file has 2000 records, and each record is 150 bytes long, what is the required physical database size?
8. How do access requirements and response time objectives affect the design of software applications and how they operate across a network?
9. What are the alternative configurations of network workstations? Why is their configuration important to the analyst?
10. What is meant by a "thin" client? a "fat" client?
11. What is the purpose of the middle tier? How do analysts interface with its configuration?

11
Internet/Intranet and Web Analysis

Intranet/Internet Development

This chapter addresses the most contemporary part of the analyst's role in the architecture of systems. Internet/Intranet development, also known as Web development, along with e-commerce processing, is one of the most important ways that today's systems are meeting the needs of the user community.

The challenge of designing Web-based systems lies in the unique requirements for graphic symbols and in the need to fulfill a wide variety of user requirements. The audience that a Web application is supposed to reach is wide and diverse. No longer are computer-based applications limited to the culture of a single organization; they must now reach out to the organization's user community. Thus, "culture" as defined in previous chapters must be expanded to include issues that relate to the way products are typically marketed to consumers. These consumers lie outside the organization, yet they need to utilize some of the internal data that has previously been seen as proprietary to the organization. The combination and interaction of internal proprietary data and externally marketed data is the essence of electronic commerce processing (e-commerce).

The responsibility of the analyst lies in three areas: (1) user interface; (2) database design; and (3) application requirements.

The User Interface

The graphic approaches to designing Web applications are unique. In fact, there are now specialized firms that concentrate on name branding, Web design and e-commerce strategies, and many companies are using such firms, rather than traditional IT staff, to design their Web sites. This development is significant, because it suggests that the relationship with external users requires personnel who are more marketing-oriented than computer-savvy. Nevertheless, the analyst continues to have the important job responsibility of ensuring that the technical and marketing aspects of Web development are properly planned and implemented. In fact, a salient issue relating to the advent of Web systems is the need to maintain traditional data processing design functions such as security, version control, and backup/restore. Indeed, many Web developers, or what are now called "Webmasters," have fallen victim to system problems due to inadequate training in data processing. On the other hand, developers have shown little ability to be pro-active with marketers, so the analyst must ensure that the needs of marketing users are met in the design of Web software. These marketing users, in effect, represent the users of the external product. A Web interface is best determined by actually including external users in the same manner that products are test marketed.

It is crucial to the success of any Web site that its user interface assume no previous knowledge of the application on the part of its users. Training users to become familiar with the interface is not relevant; the Web GUI must be intuitively obvious in that it must be usable without training, it must be powerful without being overwhelming, and it must provide information with few selections. These requirements sound straightforward, but it is a difficult task to attain all of these objectives.

There are many reasons for this difficulty. The graphics used with Web screens rely more on pictures than on the traditional icons of Windows and Apple systems. The menu bar systems are less conforming to de facto windowing, but typically follow the Microsoft Outlook format, which uses a navigator menu approach (see Figure 11.1). Most Web applications that focus on the external user work on the assumption that the user is searching for information. Thus, many screens are designed to allow for search criteria to be entered as the vehicle to interact with the user. Once the selection criteria are entered, results must be displayed in a way that allows the user to review the matching results. Once the matched results are reviewed, the screen application must allow for a modified selection to be carried out to allow the user to obtain more accurate or detailed search results. This three-step application process dictates the essential design philosophy of Web screens (see Figure 11.2). Let's take a closer look at the analysis approach to this process. I use a recent implementation of a Web-based application called *eRealtor*, created by the Corcoran Group, a major New York City apartment real estate firm.

> *Step One:* Create selection criteria using a navigation approach similar to Microsoft Outlook (Figure 11.3). Notice that users have the ability first to choose a topic; in the case of eRealtor, the topics are Index, Properties, Contacts, Advertising, Deals, Admin, and Accounting. Selecting a topic will cause the display of a different host menu to the right of the navigation list. In some cases, as with the Properties topic, there are multiple sub-subjects within the subject. In these cases, the user can navigate through these subjects by highlighting each option.

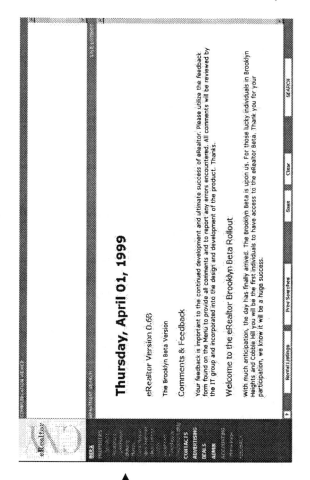

Home Page

Navigation ——▶

Figure 11.1 Microsoft Outlook menu format.

Figure 11.2 Three-step implementation process of Web applications.

How do I find a Property?

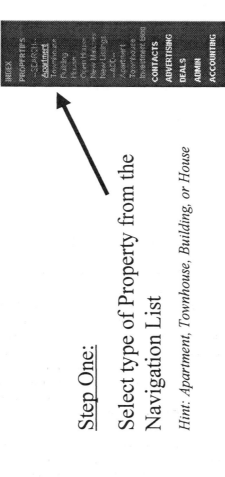

Step One:

Select type of Property from the
Navigation List

Hint: Apartment, Townhouse, Building, or House

Figure 11.3 Microsoft Outlook navigation approach.

Step Two: Once a topic or topic/subject is selected, the user is given the opportunity to select the type of search desired (Figure 11.4).

Step Three: Once the type of search criteria is selected, the user can enter the actual search criteria. The search criteria are defined as the actual data elements and values that are entered to define the domains of the selection (Figure 11.5).

Step Four: The search criteria entered in (3) result in records being retrieved by the application program from the database. All matches are displayed so that the user can select one or more of the search matches (Figure 11.6).

Step Five: The user may wish to change or update the data. The user may want to revise the search without having to reenter the original search criteria (Figure 11.7).

Web applications also differ from the traditional GUI screens in that they often have options to interface with the Web. This capability is allowed because the screens are developed as Web browsers typically using either Netscape's Navigator or Microsoft's Internet Explorer. Thus, the application screen is already operating within the environment to allow the user to interface with the Web wherever and whatever they are doing from the application (Figure 11.8). The benefits are twofold. First, users can use the Web to interface with related applications that may contain information or data relative to what they are doing in the current application. In these cases, the application program can be designed to allow the user to transfer information directly from the Web into the existing browser application. Second, users may wish to work on a completely different application on the Web without having to terminate their existing session with the product.

Another interesting aspect of Web-developed software is in its tracking abilities. In Figure 11.9, we see that the Townhouse application reflects how many "Show Sheets" have been produced. The subject of usage tracking expands to a much more important aspect of the reasons to develop Internet/Intranet software. Web-based applications, since they are developed from within a browser, can be accessed via the Web. Therefore, users may not need to be operating the software from the organization's site(s). Not only does this provide for easier access, it allows users to operate the software from a wide variety of platforms, all of which typically support Web browser software. This ability is the basis of e-commerce, and also highlights the importance of knowing which, and how many, users have accessed the software. Of course, all Web software must address the issue of security. Thus, an Intranet is a version of the Internet that allows usage only from within the company, that is, by users who are in the company. The Internet portion of the application is available to *all* users.

Figure 11.4 Web application data search process.

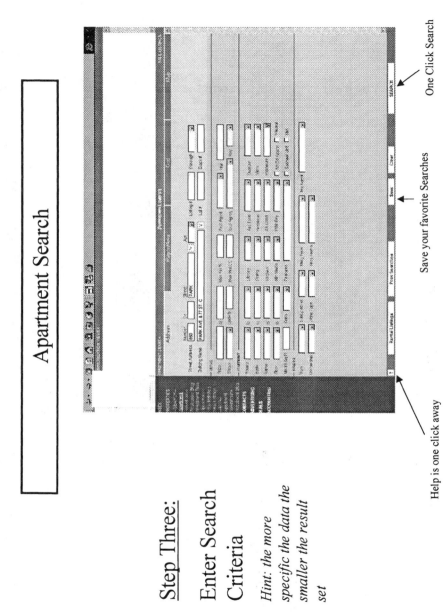

Figure 11.5 Web application search criteria.

Figure 11.6 Web search criteria results.

Apartment Search

Step Five:

Review/
Update Data

*Hint: only the
exclusive broker
may update
exclusive listings*

View Details,
Pictures, Open
House, and
Summary Info.

Return to
Search Results
without having
to re-enter
criteria

Figure 11.7 Web application update search process.

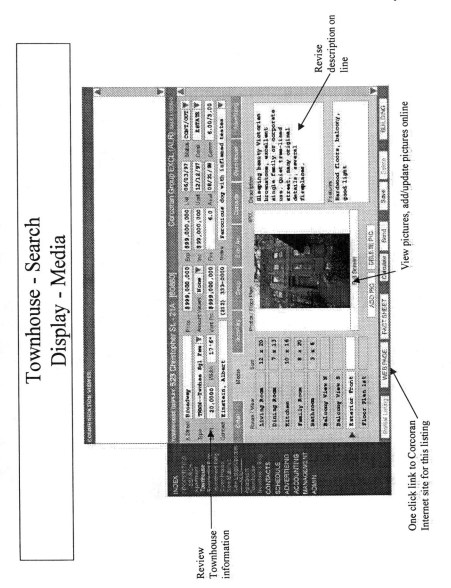

Figure 11.8 Web application interface with the Internet.

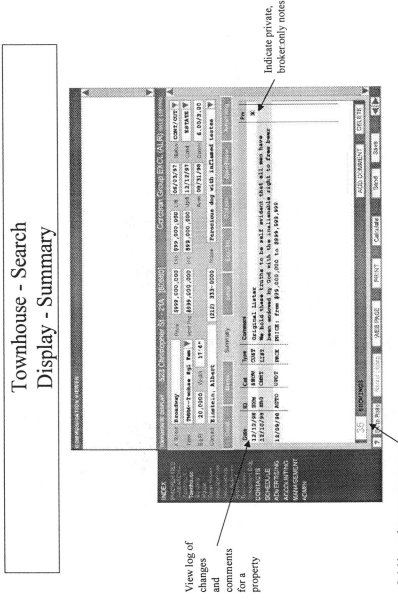

Figure 11.9 Web application tracking abilities.

Database Design

The database design of Web-based software is particularly challenging when an Internet/Intranet architecture is desired. As discussed above, security of data becomes a major issue in two areas. First, data must be encrypted in some fashion for users from within the company that are accessing internal sensitive data. While these elements are traveling via an Internet connection, they are vulnerable to illegal access. The only method to secure such data is to encrypt it, meaning that the data is scrambled using a sophisticated algorithm. Even if the data is illegally accessed or copied, it would have to be decrypted, or unscrambled, to be understood. Offenders would thus need to be sophisticated enough to know how to "break" the encryption code scheme.

Second, and more challenging, is the allowing of certain data information to be available to the general public while other data elements are secured from outside access. Data made available to the public through the Internet is said to reside outside the firewall. A firewall is a hardware server that protects organizations from illegal access from unauthorized users who could corrupt or steal data. Analysts are therefore challenged to design database systems that have data outside the firewall and available to all, and data inside and secured against those who do not have correct access security. This challenge creates a comprehensive database design issue. There may need to be a way that data on either side of the firewall can communicate. Data that resides outside the firewall may need to be refreshed from time to time with data from the internal system. There must also be a way of obtaining new data or updates from the data residing outside the firewall. Finally, and most important, there is the reality that two or more databases may indeed need to coexist. Multiple databases that contain some of the same data elements create redundancy and integrity problems. Thus, analysts need to provide a solution to what appears to be a direct design need with the concept of normalization. Further complications are the challenges of maintaining the performance of internal production data, and the impact of potentially massive amounts of access from the general public. While there is no single right answer, there are a few ways to address these issues.

1. *Maintain One Database:* This is certainly not easy, but it provides the best control over redundancies and integrity issues. The analyst has little to do with respect to design, but a lot to address as to which data may be accessed by external users. This means that data access outside the firewall must be completely controlled by an application program that filters requests to the main database server. Outside requests must be guarded by special screen programs that operate over the Internet and control which elements are available to users. Furthermore, elements that are added or updated outside the firewall must be received by the database system and handled under the auspices of the product's database manager, as shown in Figure 11.10.

Figure 11.10 Internet/Intranet central database diagram.

2. *Database Replication and Synchronization:* This provides more security over the internal data by allowing the specific database product to use its replication capabilities to generate a mirror database. Thus, all the database changes outside the firewall would need to be synchronized back to the internal copy. The external database would still allow access only to certain data elements deemed accessible to external users, as shown in Figure 11.11.

3. *Separate Databases:* This design concept creates two separate databases. The synchronization between the databases is delayed and occurs through an application that ensures that the elements are updated in a batch mode. This means that the production database, which resides behind the firewall, goes through a number of replications and updates a subset database for the general Internet user (see Figure 11.12). The second database contains only the elements that are deemed accessible to external users. The separate database method establishes two separate systems. The second, or external, database serves the Internet portion of the system and is not a copy of the latest data. This approach almost certainly requires that the external data be used only for decision support information, in that changes to the external database would be very difficult to bring back to the production system. Thus, synchronization goes only from production to external, not vice versa. External databases of this design are often implemented using data warehouses, because the data need not be in a normalized form as a read-only provider of data. Unfortunately, this design is not effective for systems that require the Internet data to update the internal production system.

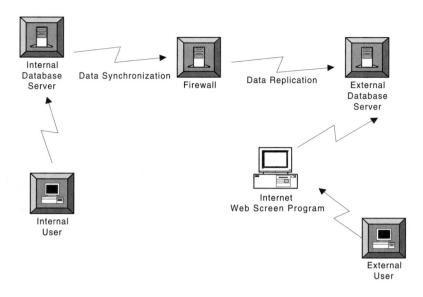

Figure 11.11 Internet/Intranet synchronized replication database diagram.

E-Commerce Application Requirements

Designing application programs that support the Internet/Intranet database design poses a major challenge for the analyst. On first consideration, it might
appear that the database design must be completed before applications analysis
begins. In fact, though, these two processes take place in a more parallel fashion. The reason for this parallel development is that decisions about the way
the database will function are inevitably shaped by the needs of the application, especially those outside the firewall. For example, if an Intranet application is required directly to update elements in the production database, then the
analyst should not prescribe the separate database design approach. Even more
important is the need to have users involved in decisions about how e-
commerce in their organization should function. User input may be ongoing
and will certainly shape the development process. However, as in other areas
of analysis, users cannot be left to determine what they want entirely on their
own. The constraints of applications, security issues, and performance limitations must be discussed with users so that they fully understand the implica-

tions of their decisions both for themselves and for other parts of the organization. Without benefit of such discussions, users may demand Web functionality that could create problems for the system as a whole.

Many Internet/Intranet development projects utilize Web applications to create a new form of business known as e-commerce (electronic commerce). E-commerce creates a virtual interface for consumers to interact with an organization, and this interface may differ from the way the business typically operates in the real world. In e-commerce analysis, the "user" becomes the "consumer." This transformation is an important issue for the analyst. The most well developed e-commerce models are usually those relating to retail operations, where defining users as consumers seems natural. Through these e-commerce retail sites, consumers can actually order, purchase, and track products from a company via the Web interface.

However, e-commerce from a data processing perspective is not just about product fulfillment via a Web interface—it also encompasses the challenges of creating a user interface that relies on forms of artificial intelligence (AI). While I am not suggesting that Web systems are full-fledged AI products, they are systems that need to allow users to enter "*what ifs*." These "*what ifs*" allow consumers to receive results about their needs based on their own input. For example, if I want to search for a particular type of exercise equipment, an e-commerce Web application might ask me to provide information about my height, weight, exercise habits, age, etc. This information would then be utilized by the application to *suggest* or *recommend* what equipment might best fit my personal needs. Thus, e-commerce systems attempt to replace the store attendant, who would typically provide this consultation to a potential buyer at an exercise storefront, with an intelligent interface. This example is certainly not limited to retail, as many e-commerce Web sites provide consulting services through a similar question and answer interface. This concept of processing is the component that represents the AI aspect of Web development.

Using AI skills, then, analysts need to develop procedures that emulate the behavior patterns of users as consumers, so that they can design systems that respond well to these behavior patterns. Unlike most traditional software development situations, it is the marketing wing of the organization that will have perhaps the greatest input in the design of the system, because of its focus on consumers. Analysts therefore need to work closely with the organization's marketing operations to gain an understanding of what consumers/users need. Rather than interviewing consumers directly, analysts will learn about their needs indirectly from the perspective of the marketing department. *This kind of learning is not an easy task.* Therefore, the following phases are recommended to help the analyst generate appropriate specifications for e-commerce systems.

Phase One of the process is to identify the types of products and services to be marketed on the e-commerce system.

Phase Two involves the prepurchase interaction with consumers. This process involves comparison shopping and/or product selection based on competitive variables and attributes.

Phase Three is the pricing, leasing, charging interface, where the consumer has the ability to understand and determine the payment plan and process of goods and/or services.

Phase Four is the consumer's actual placement of the order and its authorization and confirmation of. Delivery date is also a part of this phase of e-commerce processing.

Phase Five involves issuing the consumer some form of receipt or confirmation of the order.

Phase Six involves the postpurchase process interaction, where the customer is serviced and supported based on various plans offered by the organization.

The analyst will need to develop specifications for each of these phases by working with the marketing department to gain an understanding of the user community. The marketing department must provide an action plan to support each of these processes. Below are the proposed analysis and organizational steps that should be taken to ensure successful e-commerce development.

Phase One

This phase requires that the branding of the business's image be completed. Branding means that the marketing department must first define the image it wants the Web site to convey. Indeed, it is critical first to define the mission and image of the organization before determining the products and services that are to be offered on the Web. It is also important to have a detailed understanding of the needs and demographics of targeted consumers. Buying patterns are changing with the increasing numbers of time-strapped, two-career couples, as well as the aging American population. Recent data suggests that Americans are spending less time in shopping malls and storefronts.[31] Therefore, understanding the implications of time constraints and other issues on the way consumers shop is crucial for the development of an e-commerce site that suits this population's buying preferences. Analysts should take an active role in this research process, not so much from a market definition perspective, but rather as a manager of the on-line consumption processes. This implies that the

---

[31] Ravi Kalakota and Andrew B. Winston, *Electronic Commerce: A Manager's Perspective*, Addison-Wesley Publishing Co., 1997.

analyst will define the *kind* of information that is needed, rather than the *content* of that information.

Phase Two

This process involves determining what constitutes an effective consumer user interface. During this phase, the design of the e-commerce screens in accordance with the entire Web site must provide the features that make using the Web easy for on-line purchases. Thus, Phase Two requires the design of the features and functions that must be available to consumers, and these must be designed for effectiveness and simplicity. Software development decisions, Web browser requirements, multimedia versus dynamic screens and pictures are all components of making the appropriate design decisions.

Software product decisions must also be made during this phase. Technical architecture of the Web infrastructure, including network topology and security, use of CGI tools and interactive Web applications, as well as database integration must all be considered. Network topology decisions include selecting the hosting architecture and firewall hardware. CGI scripting will be necessary to ensure standard interfaces between other Web servers and applications. Interactivity must also address four distinct forms:

- ability to link data provided by different servers or hyperlinks and anchors.
- ability to provide customers with data from diverse sources including external systems and databases.
- ability to encompass new types of data including HTTP protocols and Internet mail extensions (MIME).
- ability to integrate new helper or plug-in applications.

The integration of a back-end database will be crucial to the overall e-commerce design. Issues surrounding the centrality of the data, and its interface with existing production systems, will require the analyst to provide an intricate design. Data warehousing alternatives for quick search results might be another alternative. In any case, a detailed database interface analysis must be completed.

Phase Three

This phase essentially creates the virtual store. The analyst must ensure that consumers are provided with systems that can determine the pricing of products and/or services, and that allow them to pursue different scenarios—in other words, an AI interface. The creation of this kind of virtual store often requires the creation of a separate business entity within the organization. This can have a profound effect on the culture of the organization. Therefore, it may be wiser to develop the Web e-commerce system as a separate and distinct business.

Some of the consumer interface design challenges involve enabling consumers to receive the answers they need to make a well-informed decision. For the selling of some items, Web sites must allow consumers to select among different options or components and thus to create different product configurations. Furthermore, the Web must offer consumers help in determining what product or service best fits their needs. This can be accomplished by creating interfaces that request specific data from the consumer. The data in turn generates advice for the online consumer. In essence, the traditional steps that typically occur during the in-store sales process need to be replicated using a virtual interface.

Phase Four

This phase requires that the new e-commerce system be incorporated into the back-end processing and delivery procedures of the organization. Again, analysts will need to decide whether to blend e-commerce processing with the existing internal system or to create a new, stand-alone, business. Analysts will also need to provide some form of on-line tracking systems that allow electronic users to receive confirmation of their orders, acknowledgment of product shipments, and a confirmed delivery date. These systems must also provide for security of on-line charge accounts.

Another challenge may be the requirement to blend production software with administrative products, such as e-mail. E-commerce transactions must be monitored and confirmations sent out to consumers. Internal e-mail accounts must be created so that a system operator responsible for the Web can receive communication from both customers and internal parties about problems and questions.

Phase Five

This process involves the actual delivery of product, and the need to have the Web interface capable of communicating this delivery. During many transactions, the normal retail issues of refunds and disputes will arise. Therefore, software must be developed that provides an e-commerce system that can handle account activity, statements, and credit handling to facilitate the resolution of postpurchase problems. Other aspects of improving delivery issues are:

- administrative software that allows staff to handle e-commerce-related issues.

- access for customers to automated support information, such as product sheets and frequently asked questions.
- providing timely information via the Web so that customers would rather check the Web page than call the office.

Also involved in this phase is the method marketing the Web site itself. This process involves developing strategies to ensure that the site receives "hits." The system must also have capabilities to capture and track user information such as the number of hits, what features and functions are being used, and how many visitors to the site are actually ordering products and services.

Phase Six

This process involves postsupport after product delivery. It addresses the issues of ongoing customer relations and activities that can be organized as installed-based sales opportunities. Existing customers and prospects represent the best opportunity for cross-selling installed customers and "upselling" product lines. The most important requirement of the technology will be to effectively gather information that aids in defining user needs. These needs can be determined by having software that records demographic information and buyer habits, and thus builds customer profiles. Such information must therefore be part of the e-commerce system. This might be a good time to discuss privacy issues with users.

Help-desk management must also interface with the e-commerce data to allow personnel to provide accurate help to callers. Calls will come in, especially from unsophisticated Web users who are not familiar with using electronic means to generate orders. Phone and e-mail interfaces should also be considered to provide maximum customer support.

We can see from the processes outlined above that constructing an e-commerce Web model involves analysts in a more expanded role than other tasks. This is why the tiered approach to analyst proficiency, as outlined in Chapter 8, is so important.

Problems and Exercises

1. Explain the challenges of Web-based development as it relates to end-user satisfaction.
2. What is e-commerce?
3. What specific advantages does using a browser product provide to software development and user operation?
4. Discuss the database design challenges for Web-based applications development.

5. What is data replication and data synchronization?
6. What is the purpose of a firewall?
7. Explain the different design techniques for developing Internet/Intranet database products.
8. What is the difference between an Internet and an Intranet?
9. How do batch updates operate within a Web-based database application?
10. Describe the six phases involved with developing e-commerce systems.
11. How are artificial intelligence (AI) concepts used in e-commerce analysis and design?

12
Documentation and Acceptance Testing

Documentation

Many IS organizations are faced with the ongoing issue of good product documentation. Documentation has been classically defined as having two components: *user documentation* and *technical documentation*. User documentation consists of the necessary instructions required for users to operate and maintain the system. Technical documentation, on the other hand, contains detailed information about the inner components of the product itself. Technical documentation should be designed to provide developers with the ability to support and maintain the system from a programming and engineering perspective.

Once analysis and design are completed, user documentation can be developed as a parallel function with the rest of the product life cycle components. This means that the screens and reports can be used from the design phase to build the documentation on the inputs, queries and output reports of the system. If the software is a GUI product, then the user documentation must also adhere to the standard Help facility which is included in these types of products. Although analysts may be involved with providing information to the documentation team, it is not their responsibility to produce user documentation.

A major part of the technical documentation should be the product of the analyst's work. All of the tools used by the analyst to formulate the logical equivalent must remain as the schematic or blueprint of the product. It is not advisable to try to provide other documentation. First, there rarely is enough time, and second, it should not be necessary. Remember, the concept of using modeling tools was compared to the creation and maintenance of an architect's blueprint in which the schematic had to be self-documenting. There are, however, other components of technical documentation. This technical documentation relates to the physical software development itself. Programming source code, product libraries and version control are examples of technical product documentation that should be the responsibility of the programming team.

Acceptance Test Plans

Acceptance Test Plans can be defined as the set of tests that if passed will establish that the software can be used in production. Acceptance tests need to be established early in the product life cycle and should begin during the analysis phase. It is only logical then that the development of acceptance test plans should involve analysts. As with requirements development, the analyst must participate with the user community. Only users can make the final decision about the content and scope of the test plans. The design and development of acceptance test plans should not be confused with the testing phase of the software development life cycle. Testing should be defined as the carrying out or execution of the acceptance test plans themselves.

The analysis and design of acceptance test plans is often overlooked in many IS organizations. This is because it is viewed inappropriately as a testing method rather than as a way of developing better systems. The question then is: Why and how do acceptance test plans improve software quality?

Quality During Analysis

If acceptance test planning is conducted as a step in analysis, then the issue of how to best test the requirements becomes part of making decisions about overall system requirements. Specifically, if a user wants something that can be difficult to test and maintain, it may force them to rethink the requirement and alter its focus. What better time to do this than when the requirement itself is being discussed? Remember, a strong part of quality software is how easy that software is to maintain.

How Much Can Be Tested?

One must work with the understanding that no new product will ever be fault-free. The permutations of testing everything would make the timetable for completion unacceptable and the costs prohibitive. The acceptance test plan is a strategy to get the *most important components tested completely enough for production*. The testing of software can be compared to the auditing of a company. Accounting firms that conduct an audit for a public company must sign a statement that the books and records of their client are materially correct, meaning that there are no significant discrepancies in the stated numbers. Accounting firms know that they cannot test everything in their client's books and records to be 100% confident that the numbers are correct. Therefore, auditors apply strategic methods like statistical sampling in order to be "comfortable" that the risk of a significant difference is improbable. Software verification is no different. Analysts and users must together decide on the minimum tests necessary to provide comfort to going live with the system. It is unfair to leave this responsibility solely with the user. Having the analyst or programmer do this alone is equally unfair. The wise strategy is to have acceptance test plans developed by the analyst along with input from the user and verification by programming as follows:

1. As each part of a system is functionally decomposed using the various modeling tools, the analyst should develop generic test plans that are based on typical standard logic tests (e.g., Account_Number must be numeric). The analyst and users should then meet to refine the test plans by focusing on how many permutations are required for each logical test. Users should also be encouraged to establish new tests that are missing from the plan. It is highly recommended that the analyst not wait for the entire analysis to be completed before working with acceptance test plan generation Tailoring an acceptance test plan specifically to the needs of a group of users is a good technique. This means that as the analyst completes the interviews with each user or user group, the acceptance test plans should be completed for the specifications developed for them. This philosophy is also good because it avoids the process of meeting again and rehashing old information.

2. The analyst develops interpart tests necessary to ensure that each component properly links with the other.

3. Once the acceptance test plans are approved by users, development must design tests that focus on product-specific validation. These include operating system and program tests to ensure that the operating environment is working correctly. Users and analysts need not be involved with this step as it represents the testing from an engineering perspective. Quality assurance personnel who are part of the development team should be involved in these test designs as these professionals are specifically trained to provide intricate testing that involves the mathematical aspects of finding errors. Once again, quality assurance and testers should not be confused or combined with the role the analyst and users play in the design of acceptance test plans.

More Efficient Development

Providing development personnel with the acceptance test plans is a somewhat controversial idea. Many IS professionals would object to doing so, arguing that the testing of software quality should not be carried out by programmers. However, programmers who are given the test plans are not being asked to do the testing but rather to understand what the user perceives as the most important operational qualities of the system. If the programmer is aware of the specific focus of the tests, then he/she should direct the development to ensure that such errors do not occur. In essence, we are trying to focus the programmer on the most important aspects of the system. To ask programmers to treat each component of a program in an equal manner is unfair, especially since they have no perspective on how to make the decision. If the programmer is

<table>
<tr><td colspan="7">

Quality Assurance

Acceptance Test Plan
This test is used to test the behavior of the program when entering data.
</td></tr>
</table>

Purpose: to ensure that contact screens operate properly when supplying new good data.	Product: Contact - Using Enter Key	Page: 1 of 4
		Number:
Test Plan #: 1G	Vendor: QA Technician:	Date:

Test No.	Condition Being Tested	Expected Results	Actual Results	Comply Y/N	Comments
1	Enter LAST NAME for a new contact; press enter key. Repeat and enter FIRST NAME; press enter key.	Should accept and prompt for COMPANY SITE			
2	Select COMPANY SITE from picklist.	Should accept and prompt for next field			
3	Enter LAST NAMEand FIRST NAME for a CONTACT that is already in the system.	Should accept and prompt for COMPANY SITE			

Figure 12.1 Sample acceptance test plan.

especially focused on the tests, there should be fewer errors detected during the test review, thus supporting a more efficient development effort. Focusing on the tests does not suggest, however, that the programmer is free to ignore the other quality areas of the program.

Now that we have established the reasons and processes of developing acceptance test plans, the analyst must provide a format for its use. The format must be user-friendly so that users can participate. The format must include a record of each iteration of the test, allowing for better documentation and audit trail. The test plans should be in a machine readable format so that changes can be made. Figure 12.1 contains a sample acceptance test plan.

The acceptance test plan in Figure 12.1 reflects a group of tests to be applied to the contact screen shown in Figure 12.2. This particular test plan assumes that no data is on the screen and that the operator will only use the enter key (as opposed to a mouse). Each condition to be tested and its expected result must be listed. The tester will then execute each test number and fill in the results along with any comments. The test plan is then reviewed for completeness. If the test plan fails, the test will be performed again after the software is fixed. Each test iteration is part of the documentation of the testing process. Users and analysts should periodically review the test plans when the system goes live. This procedure will allow the test plans to be "fine-tuned" should any critical errors occur when the system goes into production.

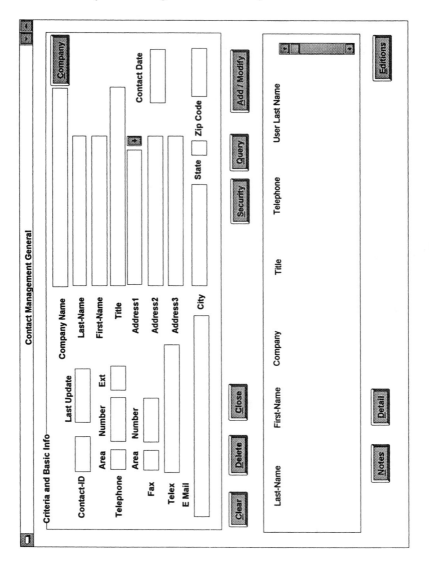

Figure 12.2 Contact Management screen.

Designing acceptance test plans is not a trivial task, for either the user or the analyst; however, good test plans can make the difference in the ultimate quality of the software. When GUI products are tested, the number of test iterations increases substantially. For example, the test plan in Figure 12.1 is focused only on data entry (as opposed to changing existing data), and when the operator uses the enter key. Because this is GUI, operators can enter data by using the enter key, a mouse or the tab key. Therefore, the analyst will need to repeat the same test plan two more times, once when the operator uses a mouse and the other when a tab key is used.

Budget Process

We have continued to expand the role of the analyst in the life cycle of systems development. Analysts must develop the ability to view an upcoming project and submit an accurate budget for their time and effort. The best approach here is to list the generic tasks that are typically performed by an analyst and then attempt to provide an estimate of the requirements not only for each task, but also for each system component within the task. Below is a step-by-step process that can be followed.

Establish the Task List

The analyst should begin the budget by listing the three standard tasks:
- interviewing;
- modeling;
- acceptance test planning.

Each of these tasks will then need to be expanded depending on the scope of the project.

Interviewing

The analyst will need to assess the number of users on the project and whether there will be a need for JAD sessions. Once this schedule is put together, the analyst should arrange for pre-meetings to assess the user skill sets, as this will affect the strategy and time frame of the user interface process. Analysts should employ a weighted criterion when budgeting time. Although there is no exact science to doing this, Figure 12.3 contains a suggested template to follow.

Task: User Interviewing

Sub-Task	Expected Hours	User Skill Set Weight .75—Knowledgeable 1.75—Amateur 1.00—Novice	Weighted Hours
Selection of Users			
Determine JAD Sessions			
Pre-Meetings			
Individual Meetings			
JAD Sessions			

Figure 12.3 User interview budget worksheet.

This table does not include the specific budget for each session, as this would require the analyst to have pre-meetings to assess the number of functions in each component and then budget the time necessary. The user interviewing tasks should take into consideration an estimate for the number of iterations. More detailed sessions can require three to four iterations before final approval is accomplished. The number of hours (or whatever time period is chosen) should be based on a novice user. Note that if the user(s) is knowledgeable, there may actually be a reduction in the budgeted time whereas amateurs (those that know a little) may substantially increase the time frame. The latter situation is due to the likelihood that amateur users will tend to get off track and in general have more questions. The ultimate budget for JAD sessions must be based on a composite of the levels of involved users for each JAD session.

Modeling

Once the interviewing budget has been determined and there is an established understanding of the scope, objectives, constraints and assumptions of the project, the analyst can begin to determine the time period for modeling the system requirements. Some guidelines are listed in Figure 12.4.

Task: Modeling

Modeling Type	Estimated Hours Based on Number of Diagrams or Data Elements	Automation Factor .75—Integrated CASE 1.00—Nonintegrated 3.00—Manual	Factored Hours
Data Flow Diagram			
State Transition			
Data Repository			
Entity Relational Diagrams			
Process Specifications			
Object Orientation			

Figure 12.4 Modeling budget worksheet.

Analysts will need to get a sense during the pre-interviews of the likely number of processes (or data elements with respect to the repository) and how many diagrams might be included. Once this is established, then the budget can be developed. Note that the weight factors are based on the level of integrated automation. Integrated automation refers to the extent of computerization (e.g., a CASE tool) that will be used to develop the models. Non-integrated, which is the non-weighted factor, represents computerized diagramming without intelligent interfaces (which would exist with a CASE product).

Acceptance Test Plans

Acceptance test plan budgeting must take into consideration two key factors: the user interviews and the type of product. The user interview portion should be based on the original budget for user interviews applying a factor based on the modeling budget (see Figure 12.5).

Task: Acceptance Test Plan

Sub-Task	10 percent of User Interview Weighted Budget Hours	Estimated Hours Based on Number of Diagrams or Data Elements (from Modeling budget)	Type of User Interface Factor 2.00—GUI 1.00—Character	Estimated Acceptance Test Plan Hours
Individual Meetings				
JAD Sessions				

Figure 12.5 Acceptance test plan budget worksheet.

Essentially the above matrix reflects that budget hours for acceptance test plans are approximately 10% of the original interview budget hours factored by the estimate of the number of diagrams and the level of automation. The 10% represents the portion of the interview time that is perceived to be spent discussing testing issues with the user. The final factor is the GUI. Because of the event-driven nature of GUI screens, the number of tests to be performed is dramatically increased. Many IS professionals would feel that a 2.00 factor is too low, since many favor 3.00.

Problems and Exercises

1. How does modeling provide the input of the system's documentation?
2. What is an acceptance test plan?
3. Comment on the statement, "Cannot test 100% of everything."
4. How does strategic testing relate to risk management?

5. What is meant by the concept of self-documentation and quality?
6. How do acceptance test plans facilitate productivity and quality of the programming phase?
7. Why is it important for the analyst to provide a budget for his/her tasks?
8. How can acceptance test plans strengthen the relationship with users?
9. Why does acceptance test planning assist the budget process?
10. When should acceptance test plans be developed and by whom?

13
Business Process Reengineering

Business process reengineering (BPR) is one of the more popular methodologies used to redesign existing applications. A more formal definition of BPR is "a requirement to study fundamental business processes, independent of organization units and information systems support, to determine if the underlying business processes can be significantly streamlined and improved."[32] BPR is not just rebuilding the existing applications for the sake of applying new technology to older systems, but also an event that allows for the application of new procedures designed around the OO paradigm. Remember, it is the OO paradigm that focuses on the essential components that were outlined in Chapter 9. The essential components first require the establishment of the core business requirements and then the mapping of the functionality of the organization or business unit to these components.

You might recall that existing applications were referred to as legacy systems in Chapter 3. Many chief information officers (CIOs) today are confronted with a corporate mission to reengineer their existing applications and apply a more sophisticated and structured approach to developing what is known as the *enterprise system*. The enterprise system is composed of one common data repository for all of the organization's data. The typical enterprise configuration includes the OO paradigm and the client/server model that was developed in Chapter 9 and is repeated here as Figure 13.1.

The mission of BPR is to take an existing system, which is typically based on older technology and developed on the basis discussed in Chapter 9 (where the analyst is on the outside looking in), and reengineer it into one integrated system. Much has been written about the approaches or methodologies to use when applying BPR, especially by Ivar Jacobson.[33] The focus of this book is to provide direction from a practitioner's perspective, that is, something that can realistically be applied within the typical resources and constraints that exist in most IS organizations of today.

---

[32] Jeffrey Whitten, Lonnie Bentley, Victor Barlow, *Systems Analysis & Design Methods*, 3rd ed., p. 238.

[33] Jacobson's book, *The Object Advantage* (1995, Addison-Wesley), focuses on business process reengineering using object technology.

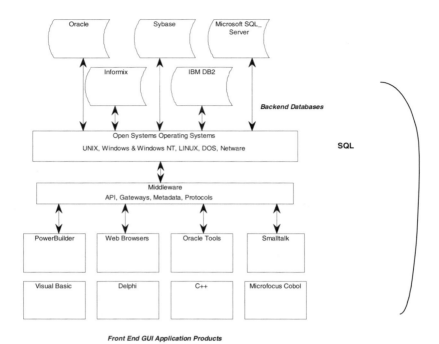

Figure 13.1 Client/server three-tiered architecture.

Analyzing Legacy Systems

The first step to applying successful BPR is to develop an approach to defining the existing system and extracting its existing data elements and applications. Once again, this is similar to the process described in Chapter 3 in that the data needs to be captured into the data repository and the applications need to be defined and compared to a new model based on essential components. Our assumption in this section is that the legacy system resides on an IBM mainframe computer. The data is stored in a VSAM format (non-database files) and the applications have been developed in COBOL. There are no central libraries or repositories of data or programs.

Data Elements

The analyst team will need to design conversion programs that will access the data files and place them in a data repository. The simplest approach is to use a repository from a CASE product. Once this has been accomplished, the analyst can utilize a reverse engineering tool to access the converted data based on the same procedures outlined in Chapter 3. Once all the data elements are loaded, the more rigorous process of identifying duplicate elements becomes the major effort. Duplicate elements may take on different forms. The most obvious is the same element with the same name and attributes. Another type is the same element name, but with different attributes. The third type, and the most challenging, is the duplicate elements that have different names and different attributes. This third type can be related to our discussion about combining user views (see Chapter 4). In any event, users and analysts will need to begin the laborious process of taking each element and building a data repository.

Applications

Application documentation is more problematic but again resembles the procedures followed in Chapter 3. This means that each existing application must be flowed and included as part of a new reengineered processes. Although this procedure may sound straightforward, it is not. BPR typically involves a methodology called Business Area Analysis (BAA). The purpose of BAA is to:

- establish various business areas that make up the enterprise.
- break down the business areas to their required data and process portions.
- reengineer the new and old requirements of each business area,
- develop requirements that provide an OO perspective of each business area, meaning that there is no need to map its needs to the existing physical organization structure,
- define the links that create relationships among all of the business areas.

A business area should be developed in the same manner as depicted in Chapter 9, where we established the essential components of a bank. Each component is a business area that needs to be reengineered into its equivalent OO and client/server enterprise system. Therefore, each essential component must be functionally decomposed to its reusable parts.

Combining Structured and Object Techniques

Once the essential components or business areas have been completed and agreed to by the user community, it is time to develop the actual architecture

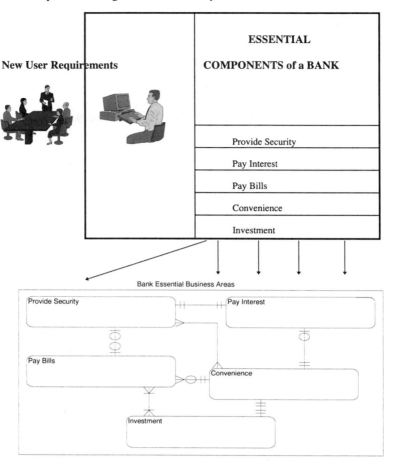

Figure 13.2 BPR modeling using the essential components of a bank.

of the new reengineered system. What modeling tools should we use? The answer is that we should be ready to use all of them when required. Figure 13.2 is a schematic of the reengineering process within a business area.

Like OO, BPR also uses the object concept to develop cohesive and reusable processes. We use the example from Chapter 9 to demonstrate how this maps to business areas. Once the business areas are defined, the structured tools should be used to define all data and processes. BPR supports the concept that the data for a business area should be determined before the processes. You may recall that the same data represented an excellent method for creating cohesive modules. By using the same data, functional primitive DFDs and STDs can be mapped to their appropriate business area.

Logical data modeling and the ERD will need to be completed prior to creating the permanent objects and classes that belong to each business area. Normalization must be applied to the required entities, which will not only have the legacy data elements but also those added as part of the reengineering analysis process.

Prior to mapping the processes and data to their logical objects, the analyst can use another tool to assist in the reconciliation that all data and processes have been found. The tool is called an *association matrix* or a *CRUD diagram*. "CRUD" stands for the four functions that can be performed on any entity: create, read, update or delete (archive). The importance of the CRUD diagram is that it ensures:

- that an object has complete control over its data,
- that a data file is accessed by at least one process, and
- that processes are accessing data.

Processes or Business Function Data Subject or Entity	New Orders	New Products	Shipping	Sales Commission
Customers	R		R,U	
Orders	C, U		U	R
Items	R	C,U,D	R	R
Inventory	R,U	C,U	U	
Expense Category				
Salesperson	R			U

Figure 13.3 Sample CRUD diagram.

The CRUD matrix in Figure 13.3 tells us a lot about the status and activities of our business area data and processes:

- Only the Items entity has enough component processes to control its objects data, that is, by spelling CRUD its processes have the minimum capabilities to control the cycle of any data element. Although this does not ensure that processes are not missing, it is a good indicator that the analysis has covered the life cycle of an entity.
- The Expense Category is not accessed by any process. This means that we have a file that the system is not using. This is an excellent indicator that processes are missing.
- The Customer, Expense Category and Salesperson data are created and deleted by some other processes or business area. This could be a

situation where the physical location of a business function is not where it logically should be processing. The analyst should look for the missing processes to complete the spelling of CRUD before finalizing both the processes and data of any business area.

Even if BPR is not used, the CRUD diagram is an excellent tool to use to determine the processes and data needed for an object. Once the CRUD diagram is finalized, the objects and classes can be created, as Figure 13.4 displays.

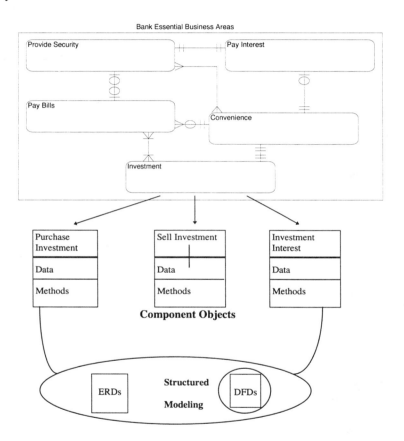

Figure 13.4 Business area component objects and diagrams.

It is important to recognize that many of the objects that are developed during BPR may become reusable components of other business area classes. If there are additions to an object as a result of reviewing a new business area, then the object's data and methods may need to be updated. The best approach to tracking these objects is through an integrated CASE tool, although any level of automation can be feasible.

Dealing with End Users

When applying BPR, analysts need to formulate a plan for how users and user groups will be interviewed. Most important, since reengineering implies change, change means discussions that must lead to decisions. Coordination of these decisions is critical, and it can get out of hand quickly. For this reason the analyst should attempt to organize BPR using multiple JAD sessions. The sessions should be focused first on each individual business area. Prior to actually holding the session, analysts and facilitators should educate users on the techniques and reasons for BPR. Analysts should not be afraid to show users the business area schematic and explain the concepts of essential components and how they eventually can become reusable objects. This means that there may be a need to hold a one-day training session for the users who will be involved in the JADs. This suggestion is consistent with the concept of having users prepared before they attend a meeting.

JAD sessions should be organized to have session leaders who can provide walkthroughs of the existing functions. While these walkthroughs take place, the adjustments and missing functionalities can be added to the business area. The issues concerning the selection of key personnel as they were outlined in Chapter 1 are extremely important, especially when selecting decision makers. Because of the volume of information being discussed, it is advisable to have more than one scribe available. This minimizes the risk of not capturing important business rules.

After each business area is completed, the links to the other business components must be handled. These should also take place via JADs and typically use the session leaders as attendees. Session leaders tend to have enough information at this point from the JAD sessions to determine the necessary links for each business area.

The use of prototypes for each JAD is highly recommended because it will provide the best vehicle to get agreement on the new system. This suggests that an integrated CASE product is almost a necessity for creating a successful BPR project.

Information Systems Issues

BPR is implemented on existing systems. Existing systems have IS staffs and constraints that must be addressed as part of the process. Since the current view of BPR is to create an open systems client/server enterprise system, the physical requirements of the network are critical during analysis. Remember, RAD means the combining of analysis, design and development into multiple iterative steps. In order to take the objects and classes developed from the JAD sessions, the analyst must start breaking up the data and methods of the classes into its related client and server functions. You may recall that if the client and server processing portions of an object must reside on separate hardware components then the object/class must be separated or further decomposed into separate physical modules (see Figure 13.5).

We have emphasized the importance of analysts being involved with the network design for client/server systems. BPR thus requires that the network design be completed as soon as possible and ideally before analysis starts. This will be difficult since many of the network decisions may be altered depending on how the objects become distributed across the network. In addition, the back-end database stored procedures (business rules, triggers, etc.) and middleware software components must be defined while the analysis specification is being finalized.

IS personnel must also be heavily involved in the JAD sessions to clarify questions about the existing system processes. This will involve discussions about the amount of data processed, as well as the difficulty or ease of getting additional information from the suggestions brought up during the JADs. IS can also disclose the details of the equipment choices and how these may affect the requirements being discussed. Such input may enable quicker decisions based on predetermined IS constraints.

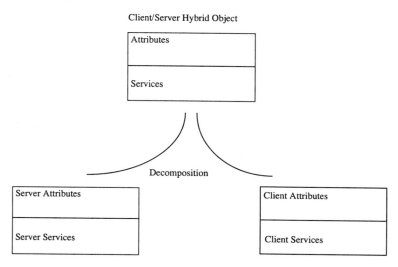

Figure 13.5 Client/server hybrid model.

Finally, IS will be required to establish the information about the existing data and processes. They will most likely be responsible for the conversion of the data as well as for clarifying the meaning of many of the data elements in question. You may assume that many of the legacy data element definitions will be unknown, and as a result analysts and programmers will be spending time together figuring out what such elements do in the system. Existing process review means looking at the current application programs and how they function in the system. Most of this work will be required from IS programmers and legacy designers (if they are still around!). Since our assumption was that the existing system was developed under COBOL, there will be a more difficult mapping of how a 3GL (third generation language[34]) is designed as opposed to today's 4GL (fourth generation language[35]) products.

System Development Life Cycle (SDLC)

BPR changes the steps in the typical IS SDLC. The traditional SDLC is based on the waterfall approach as was shown in Chapter 1 and is repeated here as Figure 13.6.

Activity		March	April	May	June	July	August	Sept	Oct
Feasibility		▭							
Analysis			▭						
Design				▭					
Development					▭				
Quality Assurance							▭		
Implementation									▭

Figure 13.6 The classic waterfall SDLC, showing each phase dependent on the completion of the previous one.

The problems with the waterfall approach are that it is unrealistic (as discussed in Chapter 1) and that it does not conform to the requirements of the OO

---

[34] A *generation language* refers to the level of the programming language. Third-generation languages were considered high-level development systems that included C, Pascal and COBOL

[35] Fourth-generation languages typically include programming languages that work directly with database systems and contain simpler program instructions than its predecessor languages.

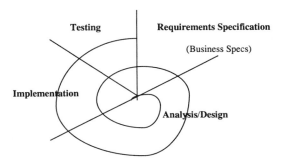

Figure 13.7 Object-oriented software life cycle.

life cycle. Therefore, IS must modify its SDLC to conform to the OO and client/server needs of BPR. The OO client/server life cycle resembles a spiral as shown in Figure 13.7.

The spiral life cycle reflects a much larger allocation of time spent on design than in the traditional life cycle, because much of the development time is spent designing the objects for product reuse. Although this may appear unduly time-consuming, there is a heavy payback in BPR if it is done correctly. Remember that the spiral life cycle is applied to the development of each object since it is a cohesive component within itself. The more reusable the object, the more spiral the effort becomes with a particular emphasis on the analysis/design phase.

Pilot Applications

Many analysts opt to have a pilot application as part of the BPR effort. The purpose of the pilot is to get users excited about the benefits of creating the new system. Because an actual application is developed, IS must be involved to ensure the pilot is successful. How can success be evaluated? The first real decision in a pilot is to select an existing application that is not working favorably and one that can demonstrate enough advantages of the OO GUI and client/server environment to pique the interest of users. Below is a suggested strategy:

- Focus on an application that can demonstrate the flexibility of the GUI front end.
- Select an application that accesses existing corporate data to show the users how easily the data can be reached. Analysts should avoid an application that gets involved with massive updates or large data queries, as this is inviting an unexpected delay in processing. Such exercises tend to involve much study and experience with the corporate network of information, and this expertise may not be available.

- Select an application that has a relatively short development time when using a GUI product. Do not try an application which might be more involved when using a client/server model.

The pilot application not only has the potential to generate more interest, but it also allows users to be more creative and understanding of the requirements of BPR.

Downsizing System Components

After the business areas and interfaces among them have been completed, the analyst and development must decide on a strategy for implementation. To attempt to convert an entire enterprise level system in one project is very dangerous and very unlikely to succeed. The user community also needs to be involved with this decision since many business units can convert only at certain times of the year due to various seasonal business requirements. Therefore, the analyst must plan to migrate applications in pieces. It is only logical to do this migration by business area and to develop temporary legacy links back to the main system. Most organizations are doing just this by purchasing open systems hardware and moving complete self-contained business areas independently onto the new platforms (see Figure 13.8).

As each business area is converted to the open systems architecture, the temporary legacy links will be deleted and incorporated in the new system.

Transactions Versus Data Warehousing

Our sample system is categorized as a *transaction-based operation*, that is, the system was designed to maximize its performance based on the processing of transactions. This type of systems must perform under the stress of many users who are using the system for production purposes. The limit of these systems is that they do not provide the end-user with on-line data comparisons and what-if analysis in a productive and robust environment. Such systems were designed in the early 1980s and were called decision support systems (DSS). Today's robust software goes even further than the awkward DSS systems, and users want the same level of flexibility with their enterprise solutions. The problem is simple: You cannot maximize your transactions performance while maximizing your DSS functionality. The result is many client/server systems have had trouble performing at the same level as the legacy systems. SQL-based queries that are issued during peak time enterprise processing can cause significant slow-down in processing. In most cases such delays are simply unacceptable. In fact, GUI applications will never outperform VSAM transaction-based mainframe systems. This sounds like a disappointing state of affairs for users. The remedy is to separate the transaction processing from the DSS functionality and improve transaction processing to an acceptable user level. This is accomplished by creating a *data warehouse environment* (see Figure 13.9). A data warehouse is an archive of the database off-loaded usually to a separate machine to provide DSS capabilities to those that need to query information.

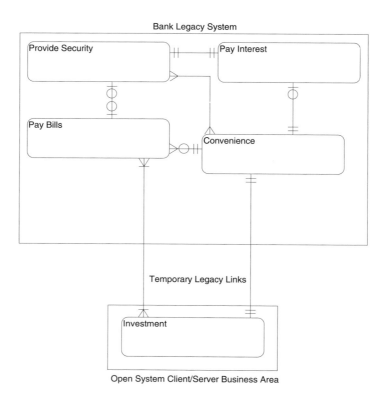

Figure 13.8 Legacy links of a business area.

The problem with data warehousing is the currency of the data, since off-loaded information is typically not performed real-time. Therefore, users must agree to use "old" data. Many organizations have provided data warehousing capabilities within hours of the input or update of information. Nevertheless, data warehousing can work only if the user community can settle on aged data that they cannot change. There are products such as SAS that provide specific tools to create data warehouse databases. Often the data is not fully normalized because the user cannot change the information. This results in a more efficient and accessible database because the information is stored in a flatter format (fewer database files). Almost every database manufacturer will be providing

Figure 13.9 Transaction/data warehouse BPR solution.

data warehouse capabilities in their next release. The analyst must be involved in determining which applications (usually reporting and inquiry operations) are candidates for the warehouse function. Analysts and IS personnel must take care in explaining the role of the data warehouse to the users so that they can use it effectively.

Problems and Exercises

1. Explain the objectives of BPR.
2. How is BPR consistent with the object and client/server models.
3. What is a business area?
4. Explain the relationship between BPR and structured tools.
5. What is a CRUD diagram?
6. How should BPR be introduced to users and IS personnel?
7. What is the SDLC? Why is it called a waterfall approach?
8. Compare the SDLC with the OOLC.
9. What is the significance of the spiral approach and how does it support the development of reusable objects?
10. Describe the procedures to implement a pilot application. Why is this so important in BPR?

11. Describe the philosophy of reengineering an enterprise system.
12. What is the difference between a transaction database and a data warehouse?

14
Concepts of ISO 9000 and the Software Development Life Cycle

Developing a System of Procedures

Perhaps one of the most significant challenges in analysis today is its role in the software life cycle. There has been much criticism of the lack of discipline applied to software development projects and personnel in general, and we continue to be an industry that has a poor reputation for delivering quality products on schedule. Although many organizations have procedures, few really follow them and fewer still have any means of measuring the quality and productivity of software development. A system of procedures should first be developed prior to implementing a life cycle that can ensure its adherence to the procedure. These procedures also need to be measured on an ongoing basis. This book restricts its focus to the set of procedures that should be employed in the analysis and design functions.

The process of developing measurable procedures in an organization must start with the people who will be part of its implementation. Standard procedures should not be created by upper management, as the steps will be viewed as a control mechanism as opposed to a quality implementation. How then do we get the implementors to create the standards? When examining this question, one must look at other professions and see how they implement their standards. The first main difference between computer professionals and members of many other professions is they lack a governing standards board like the American Medical Association (AMA) or the American Institute of Certified Public Accountants (AICPA). Unfortunately, as mentioned in previous chapters, it seems unlikely that any such governing board will exist in the near future. Looking more closely at this issue, however, we need to examine the ultimate value of a governing board. What standards boards really accomplish is to build the moral and professional responsibilities of their trade. Accountants, attorneys and doctors look upon themselves as professionals who have such responsibilities. This is not to imply that governing boards can resolve every problem, but at least they can help. With or without the existence of a standards board, analysts within an organization must develop the belief that they belong to a profession. Once this identification occurs, analysts can create the procedures necessary to ensure the quality of their own profession. Currently, few analysts view themselves as part of a profession.

If analysts can create this level of self-actualization, then the group can begin the process of developing quality procedures that can be measured for future improvement. The standard procedures should be governed by the group itself and the processes integrated into the software life cycle of the organization. In fact, analysts should encourage other departments to follow the same procedures for implementing their respective quality procedures.

Although not typically required, many firms employ ISO 9000 as a formal vehicle to implement the development of measurable procedures. ISO 9000 stands for the International Organization for Standardization, an organization formed in 1947 and based in Geneva. As of this writing, 91 member countries are associated with it. ISO 9000 was founded to establish international quality assurance standards focused on processes rather than on products.

Why ISO 9000?

ISO 9000 offers a method of establishing agreed-upon quality levels through standard procedures in the production of goods and services. Many international companies require that their vendors be ISO 9000 compliant through the certification process. Certification requires an audit by an independent firm that specializes in ISO 9000 compliance. The certification is good for three years. Apart from the issue of certification, the benefits of ISO 9000 lie in its basis for building a quality program through employee empowerment. It also achieves and sustains specific quality levels and provides consistency in its application. ISO 9000 has a number of subcomponents. ISO 9001, 9002, and 9003 codify the software development process. In particular, 9001 affects the role of the analyst by requiring standards for design specifications and defines 20 different categories of systems. Essentially, ISO 9000 requires three basic things:

1.   Say what you do.
2.   Do what you say.
3.   Prove it.

This means that the analyst needs to completely document what should occur during the requirements process to ensure quality. After these procedures are documented, the analyst needs to start implementing them based on the standards developed and agreed upon by the organization. The process must be self-documenting; that is, it must contain various control points that can prove at any time that a quality step in the process was not only completed but done within the quality standard established by the organization. It is important to recognize that ISO 9000 does not establish what the standard should be but rather that the organization can comply with whatever standards it chooses to employ. This freedom is what makes ISO 9000 so attractive. Even if the organization does not opt to go through with the audit, it can still establish an honorable quality infrastructure that:

- creates an environment of professional involvement, commitment and accountability,
- allows for professional freedom to document the realities of the process itself within reasonable quality measurements,
- pushes down the responsibilities of quality to the implementor as opposed to the executive,
- identifies where the analyst fits in the scope of the software life cycle,
- locates existing procedural flaws,
- eliminates duplication of efforts,
- closes the gap between required procedures and actual practices,
- complements the other quality programs that might exist,
- requires that the individuals participating in the process be qualified within their defined job descriptions.

How to Incorporate ISO 9000 into Existing Software Life Cycles

The question now is how to incorporate an ISO 9000-type process for the analyst function and incorporate it into the existing software life cycle. Listed below are the essential 9 steps to follow:

1. Create and document all the quality procedures for the analyst.
2. Follow these processes throughout the organization and see how they enter and leave the analyst function.
3. Maintain records which support the procedures.
4. Ensure that all professionals understand and endorse the quality policy.
5. Verify that there are no missing processes.
6. Changes or modifications to the procedures must be systematically reviewed and controlled.
7. Have control over all documentation within the process.
8. Ensure that analysts are trained and that records are kept about their training.
9. Ensure that constant review is carried out by the organization or through third party audits.

In order for ISO 9000 guidelines to be implemented, it is recommended that the analyst initially provide a *work-flow diagram* of the quality process (see Figure 14.1).

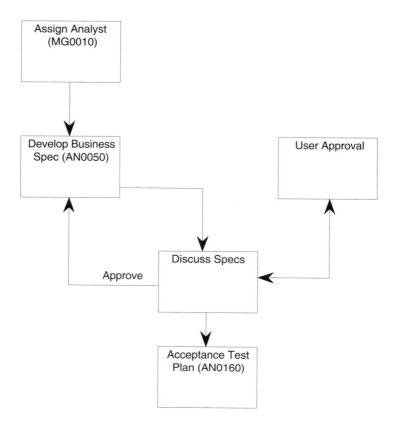

Figure 14.1 A sample work-flow diagram.

Figure 14.1 reflects some of the steps an analyst must perform in a quality process. Note that certain steps reflect that there is an actual form that needs to be completed in order to confirm the step's completion. Figure 14.2 illustrates document AN0010; Figure 14.3 shows AN0050; and Figure 14.4 displays AN0160.

These forms confirm the activities in the quality work-flow process outlined by the analyst. At any time during the life cycle, an event can be confirmed by looking at the completed form.

Project Status Report

Period Ending: / / :

| Date: | Project:

Date Delivered To Users: | Analyst: |

Previous Objectives: Objective	Previous Target Date	Act Completion Date or Status

---

New Project Objectives:

Objective		Target Date
	Start	Complete

Financial Performance:	Budget	Actual	% Remaining

\AN0010 Rev. 3/21/94

Figure 14.2 ISO 9000 Project Status Report.

Analysis Acknowledgment

User: _____

Date:	Analyst:	Date of Request	Project #

Confirmation Type	Y/N	Cost	Expected Days	Expected Delivery	Deliverable / Comments
Requirements Definition					
Conceptual Detail Design:					
Development:					
System Tested Enhancements					
User Accepted Enhancements					

\an0050 Rev. 3/21/94

Figure 14.3 ISO 9000 Analysis Acknowledgment form.

Quality Assurance

Acceptance Test Plan

Test Plan #:	Product:	Number:

Purpose:	Vendor:	Date:
	QA Technician:	Page: 1 of

Test No.	Condition Being Tested	Expected Results	Actual Results	Comply Y/N	Comments
1					
2					
3					

Figure 14.4 Quality Assurance Test Plan (AN0160).

Name: **Confirmation/Service Acknowledgment**	**Date Issued: 3/8/94**
Form Instructions	**Supersedes:**
	Revision: 1.00

The purpose of this form is to track the status of various services such as Requirements Definition, Conceptual Detail Design, Development, System Tested Enhancements, and User Accepted Enhancements.

The appropriate project # must be attached. The type of form must be checked for each type of Confirmation.

\an0050i Rev 3/8/94

Figure 14.5 An ISO 9000 form instruction page.

In order to comply with the documentation standards, each form should contain an instruction sheet, as shown in Figure 14.5. This sheet will ensure that users have the appropriate instructions. Confirmation documents can be implemented in different ways. Obviously if forms are processed manually, the documentation will contain the actual storage of working papers by project. Such working papers are typically filed in a documentation storage room similar to a library where the original contents are secure and controlled. Access to the documentation is allowed, but must be authorized and recorded. Sometimes forms are put together using a word-processing package such as

Microsoft Word. The blank forms are stored on a central library so that master documents can be accessed by the analyst via a network. Once the forms are completed, they can be stored in a project directory. The most sophisticated method of implementing ISO 9000 is to use a Lotus Notes electronic filing system. Here, forms are filled out and passed to the appropriate individuals automatically. The confirmation documents then become an inherent part of the original work flow. In any event, these types of forms implementation affect only automation, not the concept of ISO 9000 as a whole.

Interfacing IS Personnel

We mentioned earlier that ISO 9000 requires qualified personnel. This means that the organization must provide detailed information about the skill set requirements for each job function. Most organizations typically have job descriptions that are not very detailed and tend to be vague with respect to the specific requirements of the job. In addition, job descriptions rarely provide information that can be used to measure true performance. Questions such as "How many lines of code should a programmer generate per day?" cannot be measured effectively. There is also a question about whether lines of code should be the basis of measurement at all. A solution to this dilemma is to create a *job description matrix*, which provides the specific details of each job responsibility along with the necessary measurement criteria for performance (see Figure 14.6).

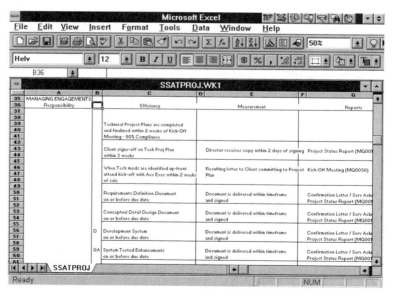

Figure 14.6 Job description matrix.

The document in Figure 14.6 is a matrix of responsibilities for an analyst. Note that the analyst has a number of efficiency requirements within the managing engagements (projects) responsibility. Efficiency here means that the analyst must perform the task at a certain indicated level to be considered productive at that task. To a degree, efficiency typically establishes the time constraints to deliver the task. Measurement defines the method used to determine whether the efficiency was met. Reports are simply the vehicle through which the analyst proves that the task was completed and on what basis.

The job description matrix represents a subset of the entire job description that focuses strictly on the procedural and process aspects of the individual's position. It not only satisfies ISO 9000, but represents a healthier way of measuring individual performance in an IS environment. Most individuals should know their exact performance at any time during the review period. Furthermore, the matrix is an easy tool to use for updating new or changed performance tasks.

Committing to ISO 9000

We have outlined the sequential steps to implement an ISO 9000 organization. Unfortunately, the outline does not ensure success, and often just following the suggested steps leads to another software life cycle that nobody really adheres to. In order to be successful, a more strategic commitment must be made. Let's outline these guidelines for the analyst functions:

- A team of analysts should meet to form the governing body that will establish the procedures to follow to reach an ISO 9000 level (this does not necessarily require that certification be accomplished).
- The ISO 9000 team should develop a budget of the milestones to be reached and the time commitments that are required. It is advisable that the budget be forecasted like a project, probably using a Gantt chart to develop the milestones and time-frames.
- The ISO 9000 team should then communicate their objectives to the remaining analysts in the organization and coordinate a review session so that the entire organization can understand the benefits, constraints and scope of the activity. It is also an opportunity to allow everyone to voice their opinions about how to complete the project. Therefore, the meeting should result in the final schedule for completing the ISO 9000 objective.
- The ISO 9000 team should inform the other IS groups of its objectives, although analysts should be careful not to provoke a political confrontation with other parts of the IS staff. The communication should be limited to helping other departments understand how these analyst quality standards will interface with the entire software life cycle.

- The work flows for the analyst tasks must be completed in accordance with the schedule such that everyone can agree to the confirmation steps necessary to validate each task. It is important that the ISO 9000 processes allow for a percentage of success. This means that not every process must be successful 100% of the time, but rather can be acceptable within some fault tolerance level. For example, suppose that the analyst must have a follow-up meeting with the users within 48 hours after a previous step has been completed. It may not be realistic to meet this goal every time such a meeting is necessary. After all, the analyst cannot always force users to attend meetings in a timely way. Therefore, the ISO 9000 step may view this task as successful if it occurs within the 48 hours 80% of the time, that is, within a 20% fault tolerance.

- All task steps must have verification. This will require that standard forms be developed to confirm completion. While we have shown samples of these forms earlier, the ISO 9000 team should beware of producing an unwieldy process involving too many forms. Many software life cycles have suffered the consequences of establishing too many checkpoints. Remember, ISO 9000 is a professional's standard and should cater to the needs of well-trained professionals. Therefore, the ISO 9000 team should review the initial confirmation forms and begin the process of combining them into a smaller subset. That is, the final forms should be designed to be as generic as possible by confirming multiple tasks. For example, form AN0010 (Figure 9.2) represents a generic project status report that was used to confirm various types of information attributable to different tasks.

- There should be meetings held with the analysis group that focus on the alternatives for automating the confirmation forms as outlined earlier in this chapter. It is advisable that this topic be confirmed by the group since their full cooperation is needed for the success of the program.

- Allow time for changing the procedures and the forms. Your first effort will not be the final one; therefore, the ISO 9000 team must plan to meet and review the changes necessary to make it work. Analysts should be aware that the opportunity for change always exists as long as it conforms to the essential objectives of ISO 9000.

- The ISO 9000 project should be at least a one-year plan, from inception of the schedule to actual fulfillment of the processes. In fact, an organization must demonstrate ISO 9000 for at least 18 months prior to being eligible for certification.

- The ISO 9000 group needs to be prepared and authorized to make changes to the job description of the analyst. This may require the submission of requests and authorizations to the executive management team or the human resources department. It is important not to overlook this step since an inability to change the organization structure could hinder the success of the ISO 9000 implementation.

As we can see from the above steps, establishing an ISO 9000 group is a significant commitment. However, its benefits can include a professional organization that controls its own quality standards. These standards can be changed on an ongoing basis to ensure compliance with the business objectives and requirements of the enterprise. Certification, while not the focus of our discussion, is clearly another level to achieve. Most companies that pursue certification do so for marketing advantage or are required to obtain it by their customers. Implementing ISO 9000 should not require that the entire company conform at once; in fact it is almost an advantage to implement it in a phased approach, department by department. The potential benefits of ISO 9000 concepts may fill the void in many of the IS organizations which lack clearly defined quality standards.

Problems and Exercises

1. Explain why ISO 9000 represents a system of procedures.
2. What are the three fundamental things that ISO 9000 tries to establish?
3. What are the overall benefits of ISO 9000?
4. How is ISO 9000 incorporated into the life cycle?
5. Why are work flows the most critical aspect of developing the ISO 9000 model?
6. Why are forms used in ISO 9000?
7. How are personnel affected by ISO 9000?
8. What is a job description matrix?
9. What steps are necessary for an organization to adopt ISO 9000?
10. Does ISO 9000 need to be implemented in all areas of the business? Explain.

Appendix A
Case Study: The Rainforest Book Company Problem

The following four events are services provided by the Rainforest Book Company:

Event I

A customer wishes to set up an account to purchase books. The Sales Department at the Rainforest Book Company receives the request and sends out a blank Account Request form. The form has space for the following information:

    Customer Name
    Customer Address
    Customer Phone Number
    Customer Fax Number
    Credit Card Information (if applicable)
    Credit Card Number
    Type of Credit Card
    Expiration Date
    Cardholder's Name
    ZIP or postal code of the billing address for this card

The customer sends back a completed Account Request form. The "for office use only" section is filled out by the Sales Group. This information includes the processor's identification, the date the account is opened, and a customer account number that is assigned. The customer account file is updated, and the Account Request form is filed. The Account Processing Department receives notification of the new account and sends the customer a confirmation letter. This letter notifies the customer of their customer account number. This number can be used to expedite the ordering process.

Event II

A customer makes a book inquiry. The customer can request a book by giving any of the following information: (book title and book author) or ISBN number. The Sales Department first verifies that the customer has a valid account. If the book is found based upon the information that was given, the customer receives the following information about the book:

Title of the book
Author of the book
Paperback/Hardcover
Price
Date Published
Availability
Reviews

If the book is not available in stock, all of the above information is returned and an out-of-stock notice is sent specifying the approximate date the book will be in stock. If the book is no longer in print and has been discontinued, an out-of-print notice is sent to the customer. This out-of-print notice includes a list of Used Book Stores in the customer's county.

Event III

A customer decides to purchase books, places the order for the books, and requests a book order form from the Sales Department. A blank book order form is forwarded to the customer. The customer account number and the date the order is being placed is entered. The following information is included in the book order:

Customer Account Number
Date Order is placed
Title of the Book
Author
Paperback or Hardcover
ISBN, if available

In addition, the customer indicates the shipping option by entering the following information:

Standard Shipping or
Second Day Air or
Next Day Air

Placed orders are sent to the warehouse, and the customer account file is updated. The warehouse issues an order confirmation when the books are shipped. The invoice is generated and then sent to the customer. The customer then sends the invoice slip and a payment or authorizes the use of a credit card on file to the Accounting Department. The Accounting Department processes the payment and updates the customer account.

Event IV

The Sales Department generates a monthly sales report and forwards it to Management.

Assignment

1. Create DFDs for the four events.
2. Decompose the four top-level DFDs into their respective functional primitives.
3. Create the data dictionary entries for all the named data flows found in the child diagrams from (2). The entries in the resulting data dictionary should be reported in alphabetical order.
4. Write process specifications for all of the functional primitives from (2).

Case Study created by Cynthia Hernandez.

Appendix B
Case Study: The CGT Rental Service Problem

The following five events represent the services provided by the the CGT rental agency:

I. Events

1. Potential renters call CGT and ask them if apartments are available for either beachfront or mountainside views. All callers have their information recorded and stored in an information folder. The most important information for CGT to obtain is the caller's maximum monthly rent limit.
2. CGT examines their database and searches for potential matches on the properties requested.
3. People call the agency to inform them that they have an apartment for rent. The agency only deals with rentals for beach fronts and mountain sides. All other calls are forwarded to their sister organization that handles other requests.
4. Fifteen days before rent is due, CGT sends renters their monthly invoices.
5. Sixty days before the lease is up, CGT sends out a notice for renewal to the renter.

II. High Level Data Elements

The following data elements should be broken down to their elementary level and added, if necessary.

Renter Name
Renter Address
Renter Phone Number
Maximum Monthly Rent
Rental Property

Rental Monthly Rent
Rental Number Bedrooms
Rental Dates
Rental Owner Information
Rental Number of Blocks from Beach
Rental Beach Side
Rental Mountain Range
Rental Mountain Ski Area
Rental Mountain Lake Site

III. Assignment

1. Draw the Data Flow Diagrams (DFD) at the Functional Primitive level.
2. From the DFD perform Logical Data Modeling and show 1st, 2nd and 3rd Normal Forms.
3. Draw the final ERD.
4. Produce a CRUD diagram.
5. What does the CRUD diagram show us?

Appendix C
Case Study: The Collection Agency Problem

I. Background

Statement of Purpose

The purpose of the ABC organization is to process customer payments on credit cards. ABC processes these payments for banks and other financial institutions. Currently, the operation is done manually, and you have been called in as a consultant to do the analysis for an automated system.

The Event List

During your analysis, you have met with departments and determined that there are essentially 8 events as follows:

Event 1

Mary gets a delivery of mail every morning from a messenger who picks up the mail at the local Post Office. Mary starts her day by opening and processing the mail. There are, however, a number of types of information contained in an envelope:

1. A check with a payment form
2. Cash only
3. Check only
4. Cash with a payment form
5. Payment form only

Note: All of the above can sometimes be accompanied with correspondence from the customer.

The information on the payment form is necessary to process the payment. The payment form is shown on Attachment I.

Mary fills in the "FOR OFFICE USE ONLY" portion and sends the Payment Form and cash/check to Joe, the Bookkeeper. Correspondence is forwarded to the Support Dept (including forms with no payment).

Payments made without a form are sent to Janet in the Research Department.

Event 2

Janet receives payments from Mary and begins a process of looking up the information that the customer has provided. This can typically include Name, Address, etc. If the customer account number is located, Janet fills out a blank Payment Form to substitute for the original and forwards the form and the check to Joe, the Bookkeeper. If the account number is not found, a substitute Payment Form is still developed with whatever information is available. These payments are also forwarded to Joe in bookkeeping.

Event 3

The Support Department receives the correspondence from Mary. The correspondence requires written response. Correspondence falls into 4 categories:
1. An error in the outstanding balance or address of a customer. This will require support to fill out a balance correction form (Attachment II). This Form is forwarded to the Correction Dept.
2. A complaint about service. The complaint is researched and a written response is sent to the customer. A monthly summary report of customers with complaints is also forwarded to the department manager.
3. A client default request, stating that the customer cannot pay due to a hardship. The Technician will send the customer a request for default form (Attachment III).
4. A request for default form (3) is received for processing. These are sent to the Correction Department.

Event 4

Joe, the bookkeeper receives payments. Payments are posted to the account master ledger. A deposit slip is prepared for identified account payments. Unknown account payments are deposited into a separate bank account called "Unapplied Payments." The payment forms are filed by account number. A daily report of payments by customer (including unapplied payments) is produced.

Event 5

The Correction Department receives balance correction forms or requests for default notices; the appropriate adjustments are made to the account master ledger. The forms are filed by type and account number. A daily and monthly report of adjustments is produced.

Event 6

The department manager receives the monthly complaint report. After analyzing the information, a summary report is produced by Complaint Type (e.g., unhappy with service, credit card problem, and wrong outstanding balance) and the department manager issues a report to management. A quarterly client survey questionnaire on service is sent to customers. This report includes statistics on client satisfaction which resulted from the previous questionnaire.

Event 7

Joe, the bookkeeper, receives bounced checks from the bank. He fills out a balance correction form and forwards it to the Correction Department such that the outstanding balance can be corrected. Joe sends a bounced check letter to the customer requesting another check plus a $15.00 penalty (this is now included as part of the outstanding balance). Checks are never re-deposited.

Event 8

Joe, the bookkeeper, issues a weekly update report on the balance of each account where there was a transaction during that week.

II. Assignment

1. Based on the above statement of purpose and event list, develop preliminary data flow diagrams (DFDs) on a separate sheet for each event.
2. Level each DFD to at least three levels. Functional primitives must be accompanied by a process specification (using psuedocode).
3. Develop the ERD in 3rd normal form.
4. Develop the data dictionary entries from the DFDs, ERDs, process specifications or other data elements. Your data dictionary should be in alphabetical order and reduced to the elementary data element level.
5. Create a CRUD diagram.
6. Map the DFD, ERDs and CRUD to an object diagram.

ATTACHMENT I

PAYMENT FORM

DATE INVOICED:__/__/__   PERIOD COVERED: __/__/__ TO__/__/__
ACCOUNT NO.:_____ (30/NUMERIC)
NAME: _____ (30/ALPHANUMERIC)
ADDRESS:_____ (30/ALPHANUMERIC)

_____ (30/ALPHANUMERIC)

STATE:_____(SELF-DEFINING) CITY:_____(15/ALPHANUMERIC)

ZIPCODE:_____ (9/NUMERIC)

_____ ADDRESS CORRECTION (Y/BLANK)

==

(A)   (B)   (C)

PREVIOUS   BAL:$_____.___   NEW   PURCH:$_____.___
PAYMENTS:$_____.___

OUTSTANDING BALANCE: $ _____._____ (A+B-C)

MINIMUM PAYMENT DUE: $ _____._____

PAST AMOUNT DUE: $ _____._____

PAYMENT DUE THIS PERIOD: $ _____._____

AMOUNT ENCLOSED: $ _____._____
==
FOR OFFICE USE ONLY
OPERATOR CODE:_____ (4/NUMERIC)

DATE RECEIVED:__/__/__ AMOUNT PAID: $ _____.____

CORRESPONDENCE:____ (Y/N)   CASH:____(Y/N)

ATTACHMENT II

BALANCE CORRECTION FORM

DATE: __/__/__

SUPPORT TECHNICIAN: _____ (30/ALPHANUMERIC)

ACCOUNT NO.:_____ (30/NUMERIC)

_____ ADDRESS CORRECTION (Y/BLANK)

NAME: _____ (30/ALPHANUMERIC)

ADDRESS: _____ (30/ALPHANUMERIC)

_____ (30/ALPHANUMERIC)

STATE:_____(SELF-DEFINING) CITY:_____(15/ALPHANUMERIC)

ZIPCODE:_____(9/NUMERIC)

==

CURRENT BALANCE: $_____.____ (A)

ADJUSTMENT AMT: $_____.____ (B)

NEW BALANCE: $_____.____ (A +/- B)

==

AUTHORIZATION CODE: _____ (10/NUMERIC)

SUPERVISOR NO: _____ (8/NUMERIC)

SIGNATURE: _____

ATTACHMENT III

REQUEST FOR DEFAULT

DATE:___/___/____

SUPPORT   TECHNICIAN: _____
(30/ALPHANUMERIC)

ACCOUNT NO.:_____ (30/NUMERIC)

NAME: _____ (30/ALPHANUMERIC)

ADDRESS: _____ (30/ALPHANUMERIC)

_____ (30/ALPHANUMERIC)

STATE:_____(SELF-DEFINING) CITY:_____(15/ALPHANUMERIC)

ZIPCODE:_____(9/NUMERIC)

==
REASON FOR DEFAULT
(CHECK ONE)

1._____ DEATH (ATTACH DEATH CERTIFICATE) NO PAYMENT REQUIRED
2._____ BANKRUPTCY (ATTACH LEGAL DOCUMENT) 180 DAY TERMS
3._____ REQUEST FOR NEW PAYMENT TERMS   60 OR 90 DAY TERMS

==
FOR OFFICE USE ONLY

OPERATOR CODE: _____(4/NUMERIC)

DATE RECEIVED: ___/___/___   ACTION CODE:_____ (1/2/3)

Appendix D
Case Study: The Mobile Telephone Company Problem

A Global System for Mobile communications (GSM) cellular telephone company provides wireless telephone equipment and services for customers. GSM telephones are packaged for sale in the form of a "pre-sale-distribution-kit" at the company's product assembly center. Each kit consists primarily of a Telephone Handset and a SIM card. (A "Subscriber Identity Module" is a credit card-like device that is inserted into digital cellular phones and identifies each customer to the telephone system.) The telephone handset manufacturer assigns each and every handset a unique International Mobile-communications Equipment Identifier (IMEI) number.

An individual may own more than one SIM, but must own at least one SIM to be considered a Customer. A customer may own more than one telephone handset; however, handset ownership is not a requisite. The SIM is interchangeable among the various handset models sold by the company. (In practice, nearly all customers own at least one telephone handset. Following the initial sale, some customers chose to "upgrade" their handset to a smaller, lighter, more functional model.)

In the back office, the company maintains an inventory of available, yet unassigned, telephone numbers. To make the technological leap from wired-telephone-number to wireless-telephone-number, each conventional Telephone Number is assigned to a Mobil Identification Number (MIN). Each unique MIN will ultimately be associated with a specific customer's SIM card when a new account is activated. A unique International Mobile SIM Identifier (IMSI) number identifies each SIM.

For billing purposes, the company maintains a record of each Call Delivery Notification (CDN) event. The unique identifier for the CDN is a concatenation of the CDN_id + IMSI.

Assignment

Using the crow's-foot notation method, prepare an Entity Relation Diagram (ERD) based on the following business case. Provide only the primary key(s) (PK) and foreign key pointers (FK) for each entity, as needed. Do not include other attributes.

Case Study created by Greg Vimont.

Glossary

Abstract object An object that is not at the lowest level in a class. Abstract objects are not executed directly.

Application server The middle tier of the three-tier client/server architecture. The application server contains common programs that are available to front-end workstation computers.

Acceptance test plans Set of tests that, if passed will establish that the software can be used in production.

Alternate key An attribute that uniquely identifies a row of occurrence in an entity. An alternate key cannot be the primary key.

Attribute A component of an entity or object. An attribute may or may not be an elementary data element.

Back-end server The top level of a tiered architecture. This tier usually houses databases that are required to support applications.

Border Also known as a "frame," defines the boundary of a window view.

Business process reengineering (BPR) A method to redesign existing applications.

Business specification A document that reflects the overall requirements of a process or system written in a prose format. The focus of the business specification is to provide the user with enough information so they can authorize the development of the technical requirements.

Cascading Multiple iterations of subtypes. A subtype entity within a subtype. A subtype that cascades is also a supertype to its cascading subtypes.

CASE (Computer-Aided Software Engineering) Products used to automate and implement modeling tools and data repositories.

Case A format for developing application logic in a process specification.

Character-based screens Support only keyboard-driven data entry. Icons and graphical symbols facilitated through the use of a mouse are not supported (or required).

Class A group of objects that have similar attributes and methods and typically have been put together to perform specific tasks.

Client An application that requests services from applications.

Cohesion The measurement of an application's self-dependence.

Concrete object The lowest-level object in a class.

Control bar Represents an array of choices and commands that need to be viewed in an accessible area of the screen and are maintained in the display area. Examples include button bars, color or pattern palettes, toolbars, rulers, and ribbons.

Coupling The measurement of an application's dependency on another application.

Crow's foot A method of showing the relationship of association between two entities.

CRUD diagram An association matrix that matches the types of data access between entities and processes. CRUD represents *c*reate, *r*ead, *u*pdate, and *d*elete.

Data dictionary (DD) A dictionary that defines data. A component of the data repository.

Data flow Component of a data flow diagram that represents data entering or leaving a process, external, or data store.

Data flow diagram (DFD) A tool that shows how data enter and leave a process. A data flow diagram has four possible components: data flow, data store, external, and process.

Data replication The process that copies data from one file to another, ensuring that all copies are synchronized with each other.

Data repository A robust data dictionary that contains information relating to data element behavior.

Data store Component of a data flow diagram that represents data that can be accessed from a particular area or file. A data store is sometimes call "data-arrest."

Data synchronization The process of ensuring that copies of the same data are equivalent.

Data warehousing A de-normalized database created to focus on decision support activities. Data warehouses hold historical information and cannot be used to update data.

Dynamic line library (DLL) An area that stores the active version of an object. Object classes are formed from DLLs at execution time.

Elementary data element A functionally decomposed data element.

Encapsulation Attributes of an object that can be accessed only through the object's methods.

Entity An object of interest about which data can be collected. Entities can consume a number of attributes.

Entity relational diagram (ERD) A diagram that depicts the relationships among the stored data.

Executive sponsor An individual at an executive level who has responsibility for a business area. The executive sponsor is a defined role in JAD sessions.

External Component of a data flow diagram that represents a provider or user of data that is not part of the system. Externals are therefore boundaries of the system.

Facilitator An impartial individual responsible for controlling the flow of JAD sessions.

Firewall A network component, usually in the form of a server, that provides access security to the network. Security is accomplished by the firewall's ability to validate data packets that attempt to enter the network.

Front-end client Workstations that function within a client/server architecture. Workstations are typically microcomputers running an operating system; however, a client can also be a dumb terminal.

Functional decomposition The process for finding the most basic parts of a system.

Functional overview A subset view of a specification. The subset usually covers a particular function of the system.

Functional primitive A functionally decomposed data flow diagram.

Gantt chart A tool that depicts progress of tasks against time. The chart was developed by Henry L. Gantt in 1917.

Graphical user interface (GUI) A screen interface that adopts the use of icons and symbols to represent functions that a user can implement.

HTTP (hypertext transfer protocol) A standard format for publishing information in a hypertext format known as HTML.

Inheritance The process by which child objects effectively retain all of the capabilities of their parents. Inheritance is implemented using an inverted tree structure.

Instantiation Independent executions of the same class.

ISO 9000 International Organization for Standardization, quality standard 9000.

Internet A cooperative message-forwarding system that links computer networks all over the world.[36]

Internet/Intranet development Application that operates within a browser product such as Netscape or Internet Explorer.

Intranet A network confined to a single organization or unit.[37]

Job description matrix The portion of an individual's job description that focuses strictly on the procedural and process aspects of the individual's position.

Joint application development (JAD) A method of developing the requirements for a system by focusing on group sessions. The sessions are typically under the direction of a facilitator.

---

[36] Douglas Downing, Michael Covington, and Melody Mauldin Covington, *Dictionary of Computer and Internet Terms*, 6th ed., Barron's Educational Series, Inc., p. 239.

[37] Douglas Downing, Michael Covington, and Melody Mauldin Covington, *Dictionary of Computer and Internet Terms*, 6th ed., Barron's Educational Series, Inc., p. 242.

Key An attribute of an entry or database that uniquely identifies a row, occurrence, or record.

Key business rules Business rules of key attributes that are enforced at the database level (as opposed to the application level).

Legacy system An existing automated system.

Leveling Functional decomposition of a data flow diagram. Each decomposition is called a "level."

LINUX Derivative UNIX operating system. Linux was developed by Linus Torvalds and was created as a free operating system.

Local area network Separate computers interacting together. A server or peer connection establishes a gateway of communication among each computer or node.

Logic data modeling (LDM) A set of procedures that examines an entity to ensure that its component attributes should reside in that entity, rather than being stored in another or new entity.

Logical equivalent An abstraction of the translation from physical requirements to software.

Long division An abstraction of the relationship of arithmetic formulas to functional decomposition.

Menu bar Is used to organize and provide access to actions that are listed horizontally across the top of the screen and below the title bar.

Metadata Data about the data being sent or received in a client/server network.

Method A process specification that invokes services in an object.

Microsoft exchange Microsoft's e-mail system, which operates under the Windows 95/98/NT and 2000 environments.

Middleware Middle tier of the three-tiered client/server architecture. Middleware contains the necessary APIs, protocols, metadata, gateways, and object messaging necessary to provide communications across client/server networks.

MIME (Multipurpose Internet mail extension) An e-mail protocol used to send messages across the Internet.

Mutual exclusivity Used specifically in relation to supertype/subtype entities. Subtypes that are mutually exclusive cannot coexist with the same supertype entity.

Network workstation Desktop computer connected to a LAN or WAN.

Normalization The elimination of redundancies from an entity.

Object A cohesive whole made up of two essential components: data and processes. The data are often referred to as attributes and processes as services.

Open systems Standards in applications software that allow such software to run across multiple operating system environments.

Persistence An object that continues to operate after the class or operation that invoked it has finished.

Polymorphism Dynamic change in the behavior of an object based on its execution circumstance.

Pre-post conditions A format for developing application logic in a process specification.

Primary key A key attribute that will be used to identify connections to a particular entity. Normalization requires that every entity contain a primary key. Primary keys can be formed by the concatenation of many attributes.

Process A function in a data flow diagram in which data are transformed from one form to another.

Process flow diagram (PFD) A tool that depicts process flow in relation to sequence and time.

Process specification A document that contains all of the algorithms and information necessary to develop the logic of a process. Process specifications can be comprised of the business and programming requirement documents. Pro-cess specifictions are sometimes called "minispecs."

Program or technical specification A technical algorithm of the requirements of a process or system.

Prototype A sample of a system that does not actually fully operate. Most software prototypes are visual depictions of screens and reports. Prototypes can vary in capability, with some prototypes having limited functional interfaces.

Pseudocode A generic or structured English representation of how real programming code must execute. Pseudocode is used in the development of process specifications.

Rapid application development (RAD) A method of application development that combines the analysis and design steps through the use of prototypes and CASE tools.

Reverse engineering The process of analyzing existing applications and database code to create high-level representations of the code.

Reusable object An object that can be a component of different classes.

Robust Software that operates intuitively and can handle unexpected events.

Schema generation CASE interface that allows a logical database to be generated into a specific physical database product.

Scribe A person who is designated in a JAD session to record minutes and decisions made by the group. In certain situations, scribes can also be responsible for data modeling.

Scroll bars Appear when all displayed information cannot be presented within the current window boundaries. The vertical scroll bar at the right of a window controls the up-and-down scrolling, while the horizontal scroll bar controls right-to-left movement.

Server An application that provides information to a requesting application.

Size grip Is a handle in a window that permits the window to be resized. The resizing is accomplished by dragging the grip and moving the window to the desired size. The grip is located in the lower right corner of the window. It is identified by three angled parallel lines.

Spiral life cycle Life cycle that focuses on the development of cohesive objects and classes. The spiral life cycle reflects a much larger allocation of time spent on design than the waterfall approach does.

Split box/Split bar Is a window that is split into two or more pieces, or panes. Split boxes can be manipulated using the split bar, which is located above the vertical scroll bar.

State transition diagram (STD) A modeling tool that depicts time-dependent and event-driven behavior.

Status bar Also known as a "message bar," provides information to the user about the state or status of the information or object inside the window.

Stored procedures Application code activated at the database level.

Structured query language (SQL) Query language and data element construct originated by IBM Corporation. SQL data descriptions are de facto standards in most relational database products.

Supertype/subtype A relational database entity construct where rows of data are divided into multiple separate entities or components. Each component or subtype is stored as a separate entity with a one-to-one relationship with its parent or supertype.

System menu button This button is located at the left corner of the title bar and is also called the "control menu" or the "window menu." This button is used as an aid to keyboard users and lists options for manipulating the window. This includes commands such as *Restore, Minimize, Maximize,* and *Close.*

Tier A level of processing in a client/server architecture. The most common client/server network environment is the three-tier model, which consists of a back-end tier, a middle or application server tier, and a client or front-end tier.

Title bar Is the top line of the window and explains the purpose or name of the window's function.

Title bar icon This icon is located in the left corner of the title bar and is used to retrieve a pull-down menu of commands that apply to the object in the window.

Triggers Stored procedures that are activated at the database level.

UNIX Operating system developed by Bell Labs in 1969, a subsidiary of AT&T. The operating system is written in the C language.

User category The conceptual view of the user from the analyst's perspective. There are three types of user categories: (1) Executive, (2) Department Head or Line Manager, and (3) Functional.

User interface The relationship with end users that facilitates the process of gathering and defining logical requirements.

User level The tier of computer project experience of the user. There are three levels: (1) Knowledgeable, (2) Amateur, and (3) Novice.

Waterfall system development life cycle A life cycle that is based on phased dependent steps to complete the implementation of a system. Each step is dependent on the completion of the previous step.

Web (World Wide Web) Loosely organized set of computer sites that publish information that anyone can read via the Internet mainly using HTTP (Hypertext Transfer Protocol).

Wide area network (WAN) A group of LANs that are connected through a gateway.

Window sizing buttons These buttons are located on the right corner of the title bar and are used to manipulate the size of the active window.

Work area The portion of the screen inside the borders of the window where the user performs tasks.

WYSIWYG (What you see is what you get) A concept that requires that what a program displays on the screen represents exactly how it will appear if printed or otherwise displayed.

References

Baudoin, Claude and Glenn Hollowell (1996) *Realizing the Object-Oriented Lifecycle.* Upper Saddle River, NJ: Prentice Hall.

Berson, Alex (1996). *Client/Server Architecture.* New York: McGraw-Hill, Inc.

Booch, Grady (1996). *Object Solutions.* Menlo Park, CA: Addison-Wesley.

Brooks, Frederick Jr. (1995). *The Mythical Man-Month.* New York: Addison-Wesley.

Brodie, Michael L. and Michael Stonebreaker (1995). *Migrating Legacy Systems: Gateways Interfaces and the Incremental Approach.* San Francisco, CA: Morgan Kaufmann Publishers, Inc.

Burd, Stephen D. (1998). *Systems Architecture*, 2nd ed. Cambridge, Massachusetts: ITP, Inc.

Connell, John and Linda Shafer (1995). *Object-Oriented Rapid Prototyping.* Englewood Cliffs, NJ: Prentice-Hall.

Date, C.J. (2000). *An Introduction to Database Systems* 7th ed. New York: Addison-Wesley.

DeMarco, Tom (1979) *Structured Analysis and System Specification.* Englewood Cliffs, NJ: Prentice-Hall.

Deutsch, Michael and Ronald Willis (1988). *Software Quality Engineering: A Total Technical and Management Approach.* Englewood Cliffs, NJ: Prentice-Hall.

Dewire, Dawna Travis (1993). *Client/Server Computing.* New York: McGraw-Hill, Inc.

Downing, Douglas, Michael Covington, and Melody Mauldin Covington (1998). *Dictionary of Computer and Internet Terms*, 6th ed. Hauppauge, NY: Barron's Educational Series, Inc.

Fleming, Candace and Barbara von Halle (1998). *Handbook of Relational Database Design.* Menlo Park, CA: Addison-Wesley.

Fournier, Roger (1991). *Practical Guide to Structured System Development and Maintenance*. Englewood Cliffs, NJ: Prentice Hall.

Gale, Thornton and James Eldred (1996). *Getting Results with the Object-Oriented Enterprise Model*. New York: SIGS Books.

Hipperson, Roger (1992). *Practical Systems Analysis: A Guide for Users, Managers and Analysts*. Englewood Cliffs, NJ: Prentice-Hall.

Jacobson, Ivar, Maria Ericsson, and Agneta Jacobson (1995). *The Object Advantage*. New York: ACM Press.

Kalakota, R., and Andrew B. Whinston (1997). *Electronic Commerce: A Manager's Guide*. New York: Addison-Wesley.

Kerr, James and Richard Hunter (1994). *Inside RAD*. New York: McGraw-Hill, Inc.

Lorenz, Mark (1993). *Object-Oriented Software Development: A Practical Guide*. Englewood Cliffs, NJ: Prentice-Hall.

Martin, James and Carma McClure (1988). *Structured Techniques: The Basis for CASE*. Englewood Cliffs, NJ: Prentice-Hall.

Martin, James and James Odell (1995). *Object-Oriented Methods: A Foundation*. Englewood Cliffs, NJ: Prentice-Hall.

Mattison, Bob (1996). *Data Warehousing: Strategies, Technologies and Techniques*. New York: McGraw-Hill, Inc.

Montgomery, Stephen (1991). *AD/Cycle: IBM's Framework for Application Development and CASE*. New York: Multiscience Press, Inc.

Microsoft Press (1994). *Computer Dictionary: The Comprehensive Standard for Business, School, Library, and Home*. Redmond, WA: Microsoft Corporation.

Muller, Pierre-Alain (1997). *Instant UML*. Birmingham, U.K.: Wrox Press.

Orfali, Robert, Dan Harkey, and Jeri Edwards (1994). *Essential Client/Server Survival Guide*. New York: John Wiley & Sons, Inc.

Perry, William (1991). *Quality Assurance for Information Systems: Methods, Tools, and Techniques*. Wellesley, MA: QED Information Sciences, Inc.

Pfleeger, Shari L. (1998). *Software Engineering: Theory and Practice*. Upper Saddle River, NJ: Prentice Hall.

Poe, Vidette (1996). *Building a Data Warehouse for Decision Support*. Upper Saddle River, NJ: Prentice-Hall.

Purba, Sanjiv, David Sawh, and Bharat Shah (1995). *How to Manage a Successful Software Project: Methodologies, Techniques, Tools*. New York: John Wiley & Sons, Inc.

Rothstein, Michael, Burt Rosner, Michael Senatore, and Dave Mulligan (1993*). Structured Analysis & Design for the CASE User*. Englewood Cliffs, NJ: Prentice-Hall.

Rumbaugh, James, Michael Blaha, William Premerlani, Frederick Eddy, and William Lorensen (1991). *Object-Oriented Modeling and Design*. Englewood Cliffs, NJ: Prentice-Hall.

Rumbaugh, James, Ivar Jacobson, and Grady Booch (1999). *The Unified Modeling Language Reference Model*. New York: Addison Wesley, Inc.

Rummler, Geary and Alan Brache (1990). *Improving Performance: How to Manage the White Space on the Organization Chart*. San Francisco, CA: Jossey-Bass, Inc.

Shlaer, Sally and Stephen Mellor (1992). *Object Lifecycles: Modeling the World in States*. Englewood Cliffs, NJ: Prentice-Hall.

Simon, Alan R., and Tom Wheeler (1995). *Open Client/Server Computing and Middleware*. Chestnut Hill, Massachusetts: AP Professional.

Sommerville, I., and Pete Sawyer (1998). *Requirements Engineering: A Practical Guide*. New York: John Wiley & Sons.

Sullo, Gary (1994). *Object Engineering: Designing Large-Scale Object-Oriented Systems*. New York: John Wiley & Sons, Inc.

Ullman, Jeffrey D., and Jennifer Widom (1997). *A First Course in Database Systems*. Upper Saddle River, NJ: Prentice-Hall.

Whitten, Jeffrey, Lonnie Bentley, and Victor Barlow (1994). *Systems Analysis and Design Methods*. Burr Ridge, IL: Richard D. Irwin, Inc.

Whitten, Neal (1995). *Managing Software Development Projects*. New York: John Wiley & Sons, Inc.

Wood, Jane and Denise Silver (1995). *Joint Application Development*. New York: John Wiley & Sons, Inc.

Yourdon, Edward (1989). *Object-Oriented Systems Design: An Integrated Approach*. Englewood Cliffs, NJ: Prentice Hall.

Yourdon, Edward, Katharine Whitehead, Jim Thomann, Karen Oppel, and Peter Neverman (1995). *Mainstream Objects: An Analysis and Design Approach for Business*. Englewood Cliffs, NJ: Prentice-Hall.

Index